WHAT THE VILLAGE GAVE ME

Conceptualizations of Womanhood

Edited by
Denise Davis-Maye
Annice Dale Yarber
Tonya E. Perry

University Press of America,® Inc.
Lanham · Boulder · New York · Toronto · Plymouth, UK

Copyright © 2014 by
University Press of America,® Inc.
4501 Forbes Boulevard
Suite 200
Lanham, Maryland 20706
UPA Acquisitions Department (301) 459-3366

10 Thornbury Road
Plymouth PL6 7PP
United Kingdom

All rights reserved
Printed in the United States of America
British Library Cataloging in Publication Information Available

Library of Congress Control Number: 2013951560
ISBN: 978-0-7618-6197-3 (paperback : alk. paper)
eISBN: 978-0-7618-6198-0

Cover artwork by Aaron Fraze.

™
∞ The paper used in this publication meets the minimum
requirements of American National Standard for Information
Sciences—Permanence of Paper for Printed Library Materials,
ANSI Z39.48-1992

DEDICATION

To...
Our foremothers
Our Mothers—Wilhelmina, Gladiola, and Demathraus
Our 12 year old selves—little miss Nini, Niecy, and Jaws
Our daughters—Daraja and Jamese
All the women of the village
We dream awake, live consciously, reach back, and move forward...so it is and so shall it be.

CONTENTS

Preface   vii

Foreword   ix

Acknowledgments   xi

Section 1: Navigating Troubled Waters: Doing Womanhood in Work Life

1. Learning to Swim with the Barracudas: Negotiating Differences   3
    in the Workplace
    Nia I. Cantey
2. Mammies, Maids &Mothers: Representations of African-   19
    American and Latina Women's Reproductive Labor in *Weeds*
    Johnanna Ganz
3. Being Black Academic Mothers   37
    Angela K. Lewis, Sherri L. Wallace, and Clarissa L. Peterson

Section 2: Too Grown for Your Own Good: Doing Girlhood

4. Combing My Kinks: A Culturally Informed Program to Strengthen   55
    Mother-Daughter Relationships
    Marva L. Lewis and Allisyn L. Swift
5. The ABCs of Doing Gender: Culturally Situated Non-Cognitive   73
    Factors & African American Girls
    LaShawnda Lindsay-Dennis and Lawanda Cummings
6. Learning Black Womanhood: An Autoethnography   91
    Denise Davis-Maye

Section 3: Turpentine, Sugar, and Pot Liquor: Black Women and Everyday Health

7. Growing Up Black and Female: Life Course Transitions and   107
    Depressive Symptoms
    Claire Norris and Paige Miller
8. Saving My Soul and Making Me Fat?: Black Mothers and the Church   123
    Annice Dale Yarber

Section 4: Speaking Change and Writing Wrongs: Representations of Activism

9. The Art of Activist Mothering: Black Feminist Leadership & Knowing   137
    What to Do
    Denise McLane-Davison
10. What *Mami* Taught Me about Empire   161
    Elizabeth Huergo

Preface

A stone in the water does not understand how thirsty the hill is.
A Hausa Proverb

At the onset of this journey, we conceptualized a volume that would provide content relevant to the experiences of women of color with respect to specific issues of increasing concern among these populations—conceptualizations of womanhood, beauty, and gender roles. The goal of this volume is to address the question of how womanhood, roles, and beauty are conceptualized by women of color and how they intersect with class, gender, and ethnicity.

What the village gave us refers to the aspects of context which influences the development of women, particularly women of color. The what, that simple word, encompasses an abundance of factors, many of which have never been discussed or identified. We, the collective "we," talk constantly about who, how, what and when women learn what they learn, know what they know, and do what they do. Unfortunately, there is a presumption because of shared humanity, that the phenomena which influences once individual in a particular way will also influence another individual similarly. Further, we rarely consider the ways in which our peers experience the same environments or how those impactful environments differ.

This volume does not serve to present normative experiences of women. In fact, these accounts, whether empirical or conceptual in nature, serve as exemplars for the heterogeneity in the experiences of women. These chapters depict experiences across the lifespan, in varied environments, and even how others miss the mark as they attempt to "know" us by creating images of us. This collection of works attempts to give readers distinct exemplars of women's experiences with working, growing up, surviving, and then serving others.

Within the Section 1, Navigating Troubled Waters: Doing Womanhood in Work Life, the focus in on women's experiences in the workplace and others' depictions of these roles. In Chapter 1, Learning to Swim with the Barracudas, Cantey highlights the challenges and lesson afforded while being "the other" in a professional space. Chapter 2, Ganz's Mammies, Maids and Mothers, describes how a particular popular television series depicts African American and Latina women in domestic roles. In Chapter 3 Lewis, Wallace, and Peterson present a poignant representation of the challenges faced by Black women attempting to fulfill their roles as mothers and academicians in Being Black Academic Mothers.

Section 2, Too Grown for Your Own Good: Doing Girlhood, focuses on the childhood. Lewis and Swift offer an innovative approach to strengthening tenuous mother-daughter relationship through grooming rituals in Chapter 4, Combing My Kinks. While Lindsay-Dennis and Cummings discuss how Black girls are further marginalized in K-12 settings as a result of differential assessment and treatment. Finally, Davis-Maye discusses the means through which and the messages she received about womanhood growing up in an urban community.

Health issues are addressed in Section 3, Turpentine, Sugar and Pot Liquor. Norris and Miller talk about emotional health and the ways that ethnicity may affect how women experience life course transitions in Growing Up Black and Female. Yarber discusses the intersecting nature of Health, Perception of Health, Religiosity and Culture in Saving my Soul and Making me Fat.

Two diverse approaches to activism are covered in Section 4, Speaking Change and Writing Wrongs. McLane-Davison discusses the nuances of Black Feminist Leadership among HIV/AIDS activists. Then in the final chapter, Huergo discusses how we must write, speak, and create our narratives, if we are to have truth and genuine representations of who WE are.

Finally, *What the Village Gave Me*, is the outgrowth of conversations about scenarios we face daily, the courses we teach, the expectations others have us, and how we wish we didn't have to reteach our individual stories with each interaction we have. Why don't people just accept that we might be different, we might hear differently, we might see differently? Well, here is the first crop of OUR stories, so folks can see for themselves. Our Village might be a bit different than your village, not better or worse, just different. Enjoy!

Foreword

The contributors to *What The Village Gave Me: Conceptualizations of Womanhood,* rely primarily on the qualitative approach of inquiry to bring us a rich discussion of the workplace experiences of women of color. Denise Davis-Maye, Annice Dale Yarber, and Tonya E. Perry have assembled a valuable collection of narratives from women of color that is interdisciplinary and intergenerational. Their narratives inspire hope and extol the power of relationships, lived experiences, personal strengths, and the efficacious use of self. These narratives draw on understandings and approaches from varied fields and disciplines. Through these narratives, the writers struggle with and coalesce around similar, yet divergent themes including mothering and motherhood, ideals of beauty, the sense of moral agency, and physical and intellectual health.

These women use narratives/stories to share their individual experiences, to reveal their identities, to educate and to address discipline specific career issues. They speak of delicate loving situations and harsh untenable events with similar passion. Their writings simultaneously communicate a sense of urgency and a dogged determination to use this writing opportunity as a weapon against the structural barriers created by the oppression of sexism, racism and heterosexism.

All of the narratives include a direct reference to mothers and mothering. Whether they are presenting content on balancing their families and their lives in the academy or using the stored arsenals of courage and fortitude that their mothers provided for them, they are steadfast in their roles as scholars, researchers and educators. Many of these women share very similar career paths and are now experiencing the thorny intersectionality of race, gender, sexual orientation, and the academic workplace. Their history of invidious and uneven encounters in the academy may hinder their ability to contribute successfully and productively. These often blatant discriminatory practices along with the constant of microaggressions create tremendous burdens, yet as their narratives reveal, these women refuse to be stopped.

In general, the challenge of narratives and stories lies in understanding the context of the storytellers' lives. In order to address this challenge, a clear understanding of the context needs to be gleaned from the participants themselves.

In this case, however, I will take some liberties since I have experienced many of the life events to which these women refer. I don't need to examine their backgrounds extensively, nor do I need to question their stories ad infinitum. I know these stories. They are familiar. These writers' stories are my stories and the stories of far too many untold women of color in the academy and other workplaces.

What My Mama Gave Me: Conceptualizations of Womanhood is a fearless book that can be useful to all women in the academy and especially to women of color. It is an excellent reader of intergenerational content on women of color. It tells stories of personal growth, coping, preparation, and possibilities. These narratives are enriching and inspire confidence. They provide that hard earned wisdom and impetus needed to forge ahead and to work toward establishing a workplace that is equitable and just and that ensures opportunities for women of color to grow, thrive, and develop their full intellectual and academic potential.

Iris Carlton-LaNey, Ph.D., Professor
School of Social Work
University of North Carolina at Chapel Hill

Acknowledgments

The book began as a vision to highlight the experiences of women of color in ways that these stories are never told. We would like to first thank the creator for providing the space, energy and spirit to embark upon this journey. As co-editors, we would like to thank each other for having the vision to create *What the Village Gave Me*. We have many people to thank for their support in this process.

Special thanks to the following people for helping to make this book a reality:

We are grateful to Laura Espinoza, Acquisitions Editor, for recognizing the value of our volume in adding to the growing literature on gender, race, health, and community. We would like to express our heartfelt appreciation to Dr. Iris Carlton LaNey for her insightful Foreword. A special thanks to Allyson Lee for her willing spirit and creative essence. Finally, a warm thank you to all our contributors for your submission of poignant, relevant and powerful works. The village is rejoicing.

And last but not least, we want to extend a very special thanks to our families…to our husbands and significant others/partners, Dwight, Fulton, and Colin; our mothers, Wilhelmina, Gladiola and Demathraus; and our children. Without your love and constant presence, our dream would never have become reality.

Section One

Navigating Troubled Waters: Doing Womanhood in Work Life

>*And so, lifting as we climb, onward and upward we go, struggling and striving, and hoping that the buds and blossoms of our desires will burst into glorious fruition ere long. With courage, born of success achieved in the past, with a keen sense of the responsibility which we shall continue to assume, we look forward to a future large with promise and hope. Seeking no favors because of our color, nor patronage because of our needs, we knock at the bar of justice, asking an equal chance.*
>
>Mary Church Terrell (Address before the National American Women's Suffrage Association, February 1898)

Chapter One
Learning to Swim with the Barracudas: Negotiating Differences in the Work Place
Nia I. Cantey

"Only the black woman can say when and where I enter, in the quiet, undisputed dignity of my womanhood, without violence and without suing or special patronage, then and there the whole...race enters with me"- Anna Julia Cooper

Introduction

The Obama era brings with it the theoretical philosophy of a post racial America. With the election of President Obama, the American nation is viewed as one devoid of racial discrimination and prejudice. Along these same lines, critics of President Obama suggest he is promoting a socialist society with the passing of equal gender wages (i.e., Ledbetter bill), publicly endorsing same-sex marriages, and the passing of the Affordable Care Act that guarantees that all citizens are medically insured. While these declarations and mandates have worked toward improving the quality of living for the American nation, regardless of differences—age, race, gender, class, and sexual orientation—these progressive steps have not changed the embedded, institutionalized forms of discrimination based on difference. Moreover, while the theoretical philosophy of a post racial America is highlighted in the age of Obama, ever present realities of racism across socio-political spaces (Harrison, 2012; Miller and Garran, 2008) may be equally highlighted thus serving to debunk the notion of a racism free society. Racism in the United States is regarded as an insidious and pervasive phenomenon which permeates socio-political interactions (West, 2008; Bell and Griffin, 1997) across three system levels (1) individual, (2) group, and (3) institutional (Miller and Garran, 2008). These three levels and other similar concepts attributed to racism are equally suitable to discrimination across differences (i.e., race, gender, age, or sexual orientation). The arguments presented in this chapter will focus on individual and institutional discrimination across differences in the workplace while illuminating the complexity involved in addressing discrimination when considering other intersecting forms of social oppression (i.e., class, gender, sexual orientation, citizenship, and other axes of identity to include disability) (Miller and Garran 2008) through an amalgam of theories and tenets (feminist standpoint theory, and feminist communication theory).

Emanating from my personal experiences of discrimination within the workplace, this chapter derives from research centered on negotiating space (Cantey, 2010) while managing intersecting marginalized identities (i.e., Black women and Black lesbians). The term space has multiple interpretations based on sociologists, environmentalists, and constructivists. Yi-Fuan Tuan (1997) discusses space in relation to the concept of place, "place is security, space is freedom: we are attached to the one and long for the other" (p. 3). Freedom is achieved when an individual feels a sense of security within her occupied place (1997). Negotiating space means making the invisible identity visible across communities and giving voice to a voiceless population in all socio-political spaces (Cantey, 2010). The findings from the research (Cantey, 2010) suggest that when an individual negotiates her space she is simultaneously negotiating differences. Negotiating differences presented by Michael Awkward (1995) is based on race, gender, and the politics of positionality. This discussion also includes the politics of age and sexuality within the workplace. Differences discussed within this chapter include an intersection of two or more of these factors with a focus on these intersections within the workplace. The literature indicates that individuals with more than one subordinate identity (i.e., Black women) experience more negative encounters within the workplace than individuals with single-subordinate identities (i.e., Black men or White women) (Rosette & Livingston, 2012, p.1162; Almquist, 1975). This chapter will expand the discourse of workplace discrimination to also include experiences of Black lesbians in an effort to examine similar experiences from two populations both with multi-layered differences. This subject is relevant for three reasons; 1) to add to the body of literature on the conceptualization of womanhood for women of color, 2) to highlight the systematic, systemic, institutionalized rejection of differences (i.e., practices of racism, sexism, ageism, and heterosexist politics) within the workplace for women of color, and 3) to illuminate how women of color manage differences within the workplace.

As a former social worker in the child welfare field for the last ten years, I have worked personally and professionally to embody what I consider two fundamental principles of social work; 1) start where the person is, and 2) be non-judgmental, when engaging others. These two principles are woven in the fabric of social work curricula and literature. However, I contend that *acknowledging* these two principles and *applying* them is distinctly different.. Moreover, these two principles are primarily used when working with populations perceived as 'the least of these' as opposed to guiding principles used to negotiate daily interactions with all. I propose applying and embedding these two principles within the fabric of our social interactions, practices, and customs. Further, I contend that these principles are essential and indispensable in recognizing, analyzing and addressing workplace discrimination.

Macro and Micro Workplace Discrimination

For the most part, workplace discrimination occurs on two levels, macro and micro. Macro level discrimination is institutionalized discrimination within the workplace while micro level discrimination is individual and direct. Individual discrimination is based on prejudices, beliefs, or actions and practiced between and among individuals (Miller and Garran, 2008, p.28). Contrary to individual discrimination, institutionalized discrimination is systemic discrimination based on various axes of social identity embedded in organizations, institutions, laws, and customs (Miller and Garran, 2008). Although the social work field is described as a helping profession guided by a code of ethics to "commit practitioners to cultural competence, nondiscrimination, and in some instances, social justice," (Miller and Garran, 2008, p.xvii-xviii) other areas such as technology, engineering, and science are without codes of ethics. Yet there remain two common interactions across all fields irrespective of the nature of business; 1) parallel relationships-employee to employee and 2) hierarchical relationships-employer to employee. Both relationships benefit from the fundamental principles of social work. These two relationships require a mutual level of respect to be supported and enforced on a macro level and embraced in micro level interactions (Robbins, Chatterjee, Canda, 2012). Consider the following excerpt from Sky, a 44 year old information technology (IT) programmer,

> I work for IT in corporate America and so for example in Atlanta, I won't say the name. But I clearly understand that I am the lowest paid with the highest production output and probably the most skilled of all the managers and employees. Just things like that. There are certain things like for example, they will steal time, they will leave like twenty minutes early, five minutes early, everyday, and over time that is... Whereas I would not do that, because I understand as an African-American woman in corporate America, and in America my Caucasian male counterparts can do things that I will get fired for. So, just those types of limitations, and then I have it in the working environment and then to top of that lesbianism, being a lesbian, at a company party, if I have a partner, it is not like I could really bring her to come to the party. I am not in the closet at work, but I am not out either, I do not wear the sign (Cantey, 2010).

Sky's excerpt illustrates an acceptance of an institutionalized rejection of differences. Through her silence she is inadvertently complicit with racism, sexism, and heterosexist politics. Sky's experience is akin to other research conducted on Black women in the workplace. Research indicates that (Center For Women Policy Studies, 1997) 69 percent of Black women have experienced some form of discrimination, 34 percent have experienced gender discrimination on the job,

42 percent believe that they must play down their race or ethnicity, and 27 percent believe they must play down their gender in order to be successful at work (Jones and Shorter-Gooden, 2003). These findings suggest that Black women have accepted the institutionalized rejection of their *otherness*.

In contrast to Sky's example of accepting institutionalized rejection of differences, Vivacious highlights accepting rejection on an individual level. She argues accepting inferiority associated with being a woman is implanted as early as childhood. She states:

> Well, for myself just growing up in the type of family I did and the type of environment that I did, early on there was always an implication that there was an inferiority that came with femaleness... Well, growing up, you know, like I said, there was some inferiority that was implied with femaleness meaning you couldn't do certain things if you're a girl. You shouldn't certain things, you shouldn't look a certain way, you know, and you should go after motherhood and wifeness and all of that stuff. I really grew up with that shit in my home and around me, that's what every woman in my family did and, you know, there was a certain... you took a backseat to your man like no matter what he said or did, or how stupid the shit was and how far out, you kind of... you took a backseat to that (Cantey, 2010).

As Vivacious' discussion mirrors acceptance of individual rejection it also supports the premise that women are subjugated and are to be seen and not heard. Vivacious' experience fortifies the discussion within Simone de Beauvoir's (1989) classical book, *The Second Sex,* which expounds upon the experiences of women's silence, being forced into otherness, the omission of their existence and experiences fraught with inequalities. Additionally, her experience underscores a larger struggle for Black women and Black lesbians in particular—a struggle with "derogatory assumptions about their character and identity" (Harris-Perry, 2011, p.5). In this same vein, Yellow (2010) states,

> I see the difference in people's awareness to the sexes, like we are in a society and it's very much great to be a male in society because you are already afforded a certain amount of privilege if you are male as opposed to being a female (Cantey, 2010).

Ultimately the experiences of Sky, Vivacious, and Yellow similarly crystalize the acceptance of rejection and how this acceptance is not only romanticized but also programmed within us. Audre Lorde (1984) suggests that we are programmed to reject differences. According to Lorde (1984)

> We all have been programmed to respond to the human differences between us with fear and loathing and to handle that difference in one of three ways: ignore it, and if that is not possible, copy it if we think it is dominant, or destroy it if we think it is subordinate.

While Sky articulates recognition of the violation of her civil rights, she also articulates an acceptance of established norms as a way of surviving. In this same spirit, the response to reject human differences *between* us is also the same conditioned response to reject differences *within* us. Rejecting our own differences is internalized oppression (Bell and Griffin, 1997) and occurs when individuals "internalize the oppressive worldviews, beliefs, values, and attitudes that stem from the durable inequalities encountered throughout society" (p. 49). Subsequently, an individual is conditioned to fear and loathe her own differences based upon established cultural norms imposed by a Eurocentric worldview. This reality is illustrated by the narratives of Vivacious and Yellow when they argue that their gender invisibility places them in a subordinate position to men. Their experiences of subordination coupled with Sky's denunciation of her orientation, suggest that they have internalized a White normative standard which rejects their *otherness*—their personhood. White America is based on majority identities (i.e., White, male, and heterosexual) and the premise that "In white America, cultural conservatism takes the form of a chronic racism, sexism, and homophobia" (West, 2001, p.42). Through internalization of a White normative standard, individuals may be conditioned to devalue, fear, and loathe their sense of being and become actors in the cycle of discrimination that sustains and perpetuates oppression. Workplace discrimination is multi-layered and complex and it has often been described as "subtle, unintentional, and unconscious" (Harrison, 2012, p.15). In the workplace, those persons who reject the White normative standard by asserting their *otherness* and vocalizing discrimination often face very negative consequences. These consequences include framed as a person who is either overly sensitive or misinterpreting the discriminatory acts in question. and Harrison (2012) further asserts, "The offended person is redefined as the 'real problem' and is made to suffer the consequences" (p.15). These consequences may include termination.

Turning Point: Learning to Swim with the Barracudas

Similarly, in my own experience of workplace discrimination, I was perceived as the 'real problem' who invited the discrimination by challenging traditional spaces based upon my physical appearance. I recall a situation that occurred during my tenure as a program manager in which I was on an elevator with two other Black female members of management when one asked about one of my visible tattoos. I explained that the tattoo was the Ghanaian Adinkra symbol, Gye Nyame, meaning 'except for God.' After sharing the meaning and significance of the tattoo, she replied, "Wow, there's some depth *down there*. I will have to come *down there* more often." Given that we both worked on the same floor, her comment was heavily value-laden. I felt extremely offended by her statement. I felt that her comments revealed her view of me as a subordinate *other* before and after our exchange. In the space of minutes, she had discounted my position, my substantive knowledge and my personhood. At the time, I wore my hair natural, cut in a Mohawk style, along with at least three visible tattoos—

including the one my co-worker questioned. In many professional spaces, tattoos and style of hair are associated with a variety of negative connotations. These perceptions are limiting and discriminatory at best. At the time of the exchange on the elevator, I was a 30-year old, with visible tattoos, an eccentric hairstyle, relaxed attire, and I was completing a Ph.D.; I certainly did not fit the traditional workplace appearance of management. The imposition of gender norms in the workplace takes on a different hue for Black women for whom race is an intersecting and oppressive dimension of body politics in a way that it not for White women.

The politics of hair for Black women is situated within a larger sociopolitical context that is inclusive of a White normative standard of beauty. Within this context, a Black woman's hairstyle is essentially a political statement, Consider the shifting dialogue and marketing surrounding Black women's hair trends which have transitioned from a preference for natural hair to chemically relaxed hair, and back to natural hair. I contend that these transitions in Black women's hairstyle preferences which are central to their conceptualization of womanhood, serve as an organic, creative and highly visible representation of her identity. Through her hair, a woman is able to define herself for herself. As she evolves spiritually, emotionally, physically, and mentally, she constructs and reconstructs her identity. Her evolution is reflected in part through her hair. This representation of selfhood for Black women is challenged in the workplace where the dominant White standard of beauty is the norm. The struggle for women of color to resist or accept imposed gender norms represents the dual conflict of maintaining their authenticity while being recognized a person of value (Harris-Perry, 2011). Along these same lines, imposed gender norms within the workplace extend beyond physical appearance to include one's demeanor. or behavior. Demeanor either supports or detracts from whether a person is viewed as being acceptable and gender-appropriate in appearance. The contribution of demeanor to perceived acceptability in the workplace is illustrated by Beige. She was forced to "develop a tougher exterior to be successful, as a physician, as a female physician" in a male dominated field (Cantey, 2010) . According to Beige, if you act like a woman (i.e., crying or being soft) in the medical field, you are not going to survive the job or be respected as a credible physician. Acceptable versus unacceptable workplace appearance is a physical, emotional, and cognitive expectation imposed by White America. A Black female lesbian like Beige working in a male dominated setting may perform and interact with others based on the established norms within the workplace by denying aspects of her identity associated with her race, gender, or sexuality. These examples along with research on identity and space from other scholars suggest that spaces are politicized, racialized, and sexualized (Kaya, 2005; Valentine, 1993).

Moreover, as Beige conformed and developed this tougher exterior in an effort to appear more credible among her colleagues, she experienced difficulty when assuming a more passive disposition in her home and personal life. Identity shifting occurs when a person possesses multiple and conflicting identities

(Settles 2004). This example echoes what occurs when a person's choices and behaviors are influenced and defined by space [workplace] which in turn informs one's identity. Black women may engage in identity shifting as a means of survival in the workplace where they are exposed to multiple oppressions (Settles, 2004; Keith and Pile, 1993). The literature further suggests that when space determines an individual's identity, consequent benefits are temporary while the negative consequences of effects psychological distress and internal conflicts are long lasting(Szymanski and Gupta, 2009; Szymanski, 2005). Consequently, Beige's inability to shift roles and behaviors from one space to another confirms the devastating impact of accepting institutionalized rejection. Conversely, when the occupied space is determined by the person's identity, shifting between modes can offer benefits for an individual (Settles, 2004; Jones and Shorter-Gooden, 2003). Allowing one's identity to determine their space is a form of liberation and a rejection of the imposed norms.

Rejection of dominant norms [institutionalized or individualized discrimination] represents a rejection of disciplinary power (Foucault, 1977). Women living outside of the norm or living on the margins of dominant society must create their own identities and spaces within society. Securing a non-disciplinary form of power is an act of resistance and a liberation strategy (Iglesias and Cormier, 2002). Resistance strategies for liberation provide a sense of unity with others that transcends age, socioeconomic status, ethnic origin, and sexual orientation. Resistance strategies are empowering in that they involve self-determination through confrontation and repudiation of oppressive attempts to demean selfhood (2002, p. 266). Women with intersecting marginalized identities must resist oppression by giving voice to their existence and empowering their lives through different forms of non-disciplinary power. Situational shifting is a non-disciplinary form of power. Situational shifting occurs when a person's intersecting, marginalized identities overlap with their insider identity (outside the norm). This shifting is space dependent

Valdes (2000) describes his experience with situational shifting:

> When I am asked which 'comes first' for me, color or sexuality, I respond 'it depends.' Thus, when I am in a people-of color situation, I find myself operating and being received as, primarily a gay man. And when I am in a sexual minority situation, I find myself operating, and being received as, primarily a person of color. In these varying settings, my mission remains constant: to interject the 'other,' and remind those who are present of those who are not (2000, p. 337).

In this situation, Valdes allows his identity to affect his space. He is liberated within the space by allowing all aspects of his identity to prevail. Valdes is able to create a positive environment to debate, challenge, explain, and transform ideas and positions about intersecting identities (Wackwitz and Rakow, 2004). Valdes has created an empowering space; however, his ability to assert his identity may not reflect the sober realities of many marginalized people. For many women, their dependency on their employment necessitates conformity to dominant normative standards.

Like the co-researchers in my study, I too conformed and did not speak up and out against workplace discrimination. As I reflect back on my experiences, I must acknowledge that my epiphany did not come until I had left my managerial position, secured an academic appointment as an associate professor, had an Equal Employment Office complaint filed against me by a graduate student for reverse discrimination and was subjected to working with colleagues with hidden agendas. This epiphany coincided with my recognition that one of my mother's adages had become manifest in my own life; she use to say that, "you need to learn to swim with the barracudas." In essence, she was encouraging me to negotiate my own space and understand how to make my presence known without becoming complicit in perpetuating discrimination against others. Moreover, she was teaching me that barracudas are everywhere and come in different forms (colleagues, bosses, subordinates, etc.) yet I resisted learning to swim with them in fear of becoming a barracuda. Nonetheless, learning to swim with the barracudas was necessary to make my voice heard while also finding my own infinite beauty once again (Harris-Perry, 2011). "To give voice to black women by acknowledging the challenges they face, not to invoke pity or even empathy" (Harris-Perry, 2011, p. 30) is a struggle but is vital for thriving within a non-affirming society. Negotiating one's space in the workplace is critical to developing a healthy sense of self. This process is experienced as a journey towards developing personal and professional self-efficacy, redefining prescribed gender roles , and managing oppressive cultural norms.

In retrospect, I was cognizant of discrimination based upon differences prior to any personal encounters and purposely sought to challenge and shift people's perceptions built on stereotypes and judgments based on commonalities and not differences. I embodied the words of sage, Dr. Maya Angelou (1993) "Human beings are more alike than unalike" (p. 11). Yet, my former workplace experiences forced me to question this mantra as I had come to understand it for myself. On the other hand, my current work place experiences while aligned with Harrison's description of experiencing subtle forms of discrimination as a Black female faculty member challenged and forced me to assert my belief; we are more alike than unalike. Harrison (2012) argues,

> ....minority faculty, who have the most direct and closest interaction with faculty of all social and political philosophies, know better. African Americans, especially sensitive to the many subtle slights and insults that reflect racial worldview, can usually recognize bigotry when it appears among their white associates" (p. 7-8).

This consciousness (Damasio, 2000) or standpoint (Swignonski, 1994) of knowing differences based on various social identities, suggests that individuals with marginalized identities are advantageously positioned to recognize social oppression with a vantage point. A vantage point of both the dominant culture's perspective and their own perspective; thereby, offering a more comprehensive view of social reality, also known as positive marginality (Hall and Fine, 2005). Swignonski (1994) argues that, "research begins from the standpoint of particular marginalized groups of human beings [and] yields less partial and distorted understandings of nature and social relations" (Brown and McPhail, 2012, p. 121). While I agree that this vantage point is useful for recognizing discrimination in the workplace, it may fall short in facilitating change at the macro level where institutionalized discrimination is pervasive.

Institutionalized workplace discrimination is cumulative, historical, and reflects contemporary social issues (Miller and Garran, 2008, p. 66) which makes eradicating it convoluted and unlikely. Institutionalized discrimination weaves a web that not only systematically prohibits marginalized groups from progressing but also reinforces patriarchal values and majority privilege (Miller and Garran, 2008). Sky's experience underscores two salient points regarding workplace discrimination; 1) she is paid less but has the highest productivity, and 2) that her white male counterparts can abuse work time without penalty; however, she would be terminated for the same act. Sky's experiences are also influenced by a systematic, systemic support of male gender privilege and race privilege. Her experience is what Peggy McIntosh (1989, 1992) refers to when she speaks of invisible knapsacks of privilege white people enjoy. Initially invisible knapsacks of privilege referred mostly to male privilege in response to sexism and then later white privilege; however, any form of privilege—age, race, gender, or sexual orientation—reinforces a privileged group to ignore their advantages based upon acceptable differences. The inability to change workplace discrimination on a macro level forces individuals managing marginalized identities to negotiate their space and ultimately change how they respond to workplace discrimination on a micro level with the potential to influence change on a macro level. For instance, Magenta asserts

> You have to know, as an African American lesbian that you are here, you deserve to be here, and you are supposed to be here. And in knowing that from within, you can then... represent that on the outside (Cantey, 2010).

Acceptance of marginalized identities is the first step in addressing micro level discrimination. Constructing one's identity is a two-fold process: it is an inward acceptance of one's multiple selves and demonstrated outwardly. Claiming one's space is an interior and exterior embodiment of authenticity and empowerment. Claiming one's space is a function of self-defining. This is akin to what Melissa Harris-Perry (2011) refers to as crafting alternative images or Audre Lorde's (1997) reconstructing one's identity. When Magenta says, "you deserve to be here, you are supposed to be here. And in knowing that from within, you can then...represent that on the outside," she is discussing a transformative process. Through this transformation, Magenta and others are negotiating their authentic selves with being recognized as citizens. This notion of accepting self is inclusive of differences based on physical appearance (hair and style of dress), disposition, demeanor, gender, sexual orientation, race, or even age.

"To be Black and conscious in America is to be in a constant state of rage"- James Baldwin

Negotiating Differences

Understanding the politics of identity is essential to this discussion of negotiating space especially with the focus on women of color with intersecting identities. Essentialists challenge the concept of identity as fluid and conceptualize identity as determined, fixed, and without change from birth. Conversely, social constructivists conceptualize identity as fluid, negotiable, reflexive, and constructed through daily interactions with others (Abes, Jones, and McEwen, 2007). A social constructionist, unlike an essentialist, considers the impact each intersecting identity as valid while seeking an understanding of the lived experiences of all aspects of identity. For example, neither Sky, Vivacious, or Magenta identified a singular experience of their identity but each of them discussed experiencing intersecting discrimination based on differences. And while identity continues to evolve and change over time and space, it is constantly being reconstructed to mend fragmented experiences of race, gender, age, and sexuality. Ultimately these experiences force an individual to make meaning of her lived experiences (Reissman, 2008) by negotiating her space.

My exploration of the experiences of women of color in managing intersecting marginalized identities illuminates a number of core findings. . Findings revealed (1)the resilience of women of color; (2) the nature of the process of negotiating space to women of color; (3) the meaning of negotiating space to women of color; and (4) the ways in which women of color negotiate space. Negotiating space is a resistance strategy in response to oppressive spaces along with an interior and exterior embodiment of accepting differences. Negotiating space occurs when women of color are absent of choices (hooks, 2000). Negotiating space also involves making the invisible identity visible across communities and giving voice to a voiceless population in all socio-political spaces, to include workspaces. For instance, Vivacious discusses how to make an invisible identity visible.

> I feel… you know, like a survivalist, you know and there's a constant drive to create ways to make sure that who you are is represented equally and fairly because it's really not in the images that we get, you know, as far as Black woman is just concerned. There is really rarely that lesbian element not included in that so, you know, you see a lot of images of what Black women are supposed to be and they're already distorted and then, you know, the lesbian element is invisible so it feels to the individual to kind of myself to really strive to create ways to feel that void and filling that blank and tell those stories that are not being told accurately so, you know, you have to kind of be a warrior when you're a Black lesbian (Cantey, 2010).

Arguably, this notion of making the invisible identity visible is relevant for any marginalized group that is not recognized on a macro or micro level. For example, Vivacious' remark of filling in the blanks is aligned with Valdes' (2000) reminder to others of the missing identity when addressing differences in a shared space. Moreover, the meaning of negotiating space is being free to be one's self and being a complete person, comfortable with self, despite the occupied space. Negotiating space means you are creating spaces for your identity while preserving all aspects of self across multiple socio-political spaces. Feminism seeks to create spaces that are open for discussion and exchange on how to achieve equality and why it is imperative to have equality for all, especially those identified as the least of these.

> Invitational rhetoric is an invitation to understanding as a means to create a relationship rooted in equality, immanent value, and self-determination. Invitational rhetoric constitutes an invitation to the audience to enter the rhetor's world and to see it as the rhetor does (Foss and Griffin, 1992, p.5).

This invitation occurs when women of color negotiate their space and normalize difference and the balance of managing marginalized intersecting identities for dominant groups. Within invitational rhetoric, women of color are able to present different ways to create and negotiate their space. The idea of creating a space to discuss the value of equality and equity is a feminist school of thought however; it is not exclusive to only those who identify as feminist. Anyone seeking to centralize and understand "the experiences of all women, especially the women whose social conditions have been least written about, studied, or changed by political movements" (hooks, 2000, p.27) reflects a feminist school of thought. Ultimately, negotiating space is negotiating differences by normalizing these differences for those who reject differences. The process of normalizing s may be best understood through the lens of feminist communications theory.

Normalizing Difference through a Feminist Communication Theory Lens

Feminist communication theory is comprised of four specific tenets; 1) political, 2) explanatory, 3) polyvocal, and 4) transformative, which theorizes "gender, communication, and social change" (Wackwitz and Rakow, 2004, p. 5-6). Analyses of both Sky's and Vivacious' narratives illustrate the power of negotiating differences through political, explanatory, polyvocal, and transformative acts as a conduit to change. These actions are universal across spaces and although efforts may be challenging to change perception of differences within the workspace it begins with the individual on a personal level. Traditionally in feminist theory, the personal is associated with the political (Wackwitz and Rakow, 2004; Cole and Guy-Sheftall, 2003). "Women's voices are silenced in so many ways that the simple act of speaking may itself become a political act . . . It is a political act to create and open a feminist floor for debate to explore elements of difference, voice and representation" (Wackwitz and Rakow, 2004, p. 6). Although Sky did not speak up about her experience within her workplace to management, she was still able to have her voice heard by sharing her narrative through research. Speaking out does not always mean directly speaking to the individuals oppressing you, it means creating a space to be heard with the potential to influence and impact change on "political and institutional levels as well as the personal level" (Brown and McPhail, 2012, p. 114). Speaking out in an effort to negotiate one's space is necessary even at the risk of being bruised or misunderstood (Lorde, 1984).

The co-researchers' narratives illuminate our understanding regarding the complexities of workplace discrimination. The goal of informing and educating others about one's struggles and lived experiences is to facilitate normalizing identities that are publicized as abnormal and different. For instance in Vivacious' narrative, she expresses a desire to provide the truth of her lived experiences towards the goal of normalizing differences that are rejected at micro and macro levels in workspaces.

Narratives which reflect the varied experiences of workplace discrimination experienced by women of color are essential to influence change even at the risk of documenting conflicting interpretations of reality (Wackwitz and Rackow, 2004). Multiple voices and experiences are required to generate macro and micro level change. The multiplicity of experiences is a form of polyvocal. Creating a space to communicate and explain experiences related to discrimination allows women of color to "speak to and from the margins, recognizing that although theory can illuminate connections between elements of lived experience, lived experience is not always common experience" (2004, p.6). However, by speaking to and from the margins, others can begin to understand the impact of oppression and strategies of resistance.. With multiple voices (polyvocal experiences) in concert with the other tenets of feminist communication theory, sociopolitical change is more likely to occur in favor of oppressed groups. For instance, the previously noted example of the passage of the Lilly Ledbetter Act reflects an achievable outcome on a macro level. The passing of this bill validates Sky's presence within her workspace and affirms that she is qualified to be paid equally to her male counterparts for the same work performed, notwithstanding gender differences and gender inequalities. This change empowers Sky on a personal level, potentially improves her relationship with her colleagues, and also establishes macro level shifts to dismantle systemic and systematic discrimination. When successful change occurs on multiple levels and benefits all involved, the change is a transformative. To be transformative is to contribute "to intellectual and spiritual growth by providing different perspectives through which to conceptualize experiences and the structures of society" (Wackwitz and Rackow, 2004, p. 6). This experience, "promotes transformation of thought and inspires action by helping individuals and groups make sense of communication practices and the realties they engender" (2004, p.6).

The narratives of the co-researchers illustrate how women of color negotiate their differences by normalizing their identities through feminist communication theory. These examples represent how social change first begins within the individual in the hopes of making socio-political changes to discriminatory policies and procedures. Women of color learn to embrace and manage their intersecting identities through storytelling as a form of social activism (Crawley and Broad, 2004) and coping with discrimination with a vantage point.

Conclusion

Negotiating space in the workplace is about liberating one's self from internalized and externalized oppression. Challenging spaces that are not accepting of differences requires courage to stand against the grain. Silver's experience expands upon value of courage and the importance of women of color negotiating their space.

> But I was telling my girlfriend who loves Starbucks, loves, loves Starbucks, and on the Starbucks sign, one of the employees that day was trying to announce, what they were trying to do. Now hiring! They're trying to get people to come to Starbucks to work at Starbucks. And what they said is, 'We don't see difference.' What? If you don't see difference, hello? You're still pressing me. You trying to say you don't see color? That means you don't see me. You don't see that I'm a female. What the hell? No, you must see all of that, and then in seeing it, you accept it. You celebrate it. So, even in those terms we use, like I don't see color, well, I don't need to be around you. You know what I'm saying? So, I think we still need to figure out what it means to... first, we need to figure out how to use words because our words, words are oppressive. You know what I mean? And so, we need to figure out how to use words. We need to figure out what is spirituality, what is humanity, and then maybe, we could work towards eliminating oppression because it's all around in the simplest things. Even women, we have been programmed to dismiss each other in our language. So, yeah, it's very... we're very much embedded in this oppression, very much. I don't know if we could help it. I think it's something that's constant, to have to constantly remind ourselves and constantly teach each other (Cantey, 2010).

Silver's comments underscore how space is negotiated. She illustrates the processes involved in negotiating space, such as educating, explaining, and normalizing. Silver's notion of being programmed to reproduce oppression is aligned with James Baldwin's notion that the world is not the oppressor but we ourselves are our own oppressors when we duplicate what the world has taught us about oppression. "You know, it's not the world that was my oppressor, because what the world does to you, if the world does it to you long enough and effectively enough, you begin to do to yourself" (N. Cantey, pers. comm.). This mindset is aligned with accepting institutionalized discrimination and internalized oppression. This mindset also paralyzes women from reaching their maximum potential; however, when space is negotiated a development of an improved authentic self is formed.

Managing multiple marginalized identities is complex and becomes even more complicated when managing these identities in spaces that are not accepting of differences. Intersecting marginalized identities is a continuous battle with self-preservation, social inequalities, and institutionalized discrimination. The ability to transform views within the workplace on a micro and possibly a macro level is linked to women of color being proactive in negotiating their space, articulating their voice, and positioning self against socio-political oppression. Negotiating one's space is a method used by women of color to gain their personal freedom and help them to develop an authentic and positive identity of self (Roberts, 2000; Wade, 1997). When women of color discuss managing multiple intersecting identities with others they are helping to remove the stigma associated with differences and normalizing these differences in both the Black community and American culture.

Workplace discrimination represents our society's continuing struggle to achieve equality for all persons. Workplace discrimination may appear invisible or undetectable; however, individuals like Sky know from personal experience that workplace discrimination is very visible and active in separating employees based on differences. Ongoing research examining women of color who manage intersecting marginalized identities within socio-political spaces is essential. In the spirit of expanding research centered on understanding negotiated spaces, it is equally imperative to remain vigilant of the illusion of a post-racial America which has been underscored by the Obama era. Through this heightened awareness, researchers, practitioners, and subsequently policy-makers can work collectively to create policies within socio-political spaces which restricting discrimination against others based upon differences. Ultimately, ongoing research will advance the literature on the conceptualization of womanhood for women of color, illuminate the systematic rejection of differences within the workplace, and identify strategies used by women of color to manage differences within the workplace.

References

Abes, Elisa, Susan R. Jones, and Marylu K. McEwen. (2007). Reconceptualizing the model of multiple dimensions of identity: The role of meaning-making capacity in the construction of multiple identities. *Journal of College Student Development*, 48, no. 1:1-22.

Almquist, E.M. (1975). Untangling the effects of race and sex: The disadvantaged status of Black women. *Social Science Quarterly*, 56, 129-142.

Angelou, Maya. (1993). *Wouldn't take nothing for my journey now.* New York: Random House.

Bell, L.A., and Griffin, P. (1997). Pedagogical frameworks for social justice education. In M. Adams, L.A. Bell and P. Griffin (eds.), *Teaching for diversity and social justice: A sourcebook* (pp. 44-58).

Beauvoir de, Simone. (1989). *The second sex.* New York: Vintage Books Edition.

Brown, B. and McPhail, B. (2012). Feminist Theory. In Robbins, S., Chatterjee, P., and Canda, E. (eds) *Contemporary human behavior theory: A critical perspective for social work* (3rd ed.). Boston: Allyn & Bacon.

Cantey, N. I. (2010). Negotiating space: African descent woman managing multiple marginalized identities. Nova Southeastern University. Published Dissertation. *ProQuest.*

Cole, Johnetta B., and Beverly Guy-Sheftall. 2003. *Gender talk: The struggle for women's equality in African American communities.* Random House Publishing Group.

Crawley, S, and K.L Broad. (2004). Be Your (Real Lesbian) Self: Mobilizing Sexual Formula Stories through Personal (and Political) Storytelling. *Journal of Contemporary Ethnography* 33, no. 1: 39-71.

Damasio, A. (2000). *The feeling of what happens: Body, emotions and the making of consciousness.* London:Vintage.

Foss, Karen, Sonja K. Foss, & Cindy L. Griffin. (2004). *Readings in Feminist Rhetorical Theory.* Thousand Oaks: Sage Publications.

Foss, Sonja K. & Cindy L. Griffin. (1995). Beyond persuasion: A proposal for an invitational rhetoric. *Communication Monographs*, 62: 2-18.

Hall, F., and Ruth Fine. (2005). The stories we tell: The lives and friendship of two older black lesbians. *Psychology of Women Quarterly*, 29: 177-187.

Harrison, Faye (2012). Racism in the academy: Toward a multi-methodological agenda for anthropological engagement. In Smedley, A. and Hutchinson, J.F. (Eds.). *Racism in the Academy: The New Millennium.*

hooks, bell. (2000). *Feminist theory: From margin to center.* New York: Library of Congress.

Jones, Charisse and Kumea Shorter-Gooden. (2003). *Shifting: The double lives of Black women in America.* Harper Collins, Library of Congress.

Lorde, Audre. (1984). *Sister outsider: Essays and speeches.* Trumansburg NY: Crossing Press.

McIntosh, Peggy. (1990). White privilege: Unpacking the invisible knapsack. *Independent School.* Vol. 49, no.2.

Miller, Joshua and Garran, A. M. (2008). *Racism in the United States: Implications for the Helping Professions.* Brooks/Cole Cengage Learning.

Perry-Harris, Melissa. (2011). *Sister citizen: Shame, stereotypes, and Black women in America.* Yale: University of Press.

Riessman, C. 2007. *Narrative methods for the human sciences.* Thousand Oaks,CA: Sage.
Roberts, Susan. 2000. Development of a positive professional identity: Liberating oneself from the oppressor within. *Advance Nursing Science*, 22, 4: 71-82.
Robbins, S., Chatterjee, P., & Canda, E. (2012). *Contemporary human behavior theory: A critical perspective for social work* (3rd ed.). Boston: Allyn & Bacon.
Rosette, Ashleigh and Livingston, R. (2012). Failure is not an option for Black women: Effects of organizational performance on leaders with single versus dual subordinate identities. *Journal of Experimental Social Psychology*, 48, 1162 1167.
Swigonski, M.E. (1994). The logic of feminist standpoint theory for social work research. *Social Work*, 39(4), 387-393.
Tuan, Yi-Fu. (1977). *Space and place: The perspective of experience.* University of Minnesota Press.
Wackwitz, A.L., and L. F. Rakow. (2004). *Feminist Communication Theory.* Edited by A.L.Wackwitz and L. F. Rakow. Sage Publications.
West, Cornel. (2008). *Hope on a Tightrope: Words & Wisdom Cornel West.* New York: Smiley Books.

Chapter Two
Mammies, Maids & Mothers: Representations of African-American and Latina Women's Reproductive Labor in *Weeds*
Johnanna Ganz

Introduction

Weeds, an award-winning cable series, provide a darkly humorous look into suburban life. Nancy Botwin and her two sons, Silas and Shane, live in Agrestic, a fictional suburb of Los Angeles, and serve as the show's primary protagonists. After her husband's sudden heart attack, Nancy finds herself unable to pay the family's bills, and as a result, she becomes a small-time marijuana dealer with big dreams. However, in her race to become a drug kingpin, Nancy's family life often interrupts her plans, as she attempts to remain the ideal Parent-Teacher Alliance member and involved mom. In a television series dedicated to looking at white, wealthy, suburban life, two women of color appear regularly as a part of the storylines within the first two seasons of the series: Heylia James and Lupita.

Heylia James plays a significant role in Nancy's life, as she is Nancy's marijuana wholesale supplier—this means that Nancy buys quantities of marijuana from Heylia to break down and sell by smaller units. *Weeds* often depicts Heylia, a Black woman, as the bustling center of the urban home in which she lives with her adult children. Importantly, Heylia does not ever appear in Agrestic but rather remains located firmly in the inner city area Los Angeles. Lupita—one of the only regularly occurring characters without a surname—is a Latina woman who prominently figures into the early episodes; Nancy employs Lupita as a live-in domestic worker. Throughout the first two seasons, viewers watch as Lupita performs household tasks and increasingly comes to care for the two Botwin boys in Nancy's business related absences.

Each of these three women represents various aspects of reproductive labor, especially reproductive labor centered on caring for children. Child rearing work can be best understood through two types of labor: Mothering and care-work, as further defined below. In order to delineate between the act of providing care to children and the ideologically privileged ideal, I use the capitalized, "Mothering" to indicate the privileged act of reproductive labor. *Weeds* rely upon problematically racialized images of motherhood that exemplify the division between care-work and Mothering. In representing reproductive labor, *Weeds* constructs white women as the ideological standard for Mothering practices and women of color as more successful in the practice of care-work. Analyzing how *Weeds* constructs Heylia and Lupita in relationship to reproductive labor reveals representations that normalize and privilege whiteness, while denigrating women of color's abilities to perform Mothering. Yet, there is more to the depiction of reproductive labor present within *Weeds*. Viewers can negotiate alternative readings, in which Heylia and Lupita embody significant challenges to the normative representation of race and gender in popular media.

The purpose of this chapter is to analyze how *Weeds* relies upon racist tropes that construct women of color as incapable of Mothering. Despite the racist tropes, however, it becomes clear that Heylia and Lupita more successfully embody both aspects of Mothering and care-work. As a result, the women of *Weeds* must be examined through both a dominant and oppositional reading of the show's content. Such research offers nuances by presenting a cross-racial analysis that examines Black, Latina, and white relationships. Additionally, such work provides ideological space to consider both a dominant and oppositional reading of cultural representations, which moves beyond reductive claims surrounding women of color's subordination or resistance. In short, I argue that the depiction of reproductive labor in *Weeds* reflects a liminal space that neither fully negates nor fully endorses racist representations, which advances discussions of media imagery of motherhood at the intersections of race and gender.

Literature Review

Sharon Hays' 1998 foundational work *The Cultural Contradictions of Motherhood* examines the competing roles working mothers face: in the public sphere they must become ruthless competitors, adopting typically masculine qualities in order to succeed in the market. In the private sphere, Hays argues that mothers must eschew all aspects of the public by fully surrendering their individual identities in order to focus on their children, altruistically caring for a child's every need. Hays' refers to this conception of the private sphere with its all encompassing mothering identity as "intensive mothering." She concludes that these conflicting norms place untenable requirements on women's lives and entrench gender role boundaries.

Importantly, Hays does not differentiate between the types of reproductive labor demands mothers face. As a result, I argue that within *Weeds*' depictions of motherhood, a hierarchical structure undergirds cultural sensibilities surrounding reproductive labor, distinguished as care-work and Mothering. Care-work represents the physical labor required in caring for a child, such as bathing or feeding. The most important fact about care-work is that *anyone* is capable of performing these tasks, which denigrates their importance. Alternatively, Mothering represents the total emotional, mental, and spiritual commitment to every need of the child; this work is endowed with a sense of higher, moral purpose. Contemporary culture places restrictions on who can successfully perform the act of Mothering often limiting the role to the biological mother, making it a specialized form of child-rearing labor. Hays' concept does not strongly critique the underlying white, middle-class norms inherent within concept of "intensive mothering." As a result, I argue that care-work and Mothering rely on norms typically attributed to white, middle class women in order to determine a woman's abilities to care for children. Analyzing Lupita and Heylia's relationship to reproductive labor reveals some of these restrictions as well as possibilities for oppositional readings.

Historically, motherhood acted as a site for public discourse surrounding gender and racial roles. The mythology of the "republican mother" set strict norms that demanded upper-middle class; white women remain within the home, performing duties that did not require hard labor. Through the industrial revolution, notions of "good" wives shifted, marking women "good" if they became dependent consumers, which served to devalue all women's reproductive labor (Boydston, 1990). Middle-class, white women's primary purpose was to maintain the private sphere and ensure their children were properly educated—both morally and intellectually—in order to be desirable citizens (Kerber, 2010). Thus, while culture devalued women's care-work, Mothering became the primary task for women as it was a virtuous endeavor. Such ideology set the stage to mark all women incapable of being stay-at-home wives as inferior mothers, which translated into narrow racial constructions of "good" womanhood.

As a direct result of racializing cultural narratives, women of color were often constructed in terms of their "depraved" sexuality, particularly Black women. By using rhetoric that positioned Black women as hyper sexualized, amoral figures—women who were the opposite of pure and virtuous white mothers—white colonists legitimated the exploitation and denigration of women of color (Morgan, 2010). As Black women struggled to cope with the bonds of slavery and the responsibilities of the family unit, whites used motherhood as a weapon against slave women. For example, Americans used the legal system to keep slave women's children in bondage, through abolishing patrilineal laws regarding slave status. In 1662 American colonists stipulated a new act focusing on matrilineal status, which condoned the practice of rape in order to increase slave holdings (Martinot, 2007). For slave women and free Black women, motherhood was not a privileged act but rather a tool for white profit.

Further, popular images of Black women served to denigrate women's experiences. Scholars have noted the role of negative representations of assertive Black women in keeping Black women oppressed (Gilkes 1981; Harris 1982). Patricia Hill Collins advanced the analysis of negative images of Black women in her work *Black Feminist Thought* where she focuses on the controlling functions depictions such as the mammy and matriarch serve (1990). Expanding on this theoretical base, Dorothy Roberts argues that media uses four primary images to control the perceptions of Black women—jezebel, mammy, matriarch, and welfare queen (1999).

Of the controlling images of Black women identified by theorists, the mammy is depicted as a fat, dark-skinned, uneducated—but experientially intelligent—woman who often wears garish clothing; she embodies a freed Black woman who happily tends to the needs of white families (Turner, 1994). Through using the mammy image, whites not only portrayed Black women as completely without family and asexualized but also placed Black women firmly within the realm of difficult care-work—innately suited to caring for others. Shirley Hill examines aspects of both the mammy and matriarch present within the cultural notions of Black womanhood through the "Black cultural ethos of motherhood." The ethos constructs Black women as innately suited to difficult reproductive labor as well as being authoritative, matriarchal figures (2005). Images of the mammy and matriarch pervade even publications designed for Black women, such as *Essence* (Hazell and Clarke, 2008). Additionally, scholars have noted the problematic construction of Black and Latina mothers in contemporary advertising (Hirshman, 2011).

Latina/o figures lack positive representation or representation at all within mainstream media, and media has played a significant role in establishing Latina/o stars in problematic ways (Beltran, 2009; Berg, 2002). Latina women have similarly experienced racialized constructions of gender roles that exclude them from desirable images of womanhood through constructing Latina women as hypersexualized (Molina-Guzman, 2010). Alternatively, media asexualizes Latina women through constructing them as domestic workers, maids, or nannies (Padilla, 2009). The imagery pervades real life, as Mary Romero discusses problematic notions of gender and race within domestic service (2002). Romero recounts the shifts in domestic work, explaining that during the 1850s middle and upper-class White women hired maids to convey social status as a "lady" rather than simply a "woman'; as noted, "Middle-class women elevated their status by supervising the work of servant and shifted to roles of 'authority and activity, rather than passivity and isolation'" (2002, p. 54). She discusses how affluent families relied primarily on stigmatizing beliefs about Mexican populations in order to exploitatively fulfill service needs, shifting difficult care-work labor to Latina women. As a result of historical and contemporary constructions of motherhood as well as racialized representations, it is necessary to further examine depictions of race, gender, and motherhood that privilege normative cultural standards.

While the literature demonstrating problematic constructions of women of color is robust, many writers have responded to such reductive claims of the total subordination of women of color. bell hooks offers a crucial theoretical concept to this study through the notion of the oppositional gaze. The oppositional gaze challenges the power of the white and male gaze, as hooks writes,

"Spaces of agency exist for Black people...In resistance struggle, the power of the dominated to assert agency by claiming and cultivating 'awareness' politicizes 'looking' relations—one learns to look a certain way in order to resist" (hooks, 1992, p. 116). The oppositional gaze creates a space of liminality in which subordinate subjects may resist the process of domination; importantly, the oppositional gaze does not wholly deconstruct power relationships but rather disrupts them. As such, authors of color have complicated traditional notions surrounding motherhood typically associated with middle-class, white women's experiences. Bonnie Thornton-Dill discusses how slave mothers created naming systems or committed infanticide to protect their families and challenge white power (1988). Similarly, Patricia Hill Collins challenges color-blind notions of motherhood by de-centering white, middle-class experience and reasserting the experience of struggles for power inherent within a white supremacist society (Collins, 1994). Based upon a brief survey of the literature, it becomes clear that the representations of Heylia and Lupita have the potential to reinforce the boundaries of racialized motherhood; however their representation also offers transgressive potential through oppositional readings of the text.

Representations

Heylia James

Viewers of *Weeds* meet Ms. Heylia James within the first three minutes of episode 1 of Season 1 entitled, "You Can't Miss the Bear." She sits in her small kitchen with three of her younger family members, marijuana, plastic bags, and scales covering the tabletop. Nancy proudly displays her purchase of a knock-off handbag, insisting no one can tell the difference. Heylia glances at the bag and points out a bad stitch that indicates it is fraudulent. Heylia taunts, "Lookin' in da dictionary de other day. Saw your pitcha sittin' up innair. Right next to 'dumbass, white bitch'" (Kohan & Dannelly, 2005). Moments later, Nancy challenges that a bag of marijuana looks "light." All four family members instantly cease what they are doing; the three younger family members' jaws drop and all look to Heylia. Heylia, in thick African American Vernacular English (AAVE), verbally berates Nancy for questioning. Each person in the room nods, and Conrad—Heylia's nephew whom Heylia raised—tells Nancy to "never question Heylia's eyeballin'."

This introduction to Heylia highlights several facets of persistently problematic portrayals of Black women. Importantly, the show establishes Heylia as a street-savvy woman, who can spot a cheap bag a mile away. The first two sentences of her language—through the use of AAVE and minimal enunciation—immediately places her outside of white-associated middle-class standards. These two qualities simultaneously work to set her apart from the "well-spoken" and dainty Nancy Botwin, which hearkens back to the historical distinction between the proper white "Republican mother" and the garish Black mammy.

Such a clear distinction immediately produces Heylia as less capable of the ideologically and morally privileged act of Mothering.

The creators of *Weeds* call upon two specific, racially charged images to establish Heylia as a definitively "Black" woman, which reinforces cultural biases around mothers of color: the matriarch and the mammy. Importantly, the show uses these two images simultaneously, and Heylia's role shifts depending upon the context: with her family she serves as a matriarch and with others she assumes the role of the mammy. Woodard and Mastin describe the markings of the matriarch, "She represents the image of the Black woman as a mother within the Black home. The 1960's Moynihan Report solidified this image within the minds of many Americans with the image of a controlling, emasculating Black woman who dictated to both her children and her man their place in her home" (2005, p. 271). The show portrays Heylia as the matriarch, as everyone immediately defers to her when Nancy challenges the amount of marijuana in the bag. Another moment later in the same episode, "You Can't Miss the Bear," exemplifies Heylia's position as the matriarch: Heylia's daughter, Vaneeta, offers to babysit for her older brother, Keeyon. Heylia points out that Keeyon does not pay Vaneeta for her time. Keeyon asks, "Is this your business?" Heylia sharply shoots back, "Everything is my business" (Kohan & Dannelly, 2005). The use of the matriarch image marks Heylia as a deficient mother; she fails to live up to white, middle-class standards of the demure housewife who dotingly cares for the children. Through constructing Heylia as a controlling matriarch, the character cannot access the more refined, normatively white associated qualities of Mothering, which reinforces racial hierarchies.

The mammy figure is also present in the depiction of Heylia James, as she is a dark-skinned, physically large woman who typically wears garish clothing, complete with a bandana covering her dred-locked hair. Within the historical depiction, the mammy is often uneducated, often speaking with a thick dialect, as typified in a minstrel show. Within *Weeds*, Heylia's speech mimics qualities of that dialect in her failure to speak using language stereotypically associated with White speakers. Another aspect that marks Heylia as a mammy is her constant cooking. The act of cooking in and of itself is not a racialized image; however, Heylia is always cooking food for her family and also for Nancy, which must be considered within the context of a dominant reading. Heylia cooks foods such as grits or cornbread, which depicts the offerings of stereotypically Southern food, widely associated with African Americans. In line with the mammy concept, Heylia constantly carries out care-working tasks for the people around her; yet, the mammy is not capable of Mothering because she—historically—is morally deficient.

American culture has historically constructed the mammy as a figure who cares more for her white charges than for her own family (Turner, 2002). As such, Heylia often serves the role of the mammy directly to Nancy, who can be read as a child within the world of drug dealing. Heylia offers care to Nancy by lending advice or forgiving mistakes that she does not offer to any other characters. An example of such behavior occurs in Episodes 8 and 9 of Season 2 when

Heylia cuts Conrad out of the family business, because he makes an unapproved (by Heylia) deal with Nancy. In this particular instance, Nancy literally outgrows Heylia; Conrad and she grow a strain of marijuana called "MILF weed" that nearly puts Heylia out of business. After Heylia discovers the betrayal, she places severe restrictions on Conrad's behaviors—simultaneously reflecting the power of the matriarch and assuming the role of the mammy—as she continues to do business with Nancy (Schepps & Zisk, 2006; Groff & Misiano, 2006). Moments such as these reflect the imagery of the mammy who is incapable of Mothering, as intensive mothering suggests that children "should" outgrow a mother's care. In a dominant reading of the text, Heylia fails to transition her adult children beyond the household and into the public sphere.

Weeds provides a final contrast within a dominant reading that constructs Heylia as a "failed" mother, which can be seen through the differences between the type of business Nancy and Heylia conduct. While both women deal marijuana, Nancy's territory remains in the gated, suburban community of Agrestic. Her work is not difficult, violent, or frightening; the show regularly depicts Nancy enacting her drug transactions while lounging in the sun at her son's soccer game. Comparatively, Heylia lives in an impoverished area with dilapidated buildings, stereotypical markings of an inner city neighborhood. Her life stands as an exemplar of the "Black cultural ethos of motherhood" as defined by Shirley Hill, which constructs Black women as fierce, independent and capable of handling anything, including violence (Hill, 2005).

An example of this imagery and the stark contrast between Heylia and Nancy appears in Episode 5 of Season 1 titled, "Lude Awakening," wherein a drive-by shooting targets Heylia's home. All members of Heylia's clan take cover, while Nancy continues standing, dumbfounded until Conrad pulls her to the ground. The camera focuses on Heylia and a pregnant Vaneeta pulling out semi-autmatic guns. Afterwards, Heylia stands up, asks if everyone is okay, and continues going about business, apparently relatively unaffected by the event. Nancy can hardly function; she falls apart (Shepard & Rose, 2005). This scene's dominant reading suggests that Heylia has socialized her children to manage the micro-assaults which are central to existing in their community environment, which makes the failure of moral Mothering clear as no mother "should" normalize violence in her children's lives. Despite this proscription, it can be argued she provides care-work, because she provides for the practical survival needs of her children.

Weeds prevent viewers from connecting to the James family by constructing such violence as normalized in their home. In a dominant reading, *Weeds* presents Heylia as a threat to her children, as she fails in her maternal duties by taking on aspects of the matriarch and mammy; she is destructive through her inability to move beyond care-work. The shooting highlights the racialized differences between Nancy and Heylia. Viewers are left with a strong sense of pity for Nancy as she is terribly shaken. However, viewers are encouraged to feel no pity for Heylia or her family, despite the fact that an eight-month pregnant woman also experienced the same shooting. Hard reproductive labor and a violent life do not seem to be of concern, as it is all in a day's work for the Black matriarch/mammy and her family.

Despite the use of racial tropes to construct Heylia, upon reading the character through an oppositional lens, Heylia more successfully embodies the aspects of Hays' intensive mothering than Nancy. Heylia is capable of managing a presence in both the public and private spheres; she maintains a successful business as a supplier—she and her family are not runners or dealers but rather have a well-developed network to minimize danger to the family unit—though with the choice to deal marijuana, the danger can never be fully eradicated as the scene in which a shooting occurs demonstrates. As such, Heylia is a smart and savvy businesswoman—an aspect of intensive mothering of which Nancy is incapable. Nancy consistently makes mistakes and tries to operate as a fun-loving, flighty dealer within her community. Consequently, Nancy fails to care for her family effectively as various characters repeatedly threaten to harm her children.

An instance of Heylia's ability to take on an effective business savvy edge appears in Episode 3 of Season 1 titled, "Good Shit Lollipop," when Heylia initially sells only low quality marijuana to Nancy; Nancy discovers this fact and is enraged. Nancy confronts Heylia by demanding a refund since she can no longer sell the low-quality product. Heylia calmly and slowly responds, "And I want an ass like Beyonce's. Ain't neither of us getting what we want." Nancy produces a list of high end product while demanding that Heylia fill the order. Nancy hands Heylia a small stack of bills and goes to grab the product; Heylia stops her informing her that, "Serious shit calls for serious cash, and your cash got a sense of humor" (Benabib & Zisk, 2005). Nancy leaves frustrated, yet Heylia proves to be the smarter businesswoman, refusing to allow Nancy's sense of entitlement to dictate the sale. Heylia does not apologize to Nancy for selling her low quality marijuana, but rather admonishes her for not asking more questions in order to learn the business better.

This interaction highlights the effectiveness of Heylia's public persona, in which she simultaneously serves as a model for Conrad and Vaneeta who watch the entire transaction. In Hays' model of intensive mothering, a "good" mother must do everything she can in the public sphere to provide the best possible experience for her children in the private sphere; mothers must adopt a calloused persona in the working world. In depicting Heylia as an unapologetic businesswoman, we see that she attempts to provide the best possible life and model for her children. Here, viewers can oppositionally read Heylia as providing not only care-work but Mothering qualities as well—though her Mothering work stands slightly outside of white cultural norms. If one reinterprets the meaning of Mothering work that recognizes social disparities and racism, then the logical conclusion is that Heylia is capable of Mothering. She provides her children with the ideological and moral tools to be effective citizens in the white supremacist system. Thus, the most important aspect of the above interaction is Heylia's refusal to apologize; it stands as a defiant moment in which the racial order is disrupted. In that scene, Heylia embodies neither the mammy who must bow to the white family nor the matriarch who damages her family through such complete control; rather, she provides a positive model of Black power for her family. In hooks' conception of the oppositional gaze, Heylia politicizes looking relations, literally and figuratively: she gazes long at Nancy as she doles out verbal admonishments and refuses to give into Nancy's entitlement. Heylia successfully negotiates racial relationships and advances her family's understanding of how to respond to privilege.

Within the private sphere, one may read against the grain to see Heylia as more successfully embodying "good" motherhood. While *Weeds* uses many markers to stigmatize Heylia, it cannot be ignored that Heylia has a tightly knit family. Heylia has successfully raised her own two children as well as a nephew, and each member of the family is loyal to Heylia. Even when Conrad makes the decision to work with Nancy against Heylia's wishes, Heylia protects Conrad when he runs into trouble as a direct result of Nancy's personal and professional blunders. Heylia provides a monetarily and emotionally stable environment for her family by maintaining a strong presence in the household. In the first season, Heylia provides her pregnant daughter with whatever care she needs; in the second season, *Weeds* consistently shows Heylia happily interacting with Vaneeta and her "grandbaby." These moments clearly demonstrate Heylia's ability to Mother and perform care-work.

In contrast, through the progression of the first two seasons, Nancy's family falls into disrepair, as her sons each become more delinquent—culminating in Silas stealing Nancy's stash, leaving her with five hostile guns pointed at her at the end of season two. Heylia's family does not leave her stranded as does Nancy's family. Quite the opposite, Heylia's family is that which Nancy so desperately desires—stable, loving, and mutually supportive. In an oppositional reading Heylia more effectively embodies the aspects of care-work and Mothering by offering her family unconditional love, support, and the tools to be effective citizens in the public sphere.

As a result of both a dominant and oppositional reading, it becomes clear that the writers of *Weeds* present conflicting messages about Black motherhood. On one hand, the show presents Heylia through the lens of two stigmatizing representations: the mammy and the matriarch. These problematic images persist in the depiction of Black women and present women of color as incapable of successfully embodying Mothering. On the other hand, one may read against the grain of the show to find that Heylia can arguably be considered a more successful mother, as she maintains her business and family.

Lupita

Nancy's personal, live-in domestic worker, Lupita, offers another example of a woman of color who performs reproductive labor within *Weeds*. The show presents Lupita as a late-middle aged, Mexican woman, and a woman with no family and very few ties outside of the Botwin household. In fact, she exists primarily in and for the Botwin family, however *Weeds* consistently undermines Lupita's contributions to the family economy by marking Lupita as a racial outsider. Within a dominant reading, Lupita appears unable to gain access to Mothering and has extremely limited access to even care-work as a result of her marginalization. However, Lupita also holds the possibility of being read as a subversive force that undermines racialized relationships with the Botwins.

To understand the limiting representations of Latino Americans, it is necessary to understand that Latinos currently suffer stronger stigma than any other "despised out-group," which promotes exploitation of subordinated populations (Massey, 2009). While not recognized as a part of the despised out-group *immediately*, the show actively marks Lupita in ways that place the out-group stigma on her. For example, throughout the first two seasons, Lupita speaks with an extremely thick Spanish accent; she often reverts to her first language when angry or upset. These actions audibly mark Lupita as an outsider, one who does not occupy the same space as the White family, placing her outside of the speaking norms associated with whiteness.

Weeds depicts Lupita as progressively more lazy, which plays on stereotypes of Mexican Americans; this subtly marks Lupita as incapable of accessing normative markers of womanhood as she cannot even perform basic reproductive labor. For example in Episode 8 of Season 1 entitled, "The Punishment Light," Nancy's brother-in-law tells Lupita to order him pizza. She throws up her hands and says out loud, "Do I look like his fucking maid" (Jones & Berlinger, 2005)? Here, the joke becomes the fact that many viewers would identify her as a maid, but Lupita does not see herself as such; this incongruity forms the joke. At the start of season two, the dishwasher is broken and Lupita refuses to wash the dishes. When Nancy threatens to fire her in Episode 1 of Season 2 titled, "Corn Snake," Lupita reminds her that she could turn Nancy into the police, effectively black mailing Nancy while refusing to do housework (Kohan & Zisk, 2006). Finally, Nancy takes all of Lupita's cleaning supplies to work on a project. When she returns, Lupita sits at the kitchen table flipping through a magazine, and Nancy apologizes. Lupita, transparently condescending, tells Nancy that she should ask before she takes the supplies because Lupita could get "nothing done." Lupita smugly smiles at Nancy, as both women understand Lupita no longer does housework (Kohan & Zisk, 2006). Depicting Lupita as progressively more lazy marks a shift, in which, Lupita's already limited access to care-work becomes irrelevant, as she no longer performs care-work tasks. Lupita fails at completing any facet of reproductive labor, thereby diminishing her contributions to the family economy. As the only Latina represented consistently during the first two seasons, *Weeds* fails to show Latina women as capable of performing reproductive labor.

Several other aspects of the dominant reading underscore Lupita's outsider and unfit status. The show also marks Lupita as untrustworthy though she lives with the family. In Episode 6 of Season1 titled, "Dead in the Nethers," when she searches the house for drugs after a discussion with her cousin, Shane (the youngest son) walks up to her and asks, "Are you stealing from us?" He goes on, "Mom said that you once stole one of her rings." Lupita, visibly shocked and hurt, replies, "What?" Shane concludes that Nancy later found the ring and bounces off to play outside (Platt, Safchik & Sanford, 2005). This accusation marks Lupita as morally unfit, foreclosing access to Mothering. Additionally, despite Nancy's insistence that Lupita "is like one of the family," Lupita rarely occupies the same leisure space as the family. Often she resides within the context of the kitchen, an area specifically marked for domestics, as Romero points out (2002). Finally, white characters consistently address Lupita by her first name. Yet, conversely, Lupita calls all white adults by more formal names, such as "Mrs. Nancy," another way that domestics show deference (2002). Examples such as these ensure that Lupita can only be read as inferior to the white family by hearkening back to the problematic historical construction of the white "republican mother" as a morally superior and women of color as morally bankrupt or unfit for Mothering.

Importantly, Lupita exists not as a housekeeper—someone who maintains a mostly clean home—but as a maid—someone who performs hard physical labor, emotional labor, shows deference, and deals with tasks that other household members could easily handle. Contradictorily, the maid is defined outside of the roles of a mother though she performs nearly identical tasks. One example occurs in Episode 3 of Season 1 when the oldest boy, Silas, gets blue spray paint on his boxers. Rather than dealing with his own mistake, he tosses them into the laundry, and Lupita repeatedly scrubs at the stain. Silas later states to a friend, "My maid thinks I fucked a smurf" (Benabib & Zisk, 2005). The operative set of words, "my maid" suggests that not only is Lupita a "maid" available for Silas' every task, but also she *belongs* to him. A typical type of interaction, this places Lupita outside of the upper-middle class family through her status as "owned" and a "maid" rather than an autonomous housekeeper. Within a dominant reading, these tactics degrade Lupita's significant reproductive labor, allowing viewers to privilege Nancy's minimal Mothering and denigrate Lupita's care-work.

Such a depiction remains consistent with white perceptions of Chicana domestic workers in Romero's study when the working relationship resembles mistress/maid. Often based on interpersonal relationships, manipulation and entitlement, the mistress/maid relationship allows whites to perceive the domestic as constantly available, ready to do "extra" work, and needing little compensation for her tasks (2002). In contrast, contemporary domestics work to develop a professionalized relationship of employer/employee by minimizing personal relationships through establishing contracts, refusing "extra" tasks, not accepting live-in positions, and cutting off distracting, one-sided conversations (2002). Clearly, Nancy and Lupita live within an unequal mistress/maid dichotomy rather than a more professionalized relationship. Such a relationship allows for the continued exploitation of Lupita's reproductive labor, which stigmatizes her contributions to the family economy and limits her access to Mothering.

The *Weeds* universe organizes reproductive labor in ways that mark Lupita as an outsider to standards associated with middle-class whiteness. Relying on racist stereotyping and conventions, *Weeds* offers little rearticulation of domestic service work within a dominant reading. Rather, the show reifies social boundaries that stigmatize Lupita; in this process, whiteness becomes reaffirmed as the desirable norm. Despite Nancy's repeated claims of "I am the mother!" she infrequently performs the more difficult tasks of reproductive labor, which American culture assigns to the domestic sphere. Her affluence allows her to shift her labor to another source—women of color. Importantly, this does not interfere with Nancy's access to reproductive labor or Mothering, because Americans readily accept the displacement of difficult, undervalued labor onto racial out-groups.

Similarly to Heylia, *Weeds* relies upon negative racial imagery to construct Lupita as a stigmatized outsider through presenting her only as a deficient, domestic worker incapable of care-work. However, as with Heylia, there is space to negotiate an alternative reading of Lupita's presence on the show. Despite the fact that *Weeds* constructs her as without a family of her own, her work with the Botwin children and her refusal to participate in racial structures of domination offer a challenge to the dominant reading of the text by renegotiating the boundaries of who can perform Mothering work.

One of the primary outcomes from Nancy's entry into the working world is the increased reliance upon Lupita for taking care of the household. While the show initially constructs Nancy as the one who Mothers Silas and Shane, she slowly drifts out of contact with her children. In her place, Lupita picks up the slack, moving beyond routine upkeep of the house. Lupita becomes more aware of the events in Nancy's children's lives than Nancy. This is most evident when Shane attempts to get his mother to pay attention to him in the episode, "Dead in the Nethers." Nancy gets ready to leave for an evening out at a dance club and quickly brushes him off. Afterwards, Shane runs to Lupita asking, "Do you want to help me build a pillow fort?" Lupita excitedly agrees to spend time with Shane, who is ecstatic to have someone to play with him (Platt, Safchik & Sanford, 2005). Lupita assumes both the role of care-work and Mothering by entertaining and emotionally supporting Shane. While there are only a few moments such as this, these moments provide an opportunity to read against the grain and see Lupita as more connected and nurturing than Nancy. Such a moment radically changes the meaning of Mothering, as within the concept of intensive mothering only a biological mother can fully assume Mothering work because of its privileged position. Lupita's participation in Mothering Shane challenges the limited images of Latina women as capable of only being care-workers.

Perhaps one of the most important moments for Lupita's public life that can be re-interpreted through hooks' oppositional gaze occurs at the moment she hands Nancy the pillowcase filled with marijuana in "Dead in the Nethers." She triumphantly drops the pillowcase into Nancy's hand, smiles coyly, and states, "Sweet dreams. I want a raise," before walking away from her white employer. While on initial reading this may be understood as a manipulative move, upon closer examination this event marks a significant disruption in the gendered and racial order. In several previous episodes, Nancy had informed Lupita that she would be unable to pay her but would do so later. This moment acts as a response to Lupita going without pay for her already undervalued reproductive labor: for the first time Lupita has a modicum of control over her life. Lupita asserts her value within the family economy opening up access to different ways of conceptualizing reproductive labor.

Additionally, from "Dead in the Nethers," Lupita demonstrates an acute awareness of the racial disparities around her. When she meets with her younger cousin who reveals Nancy is a drug dealer, at first, Lupita does not believe her. When the cousin asks, "How does she afford all of this?" gesturing around to the house, Lupita quips, "Simple, she is a skinny white lady in America" (Platt, Safchik & Sanford, 2005). This moment draws attention to the racial dynamics within not only the household but also the larger culture; the writers provide an opportunity to acknowledge racial privilege, even if just for a moment. Lupita's acknowledgement of racial privilege acts as a moment of gazing back, daring to look hard at the structures that keep her subordinated. As a result of drawing attention to the class and racial privileges that allow white women to shift their difficult reproductive labor tasks to women of color, the script of *Weeds* can subtly consider the implications of undervaluing the women who perform care-work for pay.

As a result of evaluating both the dominant and oppositional reading of Lupita, it is clear that the writers clearly construct Lupita as a racial outsider, particularly through the racial trope of a Latina woman as a domestic worker. This racist construction lends itself to the realm of reproductive labor in which Nancy overtly undervalues Lupita's contributions to the household. However, several aspects of the characterization of Lupita provide subtle opportunities to challenge the gendered and racial orders implicit within such an unequal distribution of power. Further, there are specific moments that reveal Lupita as more connected and capable of Mothering than Nancy. Despite the dominant reading, Lupita can be read as having access to Mothering despite her non-biological relationship to the boys; this significantly alters the narrow conceptions of who is capable of performing Mothering. In short, Lupita's actions and dialogue have the capacity to disrupt normative imagery of Latina women within media.

Conclusion

Imagery saturated with racial ideologies and tropes prevail within contemporary media; these images often present cultural conceptions of not only race but also gender. The depictions of the desirable or "good" mother remains based on white, upper-middle class conceptions of womanhood. These notions particularly grow out of historical constructs and cultural norms associated with Whiteness come to be the standards by which all women are judged as mothers. Such representations fail to take into account racial disparities. As a result, *Weeds* provides a unique position that offers the presentation of racial tropes that foreclose women of color's access to both aspects of reproductive labor: care-work and Mothering. However, *Weeds* also allows for opportunities to read the narrative oppositionally, which opens up the possibility of seeing women of color's reproductive labor in a positive light.

In constructing a Black mother, the show depicts Heylia using two problematic images of Black womanhood: the mammy and the matriarch. American culture has historically used the mammy figure to deny Black women access to privileged aspects of reproductive labor and to ensure that Black women's labor could be easily exploited. The image of the matriarch serves a specific purpose of undermining Black women's abilities as mothers—citing them as monstrously powerful women who damage their children. As such, white women become coded as the only ones capable of Mothering. However, in examining Heylia's character more closely, it becomes clear that Heylia is capable of effectively caring for her family. Moreover, Heylia's refusal to accept Nancy's exercise of white privilege offers further nuances to discussions surrounding the disruption of gendered and racialized norms.

Similarly, *Weeds* constructs the character Lupita through a racialized lens, one that marks her as an outsider by relying upon specific tropes about Mexican Americans women, who are often portrayed as domestic workers. Further, *Weeds* uses tropes to provide an image of Lupita as manipulative, lazy, and as failing to fit into middle-class white norms of language and behavior. As a result of this stigmatized status, Lupita's access to both care-work and Mothering becomes limited; Lupita is eternally the domestic worker who can fully participate only in undervalued care-work. Yet, *Weeds* also provides moments in which Lupita disrupts racial and gendered orders through her increased presence in the household as a positive emotional support for Nancy's children as well as explicitly acknowledging Nancy's racial privilege.

This study offers an initial entry into a larger discussion around the representation of not just gender but also race in the media representation of motherhood. By critically examining both aspects of each character—the problematic use of negative racial stereotypes as well as the defiant oppositional gaze embedded within certain moments—the opportunity to negotiate several readings allows for a better understanding of how race and gender operate within contemporary media. Importantly, each character contains the possibility of multiple readings; neither reading diminishes the importance of the other. Rather, the two readings complicate one another and offer a different way of looking at structures of domination and subordination, wherein liminality becomes an important conclusion. There is no clear-cut reading of Heylia and Lupita as entirely embracing or dispelling racialized notions of reproductive labor. Rather, Heylia and Lupita represent both negative and positive aspects of the portrayals of women of color within media and this space of negotiating difficult racial and gendered terrain mirrors women's real life experiences.

The practical implications of understanding the continual operations of racist imagery and the theoretical tools to undermine power structures provides the opportunity to renegotiate cultural meanings for all women and mothers. Learning to read media texts through an oppositional lens offers ways to de-stabilize power structures for marginalized communities and create coalitions by recognizing moments of power, privilege, and resistance. By examining the historical constructions of reproductive labor, the exploitation and devaluation of all of women's labor becomes clear; depicting women as competing for varying forms of privilege forecloses opportunities for coalition building. Constructing norms of desirable motherhood proves damaging to communities, labor systems, and interpersonal relationships. As a result, consumers of media—especially in a media saturated cultures—must continue to read oppositionally and find moments of challenge to normative depictions of racialized and gendered bodies in order to disrupt dominating power structures.

References

Beltran, M. C. (2009). *Latina/o Stars in U.S. Eyes: The Making and Meanings of Film and TV Stardom*. Chicago: University of Illinois Press.

Benabib, R. (Writer) & Zisk, C. (Producer). (2005). Good Shit Lollipop [Television series episode]. In J. Kohan (Producer), *Weeds*. New York: Showtime.

Berg, C. R. (2002). *Latino Images in Film: Stereotypes, Subversion, and Resistance*. Austin: University of Texas Press.

Boydston, J. (1990). *Home and Work: Housework, Wages, and the Ideology of Labor in the Early Republic*. New York: Oxford University Press.

Collins, P.H., (1990). *Black Feminist Thought: Knowledge, Consciousness, and the Politics of Empowerment*. New York: Routledge.

Collins, P.H., (1994). Shifting the Center: Race, Class, and Feminist Theorizing About Motherhood. In E. N. Glenn & G. Chang, & L.R. Forcey (Eds.), *Mothering: Ideology, Experience, and Agency*. New York: Routledge.

Gilkes, C. T., (1980). "Holding Back the Ocean with a Broom": Black Women in Community Work. In La Frances, R. R. (Ed.), *The Black Woman* (217-231). California: Sage.

Groff, R. (Writer) & Misiano, C. (Director). (2006). Bash [Television series episode]. In J. Kohan (Producer), *Weeds*. New York: Showtime.

Hays, S. (1998). *The Cultural Contradictions of Motherhood*. New Haven: Yale University Press.

Hazell, V., & Clarke, J., (2008). Race and Gender in the Media: A Content Analysis of Advertisements in Two Mainstream Black Magazines. Journal of Black Studies, 39 (1), 5-21.

Harris, Trudier. (1982). *From Mammies to Militants: Domestics in Black American Literature*. Philadelphia: Temple University Press.

Hill, S. (2005). *Black Intimacies: A Gender Perspective on Families and Relationships*. New York: Alta Mira Press.

Hirshman, E. C. (2011). Motherhood in Black and Brown: Advertising to U.S. Minority Women. *Advertising & Society Review*, 12 (2), np.

hooks, b. (1992). *Black Looks: Race and Representation*. New York: Routledge.

Jones, Rolin (Writer) & Berlinger, R. (Producer). (2005). The Punishment Light [Television series episode]. In J. Kohan (Producer), *Weeds*. New York Showtime.

Kohan, J. (Writer) & Dannelly, B. (Director). (2005). You Can't Miss the Bear [Television series episode]. In J. Kohan (Producer), *Weeds*. New York: Showtime.

Kohan, J. (Writer) & Dannelly, B. (Director). (2005). Free Goat [Television series episode]. In J. Kohan (Producer), *Weeds*. New York: Showtime.

Kohan, J. (Writer) & Zisk, C. (Director). (2006). Corn Snake [Television series episode]. In J. Kohan (Producer), *Weeds*. New York: Showtime.

Kerber, L. K., (2010). The Republican Mother and the Woman Citizen: Contradiction and Choices in Revolutionary America. In L. K. Kerber & J. S. De Hart & C. H. Dayton (Eds.), *Women's America: Refocusing the Past* (37-46). Oxford: Oxford University Press.

Martinot, S. (2007). Motherhood and the Invention of Race. *Hypatia*, 22 (2), 79 97.

Massey, D.S., (2009). Racial Formation in Theory and Practice: The Case of Mexicans in the United States. *Race and Social Problems*, 1 (1), 12-26.

Molina-Guzman, I. (2010). *Dangerous Curves: Latina Bodies in the Media*. New York: New York University Press.

Morgan, J. (2010). "Some Could Suckle over Their Shoulder." European Depictions of Indigenous Women, 1492-1750. In L. K. Kerber & J. S. De Hart & C. H. Dayton (Eds.), *Women's America: Refocusing the Past* (37-46). Oxford: Oxford University Press.

Padilla, Y. M.(2009). Domesticating Rosario: Conflicting Representations of the Latina Maid in U.S. Media. *Arizona Journal of Hispanic Cultural Studies*, 13(1), 41 59.

Platt, M., Safchik, B. (Writers) & Sanford, A. (Director). (2005). Dead in the Nethers [Television series episode]. In J. Kohan (Producer), *Weeds*. New York Showtime.

Roberts, D. (1999). *Killing the Black Body: Race, Representation, and the Meaning of Liberty.* New York: Vintage.

Romero, M., (2002). *Maid in the U.S.A.*. Great Britain: Routledge.

Schepps, S. (Writer) & Zisk, C. (Director). (2006). MILF Money [Television series episode]. In J. Kohan (Producer), *Weeds*. New York: Showtime.

Shepard, D. (Writer) & Rose, L. (Director). (2005.) Lude Awakening [Television series episode]. In J. Kohan (Producer), *Weeds*. New York: Showtime.

Thornton-Dill, B., (1988). Our Mothers' Grief: Racial Ethnic Women and the Maintenance of Families. *Journal of Family History,* 13 (4), 415-431.

Turner, P. A. (2002). *Ceramic Uncles and Celluloid Mammies: Black Images and Their Influence on Culture.* University of Virginia: University of Virginia Press.

Woodard, J. B., & Mastin, T., (2005). Black Womanhood: Essence and its Treatment of Stereotypical Images of Black Women. *Journal of Black Studies*, 36 (2), 264-281.

Chapter Three
Being Black Academic Mothers
Angela K. Lewis
Sherri L. Wallace
Clarissa L. Peterson

Introduction

A career in academe can be very rewarding. As Alfred (2001) surmises, it provides administrators and faculty the freedom to pursue their own research interests, autonomy and control over their work, and opportunities for stimulating, creative and intellectual development (p. 57). It also provides flexibility in raising a family. Yet, despite the flexibility, there is often conflict in balancing professional careers and family life, specifically for women scholars.

Academic mothers are members of two "greedy institutions"—the university and the family (Grant, Kennelly & Ward, 2000). Both entities demand undivided loyalty and commitment. Given these demands, research suggests that many women in the academy choose not to have families due to the traditional male-dominated structure and culture in academe, even though some studies found no significant decline in research productivity for academic mothers per se (Spalter-Roth & VanVooren, 2008). However, the most important time of a professor's career, commonly referred to as "pretenure," often occurs simultaneously with a woman's peak biological reproductive years (Wilson, 1995). Interestingly, the literature on this subject is limited and is virtually silent on Black women academic mothers.

Given that Black women constitute a small number within the academy, despite their implicit and explicit roles in education and Black life, the purpose of this work is to highlight the experiences of Black academic mothers who are successfully navigating their professional careers while raising their children. Using autoethnography, as an analytical framework, the authors discuss their roles as Black academic mothers. The authors' experiences, with their personal choices, challenges and resistance to the traditional male-dominated structure and culture in the academy, are highlighted to illustrate emerging themes that can facilitate discussion and action. Rather than a definitive study, this critical exploration seeks to heighten awareness of the impact and uniqueness of Black academic mothers in higher education and provide recommendations for understanding and improving working conditions for mothers in academe.

Literature Review

Academic Mothers

Generally, women in academe face numerous decisions which may impact career advancement. The first is whether to have a family. Mason and Goulden (2002) found that the majority of tenured women faculty across most academic disciplines are more unlikely to have children. This may be largely because the traditional six-year "tenure clock" assumes freedom from family or impending personal responsibilities (Grant, Kennelly & Ward, 2000).

The second decision women faculty face is when to have a child. Studies reveal that the timing of starting a family is often complex and can significantly impact a woman's academic career trajectory (Ackelsberg, Binion, Duerst-Lahti, Junn, Assendelft & Yoon, 2004; Assendelft, Gunther-Canada & Dolan, 2001). Although advances in medical technology may help to make the decision to delay motherhood easier for academic women, some women still decide to have children despite the structure of the academy. Those who do may utilize the "hidden pregnancy phenomenon" where they hide or minimize their maternal desires throughout their careers. They may also hide their pregnancy in an effort to accommodate unwritten professional standards (Armenti, 2004; Wilson, 1995). Others attempt to time their pregnancies to have "May babies" to lessen the "disruption" of childbirth to the academic calendar as well as not to burden their colleagues with "covering" their professional obligations (Wilson, 1999).

Despite subtle gains for family-friendly policies in the academy, there are still failures when considering the overall campus culture and the provision of family-leave policies at most universities. Many universities still do not have "tenure stop" policies for family-leave and even more have no child care facilities on campus. Additionally, in some fields, there may be a "wage penalty" for mothers, even when no statistically significant differences were found in levels of productivity (Spalter-Roth & VanVooren, 2008). Williams (2005) describes this as the "maternal wall," which is discrimination against working mothers. The lack of consistency for pro-family policies tends to create a "chilly climate" for those who wish to start families.

The academy still has farther to go to adequately address the issues of balancing work and family. In short, both sexism and "mommyism" limits advancement of women faculty prompting some women faculty to leave academe. Deciding when to have children can affect the tenure clock in terms of productivity and job obligations, which is why some women feel the need to "hide" pregnancies or plan for "May" deliveries, particularly in the absence of uniform family-leave policies. Those who have children often feel the need to increase productivity, realizing that they can be penalized on job performance reviews and receive lower wages. Still, some women faculty settle for lower ranks, term appointments or simply leave academe altogether, despite its freedom and flexibility. Overall, while motherhood may negatively impact a woman's career trajectory in the academy; the academy itself can have a negative impact on an academic mother's personal and family life. As a result, women in the academy are more likely to be single, divorced, and childless or tend to delay childbirth longer than the average woman (Mason & Goulden, 2002).

Black Women Academicians

Historically, Black women in the academy were formal educators in newly-formed Historically Black Colleges and Universities (HBCUs), who specialized in the "humbler trades" such as nursing, home economics, or moral teaching, and focused on the moral, social, and educational development of young Black women as "uplifters" of their race, families and communities (Collins, 2001, p. 32; Gregory, 1995; Harley, 2008). Today, Black women academicians hold only 3% of total faculty positions (U.S. Department of Education, National Center for Education Statistics, Integrated Postsecondary Education Data System, Fall Staff Section 2009: Table 20) and differ in experiences, background, appearances, and beliefs (Collins, 2001); however, they share some similar characteristics.

First, Black women academicians earn doctorates at rates higher than their Black male counterparts but still tend to be older than the average student and take longer to obtain their degrees, often due to the nontraditional paths taken into careers in academe (Thomas, 2001). Also, they are more often single/never married or divorced, raising children alone, and are typically first- or second-generation college graduates. Like early Black women educators, contemporary Black women scholars are most likely to earn their doctorates in education, the social sciences, and the "nurturing or serving" professions, such as nursing, administrative, social work, and the like (Moses 1997).

Second, strong ties of nuclear and extended families, flexible gender roles, and a strong sense of obligation, support and interdependence among family members traditionally characterize Black culture. In fact, Black women academicians—particularly first-generation college graduates—often must balance their careers while parenting their children in addition to serving as a caretaker to parents or other family members (Wallace, Hinton-Hudson, Moore, Hart & Wilson, 2010). Nevertheless, Black women academicians tend to revere the family, marriage, procreation, and commitment to the community as a means for survival and protection from institutional and dominant systems of discrimination and oppression (Wallace et al., 2010). Those women who grew up within the strong interconnection of the Black family and community during their early developmental experiences have a distinct sense of themselves as Black (Alfred,

2001) and female, battling against historical, negative images shaped by American popular culture that often characterize Black women, in general, in negative depictions as compared to the more positive traits attributed to White women in general. As a result, Black women academicians tend to be ever careful and cognizant about their tone of voice, facial expressions, body language, and dress in the classroom, on campus and in professional environments because these choices can have direct consequences on their perceived level of competence and authority (Gregory 2001; Jackson & Crawley 2003; Weitz & Gordon 1993).

Lastly, underrepresentation on campus, often results in Black women academicians—not being privy to mentoring, informal networks, and information—working in isolation which can have detrimental effects on morale and job satisfaction (Fries-Britt & Kelly, 2005; Wallace et al., 2010, p. 72). Being subjected to "gendered racism"—a belief that women faculty of color are better suited to work or serve in race-centered institutions or environments as opposed to Predominantly White Institutions (PWIs) (Harley, 2008)—Black women academicians continue to struggle to gain access, inclusion, and promotion to "the good life" in the academy. However, the intersections of race, gender, and class are always present as multiple levels of oppression that can and do inhibit the emotional, psychological, physical, legal, social, and even spiritual well-being of these women scholars (Wallace et al., 2010).

Methodology

This study is comprised of four Black academic mothers with tenure—three associate professors and one full professor—at three different PWIs and one HBCU located in the Midwest, the south, and on the northeast. Because it is unknown whether Black women academicians face additional challenges beyond "gendered racism," the goal of the study was to capture the experiences of Black academic mothers to highlight the choices and challenges they face in balancing work and family life. Situating their own personal narratives within the context of extant literature, the authors use their experiences to develop an analytical framework that allows them to discuss and examine their individual, yet common experiences on being Black academics *and* mothers.

Participants

Pseudonyms—*Brenda, Glenda, Linda, and Sandra*—are used to cloak the identities within the text and brief biographical descriptions are provided for contextual purposes. Although all contributors remain unidentified in the testimonials to preserve anonymity, two of the authors are participants in this study.

Brenda is an associate professor at a PWI located in the Midwest. Similar to other Black women academicians, she is a first-generation college graduate from a large family and the first in her family to earn the doctorate degree in a social science field. Although her mother passed away before she entered college, she credits her family and community for instilling in her a firm racial heritage. Brenda began her first academic position as an expectant mother. At the time, she was also the only female and only Black in her department. Her institution did not have family-leave policies. Brenda faced numerous medical challenges while pregnant, which resulted in a less than collegial environment when she returned after maternity leave.

Glenda is an associate professor at a PWI located in the South. Similar to other Black women scholars, she is a first-generation college graduate and the first in her family to earn the doctorate degree in a social science field. She grew up in a close-knit family with strong ties to the church and attended predominantly Black schools, most of her life. She began her professional career as single, never married, but later got married and had a child midway through her pretenure review.

Linda is an associate professor at a PWI located in the Northeast. Linda came from a close-knit, multi-racial and college-educated family that celebrated her racially-diverse heritage. Similar to other Black women academicians, the family, marriage and procreation are important to her as a means of survival and sense of self. She was halfway through the pretenure process when she learned that she was expecting her first child. Her university's provision for family-leave was at the sole discretion of the chair of the department. Although her institution had a family-leave policy, she encountered an overall chilly climate when she returned to work after maternity leave.

Sandra is a full professor at an HBCU located in the South. Because she spent several years outside academe, she was in her mid-thirties when she completed her doctorate degree in a professional field. Sandra shares similar characteristics with other Black women academicians in that she comes from a working-class family with strong ties to the church and grew up in a small rural town in the south. She was the first in her family to complete an undergraduate education and the first to earn the doctorate degree. Sandra spent most of her career at a PWI, but now teaches at an HBCU.

Personal Narratives

The authors decided that incorporating personal narratives in a reflective essay would be the most suitable analytical tool for examining and illustrating their individual, yet common experiences. Reflective essays involve sharing one's views and feelings about a particular subject. The goal of a reflective essay is to not only discuss what is learned, but to convey the personal experiences and findings that resulted from the experience(s). Each participant's personal narratives, written in their own voices, discuss and examine being a Black academic mother.

The oral-narrative, sometimes referred to as "autoethnographical," research method better highlights individual and collective experiences because the researcher's own experiences is a topic of investigation, and readers are asked "to feel the truth of their stories and to become co-participants" (Stanley 2006, p. 707). The personal narratives "provide a means of enfranchising and empowering people whose lives have previously been shaped by 'colonized history' written from the standpoint of outsider" (Etter-Lewis,1997, p. 83). These narratives offer an insider's view, as well as culturally determined interpretations and values of intimate and unique life circumstances (Etter-Lewis, 1997). Moreover, the narrative approach is a way by which human existence becomes meaningful.

Evaluation Procedures

For the evaluation, the authors individually and collectively examined the personal narratives to identify common themes. The recommendations discussed in the conclusion are based on the emergent themes.

Findings: The Personal Narratives

Brenda: The Dual Challenges of a New Position and a New Pregnancy

I accepted my first academic position in April and found out I was pregnant in June. This caused a great deal of panic for me and my husband because we had been told that we should NOT have a baby until after I earned tenure. I purposely chose a job at a teaching school rather than a research-oriented university because I felt it would be easier to balance work and family. However, my panic increased as I thought about how I would settle into my new job. Initially, I was afraid to reveal my pregnancy. This was our first child and I was told by my mentors and colleagues at other universities that I should not make my pregnancy a big deal, and that I should try to work as much as I could. Eventually, I made an appointment with the administration to inform them of my pregnancy. Surprisingly, the university officials communicated that they were happy about the news! In their eyes, it meant that I would likely stay at the university. Despite their positive response, there was no precedent in terms of family-leave policies or how to handle my situation. Also, given that my department was comprised of all men, the university officials expected me to structure and handle my own accommodations for maternity leave. In making my own accommodations, I suggested to the university official that I reduce my course load and that my colleagues should substitute in my courses during my maternity leave. I would return to resume my teaching responsibilities upon my doctor's release. My suggestion was accepted.

Before I could distribute and share all of my course materials with my colleagues, I prematurely went into labor one month before my due date. However, undeterred by my condition, one male colleague had the audacity to call me to ask about one of the courses while I was still in the hospital *in labor!* He even continued to call and ask questions *before* I was released from the hospital. After my release, I suffered from a medical condition that prevented me from returning to work for the remainder of the semester. Consequently, I received several calls from my male colleagues who "needed help" in finishing my courses. Although my doctor instructed me not to work, I was unable to avoid these constant telephone calls. It has been more than a decade since the birth of my first child, yet my male colleagues continue to discuss how *they did me a favor* by taking over my courses during my maternity leave.

In hindsight, asking my male colleagues to substitute my courses was the worst decision I ever made. As a new mother in an all-male department, I was made to feel "guilty" about not being able to finish my courses and handle my own teaching responsibilities. As a Black female, I was made to feel "incompetent" given their overly critical comments regarding my course layout. I was told that my teaching was "different" from how they taught their courses, with the difference suggesting less than robust instruction. Essentially, I was being devalued as a Black academic mother.

In my view, a new academic mother should never be asked to structure her own maternity leave. This is an administrative decision and there should be uniform policies already in place. When someone is out because of a heart attack, they are left alone to recover from their illness. Unfortunately, universities do not view pregnancy the same way. New and expectant academic mothers are expected to carry on their normal duties, increasing their productivity if necessary, even when the doctor says their health may be in jeopardy. Some colleagues, particularly males, tend to view maternity leave as a luxury as opposed to a natural, temporary medical condition. I was burdened with making all of own my accommodations alone, I was even told that I was "lucky" for doing so. However, the reality was that my uninformed decisions did more to cause me stress and did little to create or celebrate a family-friendly atmosphere.

Glenda: The Challenge of Navigating Tenure and Promotion as a Single Mother

I was well into my tenure track position before expecting my child. I utilized good advice from my mentors and colleagues early in my career "publish a lot quickly." Even though I was married pretenure, my husband and I did not plan for nor did we expect to have a child before tenure. I found out that I was expecting halfway through my pretenure reviews. I immediately consulted a senior female colleague, with experience in family-leave provisions, to seek advice on how to handle my professional obligations because my child would be born in the middle of the semester. The colleague and I met with my department chair, who had given me less than favorable annual reviews and who had depressed my salary despite my level of productivity and positive pretenure reviews. I have always suspected it was due to race and gender bias. I was extremely nervous because I did not want to be perceived negatively by my colleagues or students, so I asked them to keep my pregnancy confidential. In fact, I chose to conceal my pregnancy and the birth of my child from my colleagues and students.

I discovered that I was eligible for paid leave. I decided to take it, which afforded me several months to stay at home and nurse my newborn, a practice that

I was unable to continue upon my return to work. Additionally, my institution had a tenure extension policy for the birth of a child, but because I was so far along in my pretenure review when I was notified of eligibility, I strategically chose not to utilize the policy. It is often an unspoken expectation that one will demonstrate more productivity when making use of tenure extension policies, even though the policy stipulates that individuals should not be held to a higher standard.

My child was approximately eighteen-months-old when I went up for promotion and tenure. I was motivated to present a strong case because having a child changed my entire outlook. I became more efficient. By the time I submitted my dossier, I was separated from my spouse given all of life's demands and expectations. I was now a single mother so I had to earn tenure to support my child and me. I earned it!

Linda: The Challenges of Balancing Research with Motherhood

My circumstances are not unique, but I do feel both fortunate and resentful about my experiences with motherhood and academe. I gave birth to my daughter halfway through my tenure clock, and while still working on my first book manuscript. One reason I decided to have a child despite my pressing tenure evaluation was the importance of family to me. I come from a large family that regularly shared Sundays and holidays together and that I often visited during my vacation time away from school. Because having a family was so important to my sense of self, the idea of not having any children was alien and discomforting to me, which is why I took on the difficult tasks of finishing and publishing my book (and otherwise building my file) in order to win tenure—all with one and later two children in tow.

My department chair was very supportive, giving me a semester off with pay for both childbirths. On my campus, paid-leave and family-leave policies are at the chair's discretion, so I felt fortunate to have had such a supportive chair. To accommodate my teaching as a new mother, my chair allowed me to revise my schedule, which enabled me to arrive later in the morning and leave earlier in the afternoon. Both of my children were placed in daycare at 6-months so I did not have to worry about breastfeeding them, but I still needed to pump breast milk.

Unfortunately, I felt that most male and childless female colleagues did not appreciate the sort of time and energy that parenting takes or how it can affect professional productivity, even when I demonstrated performance at the same or higher levels as my childless colleagues. Their attitudes toward me were reflected in my annual pretenure reviews. I received comments like: "Where is the book contract?"; "You really need to be publishing more"; "Do anything you have to—even spinning articles from current manuscript material if you have to—to get more articles out."

In addition, I could feel the "chill" in the professional climate in which I worked and in my experience in my social interactions with colleagues. There were, of course, the looks that I have received from my colleagues. Interestingly, my female colleagues (most of whom do not have children) gave me many nonverbal cues registering critical judgment (i.e. the stares, furrowed brows, and the "OH's") when they learned I was expecting my first child. This increased with my second pregnancy. I remember feeling as though I was on the receiving end of their own frustration for choosing to limit their own lives by not becoming mothers. I noticed that my professional and intellectual input seemed less respected after becoming pregnant and having children.

I already believed my opinions as a Black academic and woman were not fully respected. For example, in department meetings I was expected to speak only when issues being discussed related to Blacks or other people of color and never to challenge or debate the agenda items—one knows this because the affirmative reactions that come so easily to white colleagues (female and especially male ones) were not expressed when I spoke. This may stem also from my being asked after only one month in my shiny, new tenure-track position to babysit for a male colleague (to take care of his daughter, that is) so that he could participate in a graduate exam. As he stood in my doorway and stated, just before asking me to babysit, "Oh, junior colleague, I know how you can impress a senior colleague." Was I approached because I was a Black woman being viewed as the stereotypical "mammy"? It is difficult to determine, but I was offended. It is why I believe, though never explicitly expressed—I have never been called by a racist or sexist term—that there is a general environment of racism and sexism at my institution. And, this is why I have interpreted nonverbal language to convey negative judgment and disapproval about my presence, my opinions, and my decision to have children as a Black academic and mother.

The insensitivity and aggressiveness of my colleagues were evident in social networks as well. One time, while speaking with a white colleague's white wife about parenting, she said to me, "Did I ever tell you that my daughter asked 'Why are Black people so mean to their children?'" I asked her how she responded to her daughter's question. She seemed taken by surprise that I would expect her to educate her daughter against racism. Clearly my colleague and his wife did what so many whites do: they participate in passive-aggressive behavior that confirms white supremacy (even in something like parenting) and negative racial stereotypes rather than vigorously challenge them. It also highlights the need for Black parents, in general, to be proactive in our parenting as well.

Probably the biggest challenge I faced, as an academic mother, was getting adequate sleep and losing mental acuity. I slept an average of 4 hours a night for about two years after my second child was born. When I finally went to the doctor to be evaluated for early Alzheimer's, he looked at me and said, "Didn't you say that you have two babies under the age of 3, that you only sleep four hours a night, and that you're working on a book, trying to get tenure? Of course your memory is shot. It's called stress." His diagnosis was a relief and a wake-up call to me as an academic and mother.

First, I realized that I wasn't going to descend into oblivion due to dementia. More importantly, I realized that *I* wasn't taking my sacrifices, hard work, stress, and efforts seriously. I hadn't learned to value all that I was doing. Yes, I was angry, angry when my husband did less than a reasonable share of childcare, when my colleagues looked at me as though I was incompetent, and that my life had been hijacked by my two precious babies. But I had to teach myself, little by little, how to take better care of myself. Fortunately, I earned tenure and took a year-long sabbatical. For the most part, the stress level receded. My kids are still more than a handful and my husband still seems oblivious to the idea of *shared* parenting, but at least I have some stability and a better sense of self as an academic and mother because there is immense responsibility, privilege and power that rest in being both.

Sandra: The Challenges of Combining Career, Childcare and Commuting

The road to full professor was daunting. I became pregnant with my youngest daughter while pursuing my Ph.D. I also got divorced and became the single mother of two minor children while pursuing my Ph.D. While most of my peers moved to the city where our doctorate program was located, I commuted each day. This reduced my participation in after-class social events because I needed to get home to relieve baby-sitters or arrive to daycare to pick up my children. Additionally, while some of my peers took more time to finish their program, I felt pressured to finish as quickly as possible to support my family.

When making a career decision about where to work, the most important thing to me was to have a family-friendly support system that I could trust given my professional demands. Although I would have preferred a university close to my home, the best offer came from an institution that was 2.5 hours away. I took it and relocated my family—comprised of two girls, ages 1 and 4, and me.

I learned during the interview process that I would be the first tenure track Black female academic in my School, a status that was not new to me. During my onsite interview, I specifically asked about evening teaching loads and childcare. I was told that there was a childcare facility onsite. However, I was not informed that the childcare facility would end its evening care program, which happened during my first semester at the university. I felt betrayed.

To make accommodations, I asked my male department chair if I could teach morning and afternoon classes. He informed me that my request was "unheard of at the university" and did not consider it further. As a result, I had to rely on people in the local community to care for my children. It was nerve-wrecking for me. I felt helpless because some baby-sitters were not the most reliable, and I did not feel very comfortable leaving my children with them. Fortunately, the wife of one of my colleagues was willing to care for my children on two evenings per week. I knew this was only a temporary solution and that I had to find something that was more permanent. Thus, by the end of my first year at the institution, I decided to move back to my home state, *a 1.5 commute each way*. Moving close to family and friends allowed me to secure a friend who would pick up my girls, take them to my home, and care for them until I arrived home at around 12 midnight. My guest room became her bedroom. This arrangement lasted for 10 years!

When it became known that I had moved my family out of the local area, the administration began to question my commitment to the university, my colleagues and students. Although I was never late for nor cancelled my classes, I had several visits with university officials who raised the issue. I sensed that my decision began to impact how I was treated as a colleague and even the opportunities that I was afforded. I was constantly defending my right to live where I wanted and to have a support system that would allow me to be successful in academe.

Throughout my tenure at the university, I felt burdened by the weight of trying to balance my roles as an academician and mother. I constantly felt I had something to prove as a woman and scholar. As the first and the only tenured Black female in my School, I felt I had to mitigate negative stereotypes of Black women in America while still maintaining my pride as a Black woman. True, I was a "single mom," but I made sure that my colleagues knew how successful my children were in school, and I brought them to campus so the faculty could get to know them personally (and see that I was doing a good job with them). I believed that if my colleagues could extrapolate my concern for own children to the students that they would come to a better understand and respect me as a professor. However, I doubt if they truly understood how motherhood informs how Black female academic mothers teach and serve our students. Our roles in the family and community impacts not only how much time we devote to our careers and families, but how we take ownership in our students' success because it reflects on us.

I earned associate professor, but I was denied the rank of full professor at the university. Given the reasons, I determined that it was best to end the conflict between my career and family after 15-years of teaching at that university. I am now at an HBCU, hold rank of full professor, and I am at a place in my life where choosing between my career and motherhood is no longer an issue for me.

Discussion and Conclusion

Although the contributors share similar characteristics as Black academicians, the findings do not reveal any particular incidents of overt race discrimination, but certainly highlight issues of gender discrimination given their roles as academic mothers. What emerge from these personal narratives are the following common themes.

The type of university—teaching vs. research—may impact the availability family-friendly policies.
Both types of institutions offer advantages and disadvantages for academic mothers. Brenda purposely chose a teaching institution because she believed it

would be easier to balance work and family issues there. However, the other participants chose research institutions and managed to successfully meet their publication expectations in addition to their family responsibilities. Based on the participants' stories, research institutions may be more likely to have family-friendly policies like paid leave and childcare centers in place to faculty and staff. For example, both Glenda and Linda's institutions had a tenure extension policy for new parents. However, neither of them chose to utilize the policy for fear of drawing more attention to their status as expectant mothers, which could have reflected negatively on their perceived level of productivity or caused them to be held to a higher standard.

1. Early communication with officials regarding pregnancy allows for proper preparation—such as reduced teaching loads, class substitutions, etc.—for maternity leave.

Three participants—Brenda, Glenda, and Linda—found themselves in situations where their pregnancies would have a direct impact on their teaching responsibilities. Although each expressed some fear in making of their pregnancies known, they all did so early in the process. Brenda's situation underlines the need for uniform family-friendly policies. Although Glenda and Linda benefited from family-friendly policies like a semester off with pay, these female scholars felt that they could not take advantage of the tenure extension policies for fear that they would have to demonstrate even more productivity or that they may be viewed by their colleagues as not being dedicated to their work.

2. In the absence of precedent or family-friendly policies, academic mothers are often pressured to make their own arrangements for their impending absence from campus, which may lead to feelings of guilt, insensitivity to parenting demands and heightened scrutiny by both male and childless female colleagues.

We learn from all participants that it is always a good idea to be familiar with not only their institutions family-leave provisions, but also with the *Family Leave Medical Act* (FMLA). FMLA allows eligible employees to take unpaid job protected leave of up to twelve weeks for the birth of a child or for care of a newborn. Given the nature of academe which demands high levels of productivity for promotion and tenure, it is unlikely that academic mothers, particularly those who are pretenure, will take a full twelve weeks for maternity leave; however, it is the law and employers are required to provide that time to employees. We also learn that family-friendly policies have done little to alter the traditional views about parenting in general. Linda's narrative demonstrates that males and childless female colleagues, particularly, can give nonverbal cues that devalue the role of academic mothers. In fact, as Linda observes, pregnancy and motherhood were just another level of oppression added to being a Black academic and woman in which she encountered and had to face.

3. Mentoring by senior colleagues, who are parents, can help new mothers negotiate and understand the range of family-friendly policies that the university offers.

Upon learning about her pregnancy, Glenda sought out advice from a senior colleague familiar with negotiating maternity leave, which allowed her sufficient time to give birth to and nurse her child without ever revealing her status to her colleagues or students.

4. Support systems, like adequate childcare, are essential and help to relieve emotional stress for academic mothers who may worry about their children's safety.

Parents should get sufficient information about childcare centers either at their institution or local facilities. This becomes even more critical for single parents. Sandra chronicles her difficulties with inadequate childcare and how it eventually caused her to move back to her home state to be close to her family and friends who provided a support network. It was the best choice to ensure her children's stability and safety, but it had a detrimental effect on her job given the reaction of her colleagues who failed to understand her role as a Black academic mother. As a Black woman, Sandra needed to raise her children in an environment that celebrated her racial heritage. Often times, other colleagues may fail to see the importance of raising children in communities that embraces their heritage while providing a means of survival and protection from dominant systems of discrimination and oppression.

5. Institutional family-friendly policies are necessary to adequately address the needs of families. In addition, professional evaluation procedures should accommodate parenting demands like providing tenure extension policies, modified duties, or special scheduling, when necessary.

The participants' narratives revealed that not all of the participant's institutions had policies that were uniform. In fact, Brenda's and Linda's accommodations were at the discretion of the department. Linda was fortunate because she had a supportive chair. This study revealed that family-leave provisions should be more uniform. Such uniformity will protect academic mothers from "disparate treatment" due to race or gender bias or "gendered racism."

To conclude, academic careers can provide flexibility and autonomy, but successful women academicians must be prudent and careful in balancing their careers with motherhood. The stories provided by these academic mothers indicate the importance of women faculty communicating with university officials the need for family-friendly policies, in general. It also highlights the necessity for Black academic mothers, in particular, to have a network of support that embraces and affirms their racial identities as they continue to struggle to gain access, inclusion, and promotion in the academy. Such affirming social networks help to balance the emotional, psychological, physical, legal, social, and even spiritual well-being of these women scholars.

References

Ackelsberg, M., Binion, G., Duerst-Lahti, G., Junn J., Assendelft L., & Yoon, B.S. (2004). Remembering the "life" in academic life: Finding a balance between work and personal responsibilities in the academy. *PS: Political Science and Politics, 37*, 879–883.

Alexander, R., & Moore, S. E. (2007). The benefits, challenges, and strategies of African American faculty teaching at predominantly White institutions. *Journal of African American Studies, 11*, 4–18.

Alfred, M. V. (2001). Reconceptualizing marginality from the margins: Perspectives of African American tenured female faculty at a White research university. *Western Journal of Black Studies, 25*(1), 1–11.

Armenti, C. (2004). May babies and posttenure babies: Maternal decisions of women professors. *The Review of Higher Education, 27*(2), 211-231.

Assendelft, L., Gunther-Canada W., & Dolan, J. (2001). The status of women in political science departments in the South: Results of the Millennium Survey. *PS: Political Science and Politics, 34*(2), 333-338.

Collins, A. C. (2001). Black women in the academy: An historical overview. In R.O. Mabokela & A. L. Green (Eds.), *Sisters in the academy: Emergent Black women scholars in higher education* (pp. 29–41). Sterling, VA: Stylus Publishing.

Etter-Lewis, G. (1997). Black women in academe: Teaching/administrating inside the sacred grove. In L. Benjamin (Ed.), *Black women in the academy: Promises and perils* (pp. 81–90). Gainesville, FL: University Press of Florida.

Fries-Britt, S., & Turner-Kelly, B. (2005).Retaining each other: Narratives of two African American women in the academy. *Urban Review, 37*(3), 221-242.

Grant, L., Kennelly, I., & Ward, K.B. (2000). Revisiting the gender, marriage, and parenthood puzzle in scientific careers. *Women Studies Quarterly, 28*(1-2), 62-85.

Gregory, S. T. (1995). *Black women in the academy: The secrets to success and achievement*. New York, NY: University Press of America.

Gregory, S. T. (2001). Black faculty women in the academy: History, status, and future. *Journal of Negro Education, 70*(3), 124–138.

Harley, D. A. (2008). Maids of academe: African American women faculty at predominately White institutions. *Journal of African American Studies, 12*(1), 19 36.

Jackson, R. L., II, & Crawley, R. L. (2003). What student confessions say about a Black male professor: A cultural contracts theory approach to intimate conversations about race and worldview. *Journal of Men's Studies, 12*(1), 25–37.

Mason, M.A., & Goulden, M. (2002). Do babies matter? The effect of family formation on the lifelong careers of academic men and women. *Academe, 88*(6), 21–27.

Moses, Y. T. (1997). Black women in academe: Issues and strategies. In L. Benjamin (Ed.), *Black women in the academy: Promises and perils* (pp. 2337). Gainesville, FL: University Press of Florida.

Spalter-Roth, R., & VanVooren, N. (2008). PhDs at Mid-Career: Satisfaction with work and family. Department of Research and Development Research Brief, *American Sociological Association*. Washington, DC: ASA.

Thomas, G. D. (2001). The dual role of scholar and social change agent: Reflections from tenured African American and Latina faculty. In R. O. Mabokela & A. L. Green (Eds.), Sisters in the academy: Emergent Black women scholars in higher education (pp. 81-92). Sterling, VA: Stylus Publishing.

U.S. Department of Education (2009). National Center for Education Statistics, Integrated Postsecondary Education Data System (IPEDS), winter 2009-10, Human Resources component, Fall Staff section, *Table 12: Employees in degreegranting institutions by race and ethnicity, gender and primaryoccupation.*

U.S. Department of Education (2009). National Center for Education Statistics, Integrated Postsecondary Education Data System (IPEDS), winter 2009-10, Human Resources component, Fall Staff section, *Table 20: Faculty in degree granting institutions by race and ethnicity, gender and academic rank.*

Wallace, S. L., Hinton-Hudson, V. D., Moore, S. E., Hart, B. G., & Wilson, L. L. (2010). African American women in predominantly White institutions: Transitions, trials, and survival strategies. In S. E. Moore, R. Alexander, Jr., & A. J. Lemelle, Jr. (Eds.), *Dilemmas of Black faculty at predominantly White institutions in the united states: Issues in the post-multicultural era* (pp. 71–94). Lewiston, MA: Edwin Mellen Press.

Weitz, R., & Gordon, L. (1993).Images of Black women among Anglo college students. *Sex Roles: A Journal of Research, 27,* 19–35.

Williams, Joan C. (2005). The glass ceiling and the maternal wall in academia. *New Directions for Higher Education Special Issue: The Challenge of Balancing Faculty Careers and Family Work, Volume 130,* 91-105.

Wilson, R. (1995). Scheduling motherhood. *The Chronicle of Higher Education* 40(26), 14–15.

Wilson, R. (1999). Timing is everything: Academe's annual baby boom. *The Chronicle of Higher Education,* 45(42), 14–15.

Section Two

Too Grown for Your Own Good: Doing Girlhood

> *I constantly felt (as I suppose many an ambitious girl has felt) a thumping from within unanswered by any beckoning from without.*
>
> Anna Julia Cooper (A Voice from the South, 1892)

Chapter Four
Combing My Kinks: A Culturally Informed Program to Strengthen Mother-Daughter Relationships
Marva L. Lewis
Allisyn L. Swift

Introduction

"Damn it! I told you to keep your stupid butt still. I'm trying to comb your nappy-ass hair." Tonya age 26

"Ok honey, mom's gonna comb your hair now and make you look all pretty. How do you want your hair, in one plait or two?" Tina, age 24

Both mothers live with their two-year old girls on the 35th floor of an urban housing development in a community with high rates of violence. Both mothers have experienced the same environmental stressors of poverty, community violence, and single parent status. Both are African American. Each mother combs her daughter's hair before sending them off to the local day care center. One mother, Tonya harshly jerks her daughter's hair while combing it, cursing and shouting at her to sit still as she combs her course hair. She wallops the squirming toddler with a brush that leaves a bruise on the side of her face. The next day, the day care center, mandated by law to report suspected child abuse, contacts Child Protective Services to report the fresh bruise on Tonya's two-year old daughter.

    The second mother, Tina lives across the hall from Tonya in the same high-risk neighborhood and sends her daughter to the same day care center. While combing her daughter's hair Tonya sings, plays and smiles at her child's antics. Her daughter gently combs her doll's hair as her mother combs her hair. She strokes and gently brushes it in the same manner that her mother brushes her hair.

These two stories illustrate the power of the hair combing ritual for young African American children (Lewis, 1999, & 2013). Powerful memories of the repeated interactions with an attachment figure during the everyday task of hair combing for little girls, or trips to the barbershop for little boys, are unrecognized factors in parent-child relationships. Within African American communities a parent is perceived as neglectful if their child appears in public with hair that is not styled. This everyday ritual must be performed by many parents regardless of the level of stress they may be experiencing. Parent-child attachment relationships are formed during the ages of zero to two years (Bowlby, 1969). During this same developmental period children under the age of four are at the highest risk for child maltreatment.

In this chapter we examine sociocultural influences on the core maternal behavioral elements necessary to foster healthy mother-child attachment relationships. The key maternal behavioral and emotional elements of what attachment theorists term *maternal sensitivity* (Ainsworth, Blehar, Waters & Wall, 1978) are critical to the formation of secure parent-child relationships. These elements include maternal warmth, nurturing physical touch, and acceptance of the individual personality of her infant, responsiveness to the cues of her infant to fulfill the child's survival needs, and prompt and accurateness in her responses. We argue that these elements occur during the interactions between African American mothers and daughters that occur during the everyday routine task of combing hair. We identify the traumatic historical origins of beliefs about skin color and hair that may impact the manner in which an African American mother approaches and carries out the hair-combing task. We propose that these unexamined intergenerational legacies about values for light skin color, rejection of dark skin tones, and what constitutes 'good hair' (silky, loosely curled, long, or straight), may be internalized by some African American mothers and impact the quality of their attachment behaviors with their young daughters.

In the next section of the chapter we will briefly describe a community-based project, titled, *Talk, Touch & Listen While Combing Hair*©, (TT&L) (Lewis, 2012). The TT&L curriculum grew out of the findings from a program of research using a cultural practices approach (Miller & Goodnow, 1995) focused on the hair-combing task. A central part of the curriculum used to address emotionally charged issues of acceptance and rejection based on skin color and hair texture are the use of children's stories about these topics. This psychoeducational group uses topics connected to the hair-combing task as a central focal point. The experiential teaching approach helps parents acquire skills and social support networks to practice the behaviors for healthy attachment relationships. The ultimate goal of the group is to help African American mothers heal from the historical traumas related to acceptance and rejection based on skin color and hair type, strengthen their individual relationships with their daughters, and re-connect in healthy ways with their community.

We conclude the chapter with recommendations for research and practice to validate the success of this innovative group approach to healing from the modern residuals of the historical trauma of slavery and strengthening mother-daughter relationships.

The Hair Combing Narrative and a Concept of Womanhood

Mother-daughter hair combing routines reflect ancient traditions rooted in practices of hair braiding within village circles of African women (Erasmus, 2000; Tyler, 1990). For African American women in the United States, issues of beauty and especially hair are tied to self-esteem, femininity, and even identity as a woman. The symbolism of hair and hairstyles compose an integral part of a woman's identity across many cultural and ethnic groups around the world (Firth, 1973). In some cultures in countries such as India, Tibet, or Morocco, the style and pattern of hair braiding communicated to others tribal affiliation, the village you were from, which age group you belong, and even social status within your tribe. Special styles or patterns were given for rituals such as marriages and coming of age ceremonies.

The intersectionality of African American hair as a political and developmental symbol.

The nomenclature of African American is used to refer to *culture* and *ethnicity*. These constructs refer to the broader culture, traditions and values created by the descendants of the enslaved multicultural Africans brought to the United States. The term "Black," capatilized and used as a proper noun, is a sociopolitical term used to categorize and identify the *race* of any person in the African Diaspora.

Black parents rear children and live in a racially stratified society in which Blacks are often overrepresented at the bottom on a multitude of social and economic indicators (Healey, 2012; Murry & Brody, 2002; Stevenson, 1994). Underlying the current challenging social and demographic reality of many Black families is the legacy of the history of enslavement and post-Emancipation inequities of African Americans in the United States (Bennett, 1967; Blassingame, 1972; Pinderhughes, 1998). This emotionally charged legacy includes a history of discrimination, stereotypes, and racism based solely on the indelible, genetically determined features of race and gender—skin color and hair texture. The intersectionality of gender, race, and hair presents another level of complexity for the formation the self-concept of African American girls as they develop into womanhood (Anderson & Collins, 2013; Collins, 1990).

The wide range of African origin physical features presented by the infant—skin color, hair texture, nose and lip size—are all associated with a complex, multi-layered social legacy of racism and stereotypes about Black people (Davis, Daniels, & See, 1998; Okazaw-Rey, Robinson, & Ward, 1987; Parmer, Arnold, Natt, & Janson, 2004; Rooks, 2001; Ryan, 1996). Young Black girls are consistently exposed to images that are not affirming of their own natural attributes, especially related to hair length and hair texture. This is primarily an issue for women of African descent. Although women of other ethnic groups may have issues associated with their hair type, there is more affirmation for straighter hair textures than there are for shorter tight curls and kinks (Altabe, 1996; Bond & Cash, 1992; Byrd & Tharps, 2001).

Many messages are communicated in the broader society about the symbolism of hair (Firth, 1979; Russell, Wilson, & Hall, 1992; Rooks, 2001). The visual media such as movies, advertisements, and television bombards families with implicit and explicit messages that coarse and kinky hair in its natural state- is unattractive, hard to manage, unfeminine, and undesirable (Akintunde, 1997; Anderson & Cromwell, 1977; Tyler, 1990). Historical pictures of African American women typically used stereotypical caricatures of exaggerated features—black skin color, thick red or white lips and a wide-eyed emotional expression. Her hair was either covered in a scarf as shown in the well-known Aunt Jemima figures, or it was tousled in its kinky state and haphazardly covered with bows. These stereotypes, widely published in the media, created negative associations between dark-skinned Black women and kinky hair, subtly promoting the idea that African origin hair needs to be subjugated. The images were rampant from the times of slavery throughout the beginning of the movies with such caricatures as the African American comedian and actor in the nineteen–twenties known as Stepin Fetchit and the large busted Mammy figures of television shows such as Beulah in the nineteen-fifties (Russell et al, 1992). The meta-message reinforced the broader stereotypes that Blacks are people not to be trusted but rather feared and who need to be subjugated (Tate, 2007; Taylor & Grundy, 1996; White & Parham, 1990).

These same multimedia outlets proclaimed European type (straight) hair as the standard of beauty for women (Brown, Johnson, Bergeron, Keeton, & Cash, 1988; Byrd & Tharps, 2001). Messages valuing a specific type of hair may become internalized as messages about ourselves (Fanon, 1968; Porter, 1991. Mothers unconsciously communicate the message to their daughters about what the gendered self looks like verbally or non-verbally during hair combing interactions (Lewis, 1999 & 2013). Further, intergenerational transmission of behaviors and values may be regularly enacted during the hair combing time. The relationship dynamics evident during the interaction between some African American women combing their young daughter's hair may reflect modern day unresolved psychological issues related to valuing lighter skin tones and straighter hair and rejecting darker skin tones that had their origins during the historical trauma of slavery and evident in persistent stereotyped images of Black women modern discriminatory and racist-based practices (Lewis, 2013). We will discuss these issues in more depth later in this chapter. In addition to the relational aspects of hair combing time, a woman's 'hair-story' may reflect her relationship with her parents and childhood experiences of early messages about self and developing self-concept.

Healthy mother-daughter relationships: The role of attachment, routines, and human touch

The first three years of a child's life are critical to the formation of a number of developmental outcomes. Their healthy physical, emotional and social development all hinge on the core process of the formation of a healthy and secure attachment relationship with a caregiver (Bowlby, 1969/1982). The relationship is formed over the first 18 months of an infant's life through their everyday interactions with a primary caregiver (Ainsworth, Blehar, Waters & Wall, 1978).

Attachment

Consistent findings from studies of early experiences of parental acceptance and rejection and adult attachment style suggest that caregiver's attachment history is associated with their caregiver behavioral responses and the quality of their child's attachment (Bretherton, 1987; Emde, 1989; Khaleque & Rohner, 2002; Hughes, Blom, Rohner, & Britner, 2005; Rohner, 1986). Ainsworth and Bowlby believed there exists within infants a built in need for "relatedness." The way in which infant's caregivers meet those needs becomes internalized, and determines how they view themselves and others, otherwise known as an "internal working model "(Bretherton, 1987). The nature of this attachment, in turn, affects a child's self esteem, personality, and the quality of her or his relationships (Emde, 1989; Stern, 1985). One of an infant's innate needs for survival is to secure a loving and stable relationship with her primary caretaker; when these basic loving and security needs are not met or thwarted, a child can feel anxious, sad and/or depressed (Bowlby, 1969/1982).

Parental attachment behaviors include verbal interaction, positive and loving touch and responsive listening. Hair combing interaction involves specific behaviors—talking, touching and listening—that may strengthen attachment relationships of parents with their children.

One of the most important evolutionary components of Bowlby's theory is proximity seeking (Karen, 1990). As the infant grows and the attachment behavioral system is consolidated, proximity seeking behaviors of the infant to the mother increases during stressful crises (Bowlby, 1969; Bretherton, 1987). Bowlby identified proximity seeking behaviors as a critical feature of the developing attachment relationship between mothers and infants. This proximity seeking and need for closeness underlies the reasoning that the attachment system is a motivational system (Lyons-Ruth, 2006). We are motivated to seek proximity to a secure base. However, attachment theory does not assume that we naturally have this motivation to seek proximity to a biological parent, rather, we are motivated to seek closeness to another who has shown us through consistent experiences that they are capable of keeping us safe physically, emotionally, and psychologically.

A unique manifestation of this parent-infant attachment relationship, the *proximity* variable, is also a distinct part of the hair-combing task and can be reliably coded (Lewis, 2013). From an attachment perspective the child's proximity to the mother during what may be a very stressful event of hair combing may provide an additional source of sensory stimulation and opportunity for physical and emotional availability of the mother to the child. But rather than the infant seeking proximity to the mother, it is the mother who determines the degree of proximity her infant will have to her during this daily ritual of combing hair (Lewis, 2013).

The concept of internal working models from attachment theory (Bowlby, 1979) also provides a theoretical framework for understanding the intergenerational transmission of skin-color issues derived from the period of enslavement throughout the history of Jim Crow segregation and discrimination devaluing features of African Americans (Boyd-Franklin, 1989; Branch & Newcomb, 1986; Stevenson, 1994). For example, attachment theory has been used to understand the developmental sequela of trauma in parent-child attachment relationships of holocaust survivors across generations (Bar-On, Eland, Kleber, Krell, Moore, Sagi, Soriano, Suedfeld, vanderVelden, van IJzendoorn, 1998).

The Importance of Human Touch

Touch is one of the key facilitators of attachment (Duhn, 2010; Heller, 2005). Increased physical contact, especially for young children, has been shown to have a positive effect on maternal responsivity and secure attachment (Anisfeld, Casper, Nozyce, & Cunningham, 1990). Even with adults, the power of touch can help lessen the effect of negative experiences (Flores & Barenbaum, 2012). In some religions traditions the 'laying on of hands' has always held a measure of power and effect of not only healing but also strengthening an individual (Duhn, 2010). As is evident in the plethora of research on the effects of touch on infants (Fields, 2001; McClure, 2000) touch is important and essential to optimal human social and neurological development. It is not just touch in general which encourages stronger attachment, but specific, nurturing touch. There is also an intergenerational effect. Mothers who have more experience in their childhood with nurturing touch are more inclined to use sensitive, nurturing touch with their children as well (Weiss, Wilson, Hertenstien, & Campos, 2000). How a child is physically touched during hair combing routines communicates the caregiver's feelings of that child's worth and respect for the body. The caregiver's hands communicate messages that the child may internalize (Lewis, 2012; Lewis, 2013). The daily task of combing hair provides mothers the opportunity to exhibit their capabilities through a routine that consistently involves physical closeness and communication through touch (Harris & Johnson, 2001; Jacobs-Huey, 2007). Hair combing interactions may reflect the mother's racial attitudes and may have long lasting effects on the daughter's self-concept and self-acceptance (McAdoo, 1985; Moore, 1985). Further, there may be biopsychosocial effects on the developing child's neurological growth, ability to self-regulate, and form future healthy attachment relationships (Murry, Bynum, Brody, Willert, & Stephens, 2001; Murry & Brody, 2002). Issues of self-efficacy and self-esteem may be developmental outcomes for the daughters that are reinforced during the daily ritual of hair combing (Straight, 2000).

Taken together the research on the development of attachment clearly indicates that sensitive nurturing touch and maternal sensitivity can encourage secure attachments. In turn, secure attachment and positive touch has also been shown to be a future indicator, particularly in women, for self-esteem, body image and even depression (Takeuchi et al, 2010). Secure attachment is also influenced by the extent to which mothers can exhibit sensitivity during tasks that may be distressing to the child (Leerkes, 2011), much like combing through knotted tightly curled hair.

Nappy-haired ghosts in the nursery: The intergenerational legacies of slavery.

Phenotypical features readily distinguish Black Americans from other racial groups as well as within their same racial group. These features vary among individuals identified as Black as well as among children within the same family. They are: skin color—ranging from very light—"high yellow," to very dark ebony; hair texture, ranging from very straight and wavy to very tightly curled, wooly, coarse and kinky; nose and lip size, ranging from broad to narrow and thick to thin; buttocks, ranging from flat to protruding and round. In addition, many Black infants' hair texture may change during these early years from straight or wavy and easy to manage to a coarse and tightly curled texture that may require different hair care techniques and a range of time and patience to style.

These features are all associated with the complex, multi-layered legacy of racism and stereotypes about Black people (Anderson & Cromwell, 1977; Davis, et al, 1998; Russell, et al, 1992; Okazaw-Rey, 1987; Pinderhughes, 1998; Rooks, 2001). Comments and messages based on these stereotypes of African racial features may have been a source of ongoing ridicule or shame within the child's network of relationships with family, extended family or school and community. Conversely, Blacks born with more stereotypically European racial features such as lighter skin color and long straight hair may have experienced rejection by other Blacks or been reinforced with socially sanctioned vanity. Therapist Elaine Pinderhughes coined the term "specialness" to describe the feelings of some lighter-skinned women who experienced this difference in treatment based on their skin color (Pinderhughes, 1998).

Within Black families, issues of skin color may be tied to important affective qualities of the relationships that evolve between parents and children (Boyd-Franklin, 1989). Children may be either prized or discounted and negative attributions made to their behavior based solely on their skin color (Lewis, 2013). Skin color is only one of the phenotypical features that readily distinguish Black Americans from other groups. The features which make up the beauty aesthetic also include hair texture and length, nose-size, hip, lip and buttock size and shape. The negative stereotypes of racial features are a direct legacy of slavery (Stampp, 1973; Stucky, 1987). A parent who has a poor racial self-concept and intense negative or unresolved emotions associated with her own features, such as skin color and hair texture, may have difficulty responding to the natural cues of her infant if her infant possesses those same features. A parent with negative internalized stereotypes about Black children may unconsciously transfer those stereotypes to their newborn child (Lewis, 2001).

The contemporary psychological residuals of chattel slavery and almost 400 years of oppression and discriminatory practices include 'colorism' and beliefs about 'good hair' in the narrative of natural African hair. The legacy of the historical trauma experienced by persons of African ancestry involve internalized oppression reflected in within group acceptance or rejection of members based on skin color. These practices grew out of destructive racial stereotypes perpetuated about enslaved Africans and their descendants (Russell, et al., 1992; Blassingame, 1972). They were designed to justify psychological terrorism and maintain submissive obedience, disunity and prevent uprisings by enslaved men and women (Bennett, 1961). Modern day legacies of this history include the disproportionate numbers of African American families separated by incarceration and foster care (Alexander, 2012).

We propose that inherent in messages communicated to children about racial features is an emotional message of acceptance or rejection. If a parent during their childhood was teased, denigrated or constantly criticized by a significant attachment figure about race-related features, they may then as adults feel some degree of stigmatization, shame or rejection. Further, they may project these feelings onto their infant who may have similar or contrasting skin tone or hair type.

Messages within the family become more salient if they are reinforced by messages outside of the family (Neal-Barnett, López, & Owens, 1996; Norton, 1993; Branch & Newcomb, 1986). The proximal and distal sources of messages of racial acceptance or rejection that developing African-American infants and toddlers may receive may come from a stranger on the street admiring their 'beautiful hair and skin color' to a grandparent who favors the lighter skinned siblings with special gifts at Christmas.

Implications of the Legacies

Attachment Relationships

Within African American communities the topic of hair and skin color has long been a focus for popular media, and interdisciplinary studies (see Byrd & Tharps, 2001; Lewis, 1999; Lewis, 2013). Other researchers in diverse regions of the world such as South Africa (Erasmus. 2000) and Puerto Rico (Neal-Barnett, et al., 1996) report the impact of hair and skin color on Black women's self concept and children's development. These emotionally toxic intergenerational legacies may permeate the everyday interactions of Black caregivers with their young children (Lewis, 2013).

Thus racial features of hair and skin color may be important flash points in the formation of African American mother-infant attachment relationships. Behavioral evidence is available from the routines and rituals involved in the everyday task of combing hair, a focus of stereotypes, racial pride and shame (Lewis, 2013; Lewis, Diaz, Turnage, 1999). The mother may perform this task in a perfunctory manner or simply assign the task to someone else if she has negative associations with kinky hair and has a young daughter with kinky hair. For other mothers the daily ritual offers a relaxing and loving time of nurturing bonding with her daughter.

These legacies may also set the stage for many developmental outcomes for young girls including the girl's self-esteem, gender and racial identity formation, and body image. The quality of relationships formed between African American mothers and daughters may create a long-lasting values associated with the hair combing routine. These values of warmth and acceptance or brusque interactions and rejections may come to be unconsciously associated with the young girls' memories of her relationship with her mother. The significance of African American hair types includes intense negative, positive or ambivalent emotions. Anthropologist and journalist Harris & Johnson (2001) compiled a book of essays by diverse African American women recalling their early experiences getting their hair combed. The emotions they recalled spanned the continuum from anxiousness to anger. For mothers, these emotions may be important determinants of the general quality of the evolving parent-child relationship. The mother may operate from a highly reified internal working model of parent-child attachment relationships triggered by the specific racial phenotype of her child. .
Hair combing interaction may contribute to the development of self-respect, self-love and self-knowledge in African American daughters despite the legacies of the negative stereotypes of hair and skin color.

Healing from the Trauma of Slavery and Modern Legacies of Stereotypes of Hair and Skin Color: Translating Research to Practice

A community-based intervention may be the best approach to ameliorate the intergenerational legacies of slavery related to skin color and hair. The task of hair combing and literacy provide a strengths and relationship-based framework for parent education and support. The task of hair combing offers a culturally valid and naturalistic method to strengthen the bond and attachment between a young child and his or her mother. For example, African American caregivers may comb both boys' and girls' hair on a daily basis for about 10 minutes to half-hour or more. When a mother combs her child's hair each day there are multiple opportunities to practice talk, touch, and listening. There are a variety of parenting skills required during this task that ranges from behavioral management to expert styling skills needed depending on the length of time of the hair combing task and the temperament of the child.

The findings from research on hair combing interaction has been translated into a parent support group titled, *Talk, Touch, and Listen While Combing Hair*© (TT&L). This curriculum is a culturally relevant group intervention for enhancing caregivers' interactions through the routine task of combing hair. These guided interactions compliment traditional clinical parent-child therapeutic approaches and case management services. The goal of this intervention is to build on the everyday opportunity of hair combing interaction as an existing skill to enhance the quality of relationships between caregivers and their young children. By addressing the issues associated with the task of hair combing families may begin to overcome the intergenerational legacies of the historical trauma of slavery including the modern day internalized oppression where adults and children may be valued based on their skin color and hair texture.

A Community-based, Culturally-Centered, Visualization Approach to Parent Education.

The hair-combing task provides a vehicle that reclaims a cultural practice for reunification of African American families and communities separated by incarceration and foster care. It builds on the strengths of African American families that value the social support of the collective (Hill, 1972). The journey of reconnection of parents with their young children is done through a community-based psycho-educational, peer support curriculum titled, *Talk, Touch & Listen While Combing Hair*© (TT&L). TT&L works to emotionally re-connect African American families and communities psychologically separated through practices of acceptance or rejection based on *colorism*—valuing light skin color and rejection of dark skin and kinky hair. Social support from peers helps parents reconnect to community recognizing the individual strengths of their child and self (McLeister & Barnett, 1999). A strong positive emotional connection based on love and acceptance of young children regardless of their skin color or hair texture by their parents, families and communities serves as the primary means to heal from these specific psychological residuals of slavery.

Development of the curriculum Talk, Touch & Listen While Combing Hair©

The findings from a series of research studies explored the interaction between a parent and child that takes place during the hair combing task as a context for assessment and intervention with low-income African American mothers and children (Lewis, Turnage, Taylor & Diaz, 1999). Our research using the HCT identified a number of significant activities occur during this task: verbal exchanges and negotiation between the mother and child, physical touch, and caregiver responsiveness to the nonverbal gestures and cues of the infant. The time spent together during the HCT may range from a few minutes to hours depending on the style the mother has selected. The infant must sit compliantly for the mother to accomplish this task.

This curriculum compliments traditional court ordered parent groups, agency-based substance abuse, probation, and case management services. The curriculum begins with helping the parent understand each of their children's temperaments and age-appropriate developmental needs. The overall goals are to increase the quality of acceptance and the attachment-related behaviors during the hair-combing task. These behaviors involve intimate and nurturing touch, verbal interaction (talk), and responding appropriately to the cues of the infant (listen). These behaviors are critical to the formation of healthy parent-child attachment during the developmental period six months to 18 months (Ainsworth, et al., 1978; Bowlby, 1969). These behaviors also contribute to the infant and toddler's ability to regulate their emotions. By understanding the underlying physiology of emotionality, emotions, and temperament, their child's behavior will be more normalized. Thus, the parent will be better able to respond to each child's needs more accurately and be more accepting of their child.

This curriculum is built around the everyday task of hair combing and storytelling to address parent-child relationship dynamics. The behavioral goals of this group are to increase parental responsiveness and acceptance of children, the parents' sense of self-efficacy, their literacy skills, and use of peer social supports available in the community. These behaviors are the fundamental ways that parents use to express and teach emotions to children. Parents will be taught to recognize and increase the type of talk to children that enhances self-esteem in children and communicates warmth and acceptance. They will be reminded of how physical touch may be experienced as positive or negative. They also learn is how to use active listening to hear all the ways that infants and young children communicate verbally and non-verbally.

A primary goal of the curriculum is to help the parent be aware of emotional responses to off-handed remarks about hair and skin color they may have experienced as a child and may be unconsciously communicating to their child. With positive feedback from videotaped interaction from a community of peers the parent may use the hair-combing task as an opportunity for strengthening their relationship with their child.

The Curriculum

The *Talk, Touch & Listening While Combing Hair*© curriculum is designed to be administered in a group format of approximately 10-12 parents divided into three topical modules. The topical areas of the curriculum—talking, touching & listening—parallel the core component behaviors that create a child's feeling of acceptance and development of secure attachment relationships. The 8-week curriculum uses a community-based parent psychosocial support model. It has been piloted in local shelters for homeless adolescent and adult women and a residential treatment facility for substance abusing women (Lewis, 2012). The primary goals of the group are to strengthen parent-child relationships, promote literacy behaviors of the mother and strengthening community connections. Throughout each session a number of didactic and experiential approaches are used to teach topics such as normal child development, racial and family legacies, active listening, attachment, values, and emotions. Each session provides opportunities to practice routines for story time and hair combing routines. The structure for each session includes psychological rules for safety, an opening ritual, a mini-lecture on a topic related to hair combing and attachment, a group or dyad exercise, a 'go-round' which is an opportunity for all participants to respond to a specific question, and a closing ritual called, 'pass the comb' where participants express the wishes for their children in the future related to the topic of the session.

Table 4.1 provides examples of sessions and the coordinated experiential exercises. For example in one of the early sessions on valuing individual differences we have mothers identify their child's temperament and then have them rate their own temperament. To tie the topic to hair we have them rate their child's degree of being 'tender-headed' (where the scalp is sensitive to touch) and report their own level of tender headedness. This evidence of inborn personality differences—temperament and tender-headedness—normalizes their child behaviors and responses during the hair combing task.

The visualization approach uses peer feedback and guided interaction during the task of combing natural hair, and oral traditions of story-telling to compliment traditional clinical parent-child therapeutic approaches and community-based case management services. The goal of this intervention is to *strengthen* emotional attachment relationships between parents and their young children ages zero to twelve. Further, the narrative therapeutic approach combined with the hair-combing task serves as a context for community, family and individual *healing* from the psychological residuals of the historical trauma of slavery.

Table 4.1—Examples of Topics and Experiential Exercises Used in *Talk, Touch & Listen While Combing Hair*© Curriculum.

Examples from 8-Week Session	TOPIC	Examples of Experiential Exercise Used During Session
#1 — Introduction & Overview	The value of parent-child Relationships.	"Hair Story" — Draw a picture of your hair during childhood & write one emotion word.
#2 — LISTEN	Individual differences: Temperament & Tender-headedness.	Telegraph game: *"What proverb do you remember hearing as a child about hair."*
#5 — TALK -	Why Hair? Legacies of slavery — CERAR, 'colorism' — valuing	HCI-VISUALIZATIONS Group reviews one of

	light skin, and straight hair and rejecting dark skin and short, kinky hair.	each mother's initial HCI tape & comment on the positive qualities of talk that occurs during HCI. The group focuses on the positive response of the daughter to the mother's verbal and non-verbal cues.
#7 — TOUCH	What did I learn about different kinds of touch from my family?	HCI-VISUALIZATIONS Group reviews one of each mother's initial HCI tape & comment on how the positive touches she performs during HCI.
#8 — Closing Rituals & Celebration — Intergenerational Legacies	What messages do I want my children to remember about our HCI?	Group Story Circle time. Parents act out *Miranda's Green Hair*, with children in the room. Certificate of Completion Awarded

Parent Whisperers (Parent-Peer Coaches)

In addition to a trained group facilitator, graduate level students are given training and supervision to participate in the group as parent coaches called "parent whisperers." The role of *parent whisperers* in TT&L groups is to provide modeling for participation, individual support and encouragement to each mother during the sessions (Lewis, 2012). These parent-peer coaches are teachers, role models, cheerleaders, and advocates (Biswas-Diener, 2009). The goal is to support participants with experiences where they feel understood, accepted, encouraged, and empowered similar to how their child needs to be listened to, accepted, and encouraged.

Conclusions

In this chapter we examined how sociocultural factors may influence maternal attachment behavior necessary for healthy mother-child attachment relationships. These elements include maternal warmth, nurturing physical touch, and acceptance of the individual personality of the infant, responsiveness to the infant's cues, and prompt and accurateness in her responses. We presented findings from research identifying the interactions during the hair-combing task as a site for these elements to occur between African American mothers and daughters. We discussed the intersectionality of gender, race, and the traumatic historical origins of beliefs about skin color and hair that may impact the manner in which some African American mothers may interact with their daughter during the hair-combing task. We argued that the unexamined intergenerational legacies about light skin color and what constitutes 'good hair' may be internalized by some African American mothers and impact the quality of their attachment behaviors with their young daughters.

We then briefly described a community-based curriculum titled, *Talk, Touch & Listen While Combing Hair,* designed to support parents. The topics, exercises and information all center on the hair-combing task. We proposed that a culturally valid curriculum is needed to strengthen parent-child relationships as well as re-connect mothers with supportive community members. The primary goal of the group is premised on the belief that a strengthened parent-child attachment relationship also serves to prevent child abuse and the rejection of children based on racial features.

Validating the narrative—The need for research

Longitudinal research needs to be conducted on the increased parental acceptance of children, family routines, literacy behaviors, enhanced parental self-efficacy and social support as outcomes of healthy hair combing interaction routines. With strengthened attachment relationships, parents may interact with their children with increased emotional connection and acceptance that includes breastfeeding, and everyday routines that include literacy behaviors and the oral traditions of story telling. These healthy interactions involving talk, touch and listening that strengthen mother-daughter attachment begin during the everyday task of combing natural hair.

References

Ainsworth, M. D., Blehar, M. C., Waters, E., & Wall, S. (1978). *Patterns of attachment: A psychological study of the strange situation.* Hillsdale, NJ: Lawrence Erlbaum associates.

Ainsworth, M. D., & Bowlby, J. (1991). An ethological approach to personality development. *American Psychologist, 46,* 333-341.

Akintunde, O. (1997). Light skinned with good hair: The role of the media and Christianity in the maintenance of self-hatred in African Americans. *Vision Quest: Journeys toward Visual Literacy. Selected Readings from the Annual Conference of the International Visual Literacy Association, 161-163.*

Alexander, M. (2012). *The new Jim Crow: Mass incarceration in the age of colorblindness.* New York: The New Press.

Altabe, M. (1996). Issues in the assessment and treatment of body image disturbance in culturally diverse populations. In J. K. Thompson (Ed.), *Eating disorders, obesity, and body image: A practical guide to assessment and treatment.* Washington, DC: American Psychological Association Books.

Anisfeld, E., Casper, V., Nozyce, M. & Cunningham, N. (1990). Does infant carrying promote attachment? An experimental study of the effects of increased physical contact on the development of attachment. *Child Development, 61,* 1617-1627.

Andersen, M.L. & Hill-Collins, P. (2013). *Race, class and gender: An anthology.* (8th Edition). Belmont, CA: Wadsworth.

Anderson, C., & Cromwell R.L. (1977). Black is beautiful and the color preferences of Afro-American youth. *Journal of Negro Education, 46,* 76 88.

Bar-on, D., Eland, J., Kleber-Rolf, J., Krell, R., Moore, Y., Sagi, A., Soriano, E., Suedeld, P., van der Velden, P. G., & van Ijzendoorn, M. H. (1998). Multigenerational perspectives on coping with the Holocaust experience: An attachment perspective for understanding the sequel of trauma across generations. *International Journal of Behavioral Development, 22,* 315-338.

Benasich, A. A., Brooks-Gunn, J. (1996). Maternal attitudes and knowledge of child rearing: Associations with family and child outcomes. *Child Development, 67,* 1186-1205.

Bennett, L., (1961). *Before the Mayflower: A History of Black America.* Chicago, IL: Johnson Publishing Company.

Biswas-Diener, R. (2009) Personal coaching as positive intervention. *Journal of Clinical Psychology: In Session.* 65(5), 544-553.

Blassingame, J. W. (1972). *The slave community: Plantation life in the antebellum south.* New York: Oxford University Press Books.

Bond, S., & Cash, T. (1992). Black beauty skin color and body images among African American college women. *Journal of Applied Social Psychology, 22,* 874-888.

Bowlby, J. (1969/1982). *Attachment and loss: (Vol. 1). Attachment.* New York: Basic Books.

Bowlby, J. (1988). *Parent-Child Attachment and Healthy Human Development.* London: R. P. L. Bowlby/Basic Books, Inc.

Boyd-Franklin, N. (1989). *Black families in therapy: A multi-systems approach.* New York: Guilford Press.

Branch, C. & Newcombe, N. (1986). Racial attitude development among young black children as a function of parental attitudes: A longitudinal and cross-sectional study. *Child Development, 57,* 712-721.

Bretherton, I. (1987). New perspectives on attachment relations: Security, communication and internal working models. In J. D. Osofsky (Ed.), *Handbook of infant development*, pp.

Brown, T. A., Johnson, W. G., Bergeron, K. C., Keeton, W. P., & Cash, T. F. (1988). Assessment of body-related cognitions in bulimia: The Body Image Automatic Thoughts Questionnaire. Paper presented at the Association of the Advancement of Behavior Therapy, New York.

Byrd, A. D. & Tharps, L. L. (2001) *Untangling the roots of Black hair in America*. New York: St. Martin's Press.

Collins, P. H. (1990). Black women and motherhood. *Black feminist thought*. Boston: Hyman.

Davis, K. B., Daniels, M. See, L. A. (1998). The psychological effects of skin color on African Americans' self-esteem. *Journal of Human Behavior in the Social Environment* (2/3), 63-90.

Duhn, L. (2010). The importance of touch in the development of attachment. *Advances in Neonatal Care, 10,* 294-300.

Emde, R. N. (1989). The infant's relationship experience: Developmental and affective aspects. In A. Sameroff & R, N. Emde (Eds.), *Relationship disturbance in early childhood: A developmental approach* (pp. 33-51). New York: Basic Books.

Erasmus, Z. (2000). Undoing the locks: the politics of black hairstyles in South Africa. In Nuttail, S. & Michael, C. *Senses of Culture*. Cape town: Oxford University Press.

Fanon, F. (1968). *The wretched of the earth*. New York: Grove Weidenfeld.

Firth, (1979). *Hair as Symbol*. Basic Books.

Fields, T. (2001). *Touch*. Cambridge, MA; London: MIT Press

Flores, L. E. & Berenbaum, H. (2012). Desire for emotional closeness moderates the effectiveness of the social regulation of emotion. *Personality and Individual Differences, 53,* 952-957.

Harris, J. & Johnson, P. (Eds.) (2001). *Tenderheaded: A comb-bending collection of hair stories*. New York: Pocket Books.

Healey, J. (2012). *Race, ethnicity, gender, and class: The sociology of group conflict and change* (6th edition). Thousand Oaks, CA: Pine Forge Press.

Heller, S. (1997). *The vital touch: How intimate contact with your baby leads to happier, healthier development*. New York: Henry Holt and Company.

Hill, R. (1972). *The strengths of Black families*. New York: Emerson Hall.

Hughes, M. M., Blom, M., Rohner, R. P., Britner, P. A., (2005). Bridging parental acceptance-rejection theory and attachment theory in the preschool strange situation. *Ethos*, Vol. 33, No. 3, pp. 378-401.

Jacobs-Huey, L. (2007), *From the Kitchen to the Parlor: Language and Becoming in African American Women's Hair Care*. New York: Oxford University Press.

Karen, R. (1990). Becoming attached. *The Atlantic Monthly*. 265 (2), 35-69.

Khaleque, A., & Rohner, R. P. (2002). Perceived parental acceptance-rejection and psychological adjustment: A meta-analysis of cross-cultural and intracultural studies. *Journal of Marriage and Family* 64, 54-64.

Leerkes, E.M. (2011). Maternal sensitivity during distressing tasks: A unique predictor of attachment security. *Infant Behavior and Development, 34,* 443-446.

Lewis, M. L. (2013). The historical roots of African American mother daughter relationships and the psychology of hair combing rituals. In H. Jackson Lowman, editor. *Afrikan-American Women: Living at the crossroads of race, gender, class, and culture*. Cognella Press/University Reader.

Lewis, M. L. (2012). *Facilitator Training Manual for the Talk, Touch & Listen While Combing Hair© Parent Support Group.* Unpublished manual, Tulane University, New Orleans, Louisiana, USA.

Lewis, M. L. (1999). The hair-combing task: A new paradigm for research with African American mothers and daughters. *American Journal of Orthopsychiatry,69*,1-11.

Lewis, M. L, (April, 2001). *The Childhood Experiences of Racial Acceptance and Rejection scale: Development, reliability and validity.* Poster symposium presented at the Biennial Meeting of the Society for Research in Child Development, Minneapolis, Minnesota.

Lewis, M. L., Diaz, L., Taylor, S., & Turnage, B. (1999). *Ethnicity predicts parenting styles in African American mothers.* Poster session presented at the Biennial Meeting for the Society for Research in Child Development, Albuquerque, New Mexico.

Lyons-Ruth, K. (2006). The interface between attachment and inter-subjectivity: Perspective from the longitudinal study of disorganized attachment.*Psychoanalytic Inquiry, 26,* 595-615.

McAdoo, H. P. (1985). Racial attitude and self-concept of young Black children over time. In, H. P. McAdoo & J. McAdoo, (Eds.) *Black children*, (pp. 213-242). Beverly Hills, CA: Sage.

McClure, V. (2000). *Infant Massage: A handbook for Loving Parents.* New York: Bantam Books.

McLeister, A., and Barnett, D. (1999). Perceived social support mediates between prior attachment and subsequent adjustment: a study of urban African American children. *Developmental Psychology,* 35 (5), 1210-1222.

Miller, P. J. & Goodnow, J. J. (1995). Cultural practices as contexts for development. New directions for child development, No. 67 (pp. 5-16). San Francisco, CA: Jossey-Bass.

Moore, E. G. (1985). Ethnicity as a variable in child development. In M. B. Spencer, and G. K. Brookins, (Eds.). *Beginnings: The social and affective development of black children*, (pp. 101-115). Hillsdale, NJ: Lawrence Erlbaum Associates, Inc.

Murry, V. M. & Brody, G. (2002). Racial socialization processes in single mother families: Linking maternal racial identity, parenting, and racial socialization in rural, single-mother families with child self-worth and self-regulation. In H. P. McAdoo, (Ed.) *Black children: Social, educational, and parental environments* (2nd ed.) pp. 97-118. Thousand Oaks, CA: Sage.

Murry, V. M., Bynum, M. S., Brody, G. H., Willert, A., & Stephens, D. (2001). African American single mothers and children in context: A review of studies on risk andresilience. *Clinical Child and Family Psychology Review, 4,* (2), 133-155.

Neal-Barnett, A. López, I. & Owens, D. (1996, August). Neither Black Nor White. The impact of skin color in the Puerto Rican community. In A. Neal Barnett (Chair), *Women of Color on Color: Healing wounds, and building legacies.* Round table discussion conducted at 104th annual meeting of the American Psychological Association, Toronto, Canada.

Norton, D. (1993). Diversity, early socialization, and temporal development: The dual perspective revisited. *Social Work, 38,* 82-90.

Okazaw-Rey, M. Robinson, T. & Ward, J. V. (1987). Black women and the politics of skin color and hair. *Women and Therapy, 6* (1-2), 89-102.

Parmer, T., Arnold, M. S., Natt, T. & Janson, C. (2004). Physical attractiveness as a process of internalized oppression and multigenerational transmission in African American families. *The Family Journal,* 12, 230.

Pinderhughes, E. (1989). *Race, ethnicity and power: The key to efficacy in clinical practice.* New York: The Free Press.

Porter, C. P. (1991). Social reasons for skin tone preferences of Black school age children. *American Journal of Orthopsychiatry,* 61 (1), pp. 149-154.

Rohner, R. P. (1986). *The warmth dimension: Foundations of parental acceptance-rejection theory.* Newbury Park, CA: Sage.

Rohner, R.P. (1994). Patterns of parenting: The warmth dimension in cross cultural perspective. In W. J. Lonner & R. S. Malpass (Eds.) *Readings in psychology and culture.* Needham Heights, MA: Allyn and Bacon.

Rooks, N. (2001). Wearing your race wrong: hair, drama, and politics of representation for African American women at play on a battlefield. In M. Bennet & V. D. Dickerson, (Eds.), *Recovering the Black female body: Self-representations by African-American women* (pp. 279-283). New Brunswick, NJ: Rutgers University Press.

Russell, K., Wilson, M., & Hall, R. (1992). *Color Complex: The politics of skin color among African-Americans.* New York: Anchor Books/Doubleday.

Ryan, C. S. (1996). Accuracy of black and white college students' in-group and out-group stereotypes. *Personality and Social Psychology Bulletin,* 22, 1114-1127.

Stampp, K. (1956/1989). *The peculiar institution: Slavery in the antebellum south* pp. 144-48. New York: Vintage Books, Random House.

Stern, D. N. (1985). The representation of relational patterns: Developmental considerations. In A. Sameroff & R. N. Emde (Eds.), *Relationship Disturbances in Early Childhood. New York: Basic Books, pp. 52-69.*

Stevenson, H. C. (1994). Racial socialization in African American families: Balancing intolerance and survival. *The Family Journal: Counseling and Therapy for Couples and Families,* 2, 190-198.

Straight, S. (December, 2000). Talking heads: With this simple ritual we braid our lives together. *Reader's Digest,* 59-64.

Stuckey, S. (1987) *Slave culture: Nationalist theory & the foundations of Black America* New York: Oxford University Press.

Takeuchi, M.S., Miyaoka, H., Tomoda, A., Suzuki, M., Liu, Q., & Kitamura, T. (2010). The effect of interpersonal touch during childhood on adult attachment and depressions: A neglected area of family and developmental psychology? *Journal of Child and Family Studies,* 19, 109-117.

Tate, S. (2007). "Black Beauty: Shade, Hair and Anti-Racist Aesthetics." *Ethnic and Racial Studies,* 30.2, 300-319.

Taylor, J., & Grundy, C. (1996). Measuring Black internalization of White stereotypes about African Americans: The Nadanolitization Scale. In R. L. Jones, (Ed.) *Handbook of Tests and Measurements for Black Populations,* Vol. 2, pp. 217-226. Hampton, VA: Cobb & Henry.

Tyler, B. M. (1990). Black hairstyles: Cultural and socio-political implications. *Western Journal of Black Studies,* 14 (4): 235-247.

Weiss, S.J., Wilson, P. Hartenstein, M.J., & Campos, R. (2000). The tactile context of a mother's care giving: Implications for attachment of low birth weight infants. *Infant Behaviors & Development,* 23, 91-111.

White, J. L., Parham, T. A. (1990). *The psychology of Blacks: African American perspective,* 2nd Ed. Upper Saddle River, NJ: Prentice Hall.

Chapter Five
The ABCs of Doing Gender: Culturally Situated Non-Cognitive Factors & African American Girls
LaShawnda Lindsay-Dennis
Lawanda Cummings

Introduction

There is a dichotomy in the roles that emerges in educational research where African American girls are depicted as either having immense academic capacity (cognitive factors) or deficits in psychological and social navigational skills (non-cognitive factors; Chavous & Cogburn, 2007; Evans-Winters, 2005; Evans, 1988; Fordham, 1993). For instance, one dimension of the literature creates an image of academic excellence based on findings that African American girls are more likely than African American boys to have positive academic identities, participate in college preparatory programs, graduate from high school, and attend college (Ford, 1995; Saunders, et al, 2004; Thomas & King, 2007; Williams et al, 2002). Another domain of scholarly literature reveals this population's at-risk status. Henry (1998) describes the status of African American girls:

> African American girls are expected to adopt female roles of passivity and complacency; they are invisible to teachers as serious learners; they receive less encouragement and rewards; they are assessed for their social skills rather than academic achievement; and they are evaluated by their physical characteristics (hair texture and skin color) (Henry, 1998, p. 154).

Scholars have focused predominately on the cognitive factors that emphasize the two dichotomous realities without acknowledging non-cognitive factors. This lack of acknowledgment is problematic given that the characteristics associated with these two roles are based on non-cognitive skills that advance or impede performance. There is a need to understand how non-cognitive factors influence the construction of these co-joined realities.

Non-Cognitive Factors Defined

Within this dialogue about how African American girls are perceived, there is a need to clarify what cognitive and non-cognitive factors entail. Within the literature, cognitive factors are defined as school readiness, test scores grades, and other academic/cognitive measures (Cuasay, 1992). Non-cognitive factors are defined as attributes that both advertently and inadvertently affect academic performance including personality characteristics, motivation, and other factors which aid in student functioning within the school context (Rosen, Glennie, Dalton, Lennon, & Bozik, 2010). Furthermore, Heckman and Rubinstein (2001) contend that the current focus on cognitive skills is based on the belief that measured constructs on standardized tests are essential to academic achievement. In recent research, the connection between non-cognitive factors and educational/occupational outcomes has spurred renewed interest in the impact of these factors on school success and the potential for intervention development (Rosen et al, 2010).

Rosen and colleagues (2010) identified seven non-cognitive factors that contribute to academic success including: 1) motivation, 2) effort, 3) self-regulated learning, 4) self-efficacy, 5) academic self-concept/identity, 6) anti-social/pro-social behavior, and 7) coping and resilience. A student with developed non-cognitive skills benefits within the classroom and school context by being perceived as an invested learner that knows how to navigate schools, relationships, and authority structures. Sub-optimal non-cognitive skills often translate into fewer educational and occupational opportunities well into adulthood (Farkas, 2003; Kerckhoff & Glennie, 1999).

Although the study of non-cognitive factors is a growing area of inquiry, research on the role of non-cognitive factors on African American girls' academic experiences and performance is limited. As African American female researchers with a thorough understanding of the literature and lived experiences within the school context as both students and educators, we can begin the process of understanding the cultural underpinnings of the dichotomous roles assigned to African American girls. The overall goal of this paper is to create dialogue about the non-cognitive factors affecting African American girls in schools. Additionally, this paper will situate this occurrence within the multiple-worlds framework (Phelan, Cao & Davidson, 1994). This framework acknowledges the conflict that students experience when negotiating culture-based and mainstream norms within the school context. Contextualizing African American girls' experiences through this framework can lead to a better understanding of how non-cognitive factors advance and/or impede academic performance.

Theoretical Framework: The Multiple Worlds Framework

Scholars have begun to understand the incongruence between specific cultural strengths and non-cognitive factors that facilitate academic success. The behaviors and conceptualizations within non-cognitive factors have their foundational value within culture. Cultural knowledge and behaviors found within the African American community often include culturally bound non-cognitive factors that conflict with mainstream ideals. Phelan, Cao and Davidson's (1994) research on high school youth demonstrated that many students from diverse ethnic groups have trouble negotiating the boundaries between their multiple worlds. The concept of 'worlds' encompasses "the cultural knowledge and behaviors of students' particular families, peer groups, and schools in which we presume that each world contains values and beliefs, expectations, actions, and emotional responses familiar to insiders" (Phelan et al., 1994, p.53). The multiple-worlds framework describes the movement between students' family, peer, and school worlds as an active negotiation process.

Students from diverse backgrounds are required to learn how to cope and negotiate educational systems that propagate the majority culture as the only 'right' way to be intellectual. In Phelan and colleagues' (1994) multiple-worlds framework; negotiating school, family and peer contexts is viewed as a necessary part of minority adolescents' life. For this framework, four categories emerged: First the *congruent world/smooth transitions* occur when there is congruence between the students' values, beliefs, and expectations with mainstream culture making transitions harmonious and uncomplicated. Next the *different world/border crossing managed* encompasses students using strategies to successfully negotiate differences in family, peer, and/or school worlds (with respect to culture, ethnicity, socioeconomic status and/or religion). These students appear well-adjusted and high performing despite some costs in authentic connections with their cultural base. Then *different world/borders crossings difficult* status includes students with distinct differences between their home and school worlds. The students may not have mastered or embraced the strategies needed for successful transitions. The struggle of reorienting across settings leaves students frustrated and academically isolated. Finally, the *different worlds/borders crossing resisted* status endorse a distinctly discordant reality between students' worlds that they perceive as insurmountable. Low and high performing students actively or passively resist transitions and express a bleak expectation for their future opportunities due to systemic barriers.

Minority students usually fall within the last three categories as their cultures are not usually parallel with mainstream culture. The level of proficiency that students transition between these worlds is predictive of their academic success and level of school connectedness (Phelan et al., 1994; Blum, 2005). Academically successful African American girls must learn to navigate these worlds but many times at a cost to their personal and ethnic identities (Phelan et al., 1994).

Learning to transition between these worlds during adolescence is imperative for academic and social success (Phelan et al., 1994). The ability to 'cross the borders' of these worlds and negotiate the expectations and values within each world requires highly developed non-cognitive skills. Phelan and colleagues (1994) identified six types of borders that students navigate.
Psychosocial borders emerge when students experienced anxiety, fear, or apprehension in the setting preventing them from establishing relationships with teachers or peers. *Sociocultural borders* are erected when the cultural characteristics of one's world is viewed as less important than another world. This manifests in schools when the cultural values and expressions of minority groups are portrayed in a negative light. *Linguistic borders* result when communication between students words is obstructed, not become of different language per se, but become one group regards another group's language as unacceptable or inferior. *Socioeconomic borders* emerge when economic circumstances create serve limitations. This border can result from students' community and neighborhood conditions that contrasts with their school environment. *Gender borders* are created when the roles, aspirations, and norms of one gender group is valued over the other gender group. This border undermines self-confidents and block students' perceptions of what is possible of themselves and others. *Structural borders* are features in school environments that prevent, impede, or discourage students from engaging fully in learning. The described type of border crossing aligns with various non-cognitive factors which may impact African American girls' academic experiences.

Contextualizing Non-Cognitive Factors of African American Girls

Although Rosen and colleagues identified seven non-cognitive skills, upon review of the educational research literature about African American girls, three non-cognitive factors emerged; academic self concept/identity, effort, and anti-social/pro-social behavior. Motivation is a complex phenomenon that encompasses key aspects of the above identified factors which influence African American girls' school experiences in cognitive and non-cognitive domains. Defining and contextualizing these factors through a cultural lens can help educators and researchers move non-cognitive behaviors from the margins and localize them within the appropriate cultural context (Tilman, 2002).

Academic self-concept/identity

The first non-cognitive factor that emerged in the literature for African American girls was academic self-concept/identity. This factor is defined as "a student's self perception of academic ability formed through individual experiences and interactions with the environment" (Rosen et al., 2010, p. 118). Student who have a positive academic self-concept/identity are more likely to engage in scholastic behaviors such as completing homework, studying for tests, and participating in class. These scholastic behaviors directly influence cognitive factors and proficiencies that are used to measure academic success. An engaged learner has the skills to navigate across borders and function within their social and academic worlds.

Many scholars suggest that African American girls develop "anti" academic identities as a means to maintain their racial and cultural identities. Ogbu's cultural ecological theory argues that experiences of historical oppression and negative societal treatment shape ethnic minorities' identity (Ogbu, 2003). For African Americans, enslavement, subsequent relegation, and involuntary minority status has produced an oppositional consciousness that manifests as culturally resistant attitudes toward mainstream European American culture, including education. The presence of these culturally resistant attitudes may result in the rejection of school and/or underperformance by some African American students. Students who do not reject school and accept mainstream cultural values are often accused of "acting white" and rejecting their racial identities (Ogbu, 2003). Some African American girls actively withdraw from academic pursuits while others withdraw from their peer and families groups in order to cross psychosocial and sociocultural borders. Many African American girls do not fall in either category because they have developed the non-cognitive skills necessary to cross multiple borders.

From observation and interviews with African American female students, Fordham (1998) indicates that many girls create two divergent identities, a school and a home persona. Home and school life represent two different worlds that require girls to alter their speech, behavior, appearance, abilities and feelings to cross psychosocial, sociocultural and linguistic borders. At home, many African American girls use African American dialect, demonstrate culturally situated behavior, and dress. However, the school persona, especially among girls who attend predominantly White schools, is more reflective of mainstream cultural values (Horvat & Antonio, 1999). An adoption of a de-culturalized identity means that African American girls must "drop their accents or change their patterns of speech" (Horvat & Antonio, 1999, p. 334) to assimilate into the school culture.

Many African American girls experience difficulty maintaining positive academic self-concepts within the racist and sexist context of schools (Chavous & Cogburn, 2007). African American girls often experience challenges due to faulty perceptions about who they are, how they should behave, and their style of dress (Lindsay-Dennis, 2010; Horvat & Antonio, 1999; Archer-Banks & Behar-Horenstein, 2012). School often represents a place that points out their deficiencies and tries to rectify perceived inadequacies without understanding their background. Many of these faulty perceptions manifest in formal and informal exclusion from the academic learning process. Horvat and Antonio (1999) found that African American girls are often ostracized in educational settings where negative stereotypes influence their teachers' perceptions about their value and potential. For example, a participant within a study examining the school experiences of African American adolescent girls, expressed concerns about the gender stereotypes perpetuated in schools, stating, *"one of our teachers told us toward the beginning of the semester that many of us would get pregnant before the semester was over...They don't talk to the White girls like that"* (Archer-Banks & Behar-Horenstein, 2012, p. 209). These types of experiences reflect one of the pejorative images that are held of African American girls and women as hyper-sexualized.

Many African American girls are able to successfully cross various borders by developing bi-cultural competence. Bi-cultural competence refers to their ability to modify speech, behavior, and appearance to navigate multiple worlds (Jones & Shorter-Gooden, 2003). This type of competence is an unacknowledged non-cognitive skill that requires the cultivation of border crossing strategies that enables one to be successful in school while maintaining an authentic connection with family and peers. One researcher reflects on having to learn how to negotiate the different contexts of home and school saying:

> I remember being selected for a magnet program that was supposed to be for the brightest students in our district. My parents applied and my name was literally selected from a bingo-ball turner. I remember the first week I was there; I met a few Black girls who were very outspoken and always in trouble. I chose to stay away from them so that my teacher would know I was a serious student, not like 'those Black girls'. In a very culturally diverse school, I strove to be raceless by changing my speech, my clothes, even the music I listened to fit the school norm. When I left school each day, I would have to flip my speech from 'proper English' back to the comfortable dialect of my southern parents. I felt like I woke every morning and put on my uniform of whiteness to be successful in school (L. Cummings, personal communication, September 12, 2012).

The presence of various borders (psychosocial, sociocultural, gender, and linguistic) requires that African American female students develop strategies to sustain positive academic identities in hostile learning environments. Becoming bicultural may help girls to make smoother transitions especially when faced with borders that threaten their academic and cultural selves. Bicultural competence may also help them overcome challenges and engage in the learning process despite personal and social costs.

Effort

The second non-cognitive factor, effort, has been described as a component of school engagement. Kindermann (2007) defined effort as "students' energized, enthusiastic, emotionally positive, cognitively focused interactions with academic activities" (p.1186). Effort includes two distinct components; cognitive engagement and behavioral engagement. Cognitive engagement consists of the psychological investment and determination to accomplish mastery of a task or activity. Behavioral engagement is the actual observable actions in completing or mastering a task or activity (Rosen et al., 2010). Research has shown that a teacher's beliefs about a student's ability and performance are significantly predictive of student engagement and performance. African American girls are often not viewed as serious learners (Henry, 1998). Many African American girls are routinely perceived by teachers as being cognitively and behaviorally disengaged in the classroom setting. These judgments often place girls at-risk for academic underperformance. For example, Gilmore (1991) reported that African American girls whom were perceived as being disengaged in the learning process are often tracked into lower ability courses.

It is possible that cultural differences between teachers and African American girls create a hostile learning environment where it is communicated that there is only one acceptable way to be engaged in the learning context. Many girls respond to hostile environments by "not learning." Not learning tends to take place when someone has to deal with unavoidable challenges to their personal and family loyalties, integrity, and identity. In such situations, there are forced choices and no apparent middle ground. To agree to learn from a stranger who does not respect your integrity causes a major loss of self. The only alternative is to not learn and reject their world (Kohl, 1994, p. 134-135).

"Not learning" may function as a coping mechanism for some African American girls that experience difficulty reorienting across home and school borders. A refusal to learn may also help girls resolve dilemmas regarding a potential denial of their cultural selves. One researcher vividly recalls an incidence where refused to learn from a teacher. She reflects on an altercation with a teacher saying:

> During 11th grade year, my Spanish teacher wanted her all-black class to adopt Spanish names for the semester. I refused to adopt a Spanish name and openly rebelled in class. For example, I told the teacher her name change request was "what the white people wanted ...to change us." The teacher proceeded to assign me a name "LaSanja." The teacher would mark me absent because I would not answer to my assigned name during her roll call. My refusal to respond and participate in class was viewed a disengagement. I barely passed the class (L. Lindsay-Dennis, personal communication, September 10, 2012).

For this researcher and many other African American girls, engaging in school is more difficult when they feel devalued by teachers and administrators. A rigid approach to student learning and engagement that is based in European cultural values dismisses the cultural behavioral norms that African American girls bring to classrooms. The lack of value for non-traditional modes of engagement presents sociocultural, psychosocial, and structural borders that may cause African American girls to disengage from the academic process and exhibit purposeful 'not learning' (Lindsay-Dennis, 2010).

School policies and discipline procedures often prevent African American girls from being present and active participants in class. These structural borders include dress code violations, punitive tardy policies, and other disciplinary actions for minor nonviolent infractions. An example of a structural border threat can be drawn from the personal experiences of one researcher.

During my senior year in high school, I was often tardy for 1st period class (senior English). The school tardy policy mandated that tardy students report to the "tardy tank" upon late arrival. As a result, I missed a significant amount of class instruction even when I missed the bell by a few seconds. My repeated tardiness also resulted in school suspension. Being kept out of class for minor infractions impaired my ability to remain academically engaged (L. Lindsay-Dennis, personal communication, September 12, 2012).

Research findings have shown that many African American girls experience exaggerated consequences for similar violations of school policies. Other minor infractions that act as sociocultural and structural barriers include dress code violations, verbal conflicts, and issues with authority (Blake, Butler, Lewis, & Darensbourg, 2011). While it is important for African American girls to understand and adhere to school policies it should not be at the cost of their academic engagement and success. Overall, evidence has suggested that effort (i.e. cognitive and behavioral engagement) influences African American girls' ability to be successful and utilize effective border crossing strategies.

Anti-Social/Pro-Social Behavior

The anti-social and pro-social behavior represents another non-cognitive factor that has negative and positive effects on social and contextual engagement. Anti-social behavior includes physical violence, verbal abuse and social rejection. In more subtle forms, anti-social behavior includes social withdrawal and a refusal to share or help others (Bandura, 1973; Rosen et al., 2010). The purpose of this aggressive behavior is to directly and indirectly intimidate others. The anti-social behaviors that have been associated with African American girls include confrontation, aggressiveness, and lack of respect for authority figures (Evans, 1988; Fordham, 1993). Pro-social behaviors, on the other side of the behavioral spectrum, represent acts that show a level of positive social regard and cooperativeness (Rosen et al., 2010). These behaviors go beyond friendliness to include helping behaviors such as encouragement, sharing, providing leadership, and expressing empathy. In our review of the literature, incidences of both anti-social and pro-social behaviors emerged as descriptors of African American female students.

Anti-social behaviors emerge throughout the literature and include social confrontation, aggressiveness, and defiance of authority figures. African American girls are perceived by teachers as exhibiting elevated levels of aggression and defiance (Blake, Butler, Lewis & Darensbourg, 2011). Evans (1988) provides a vivid example of this phenomenon:

> In staffrooms a common cry to be heard from white teachers—usually women, for male teachers seldom revealed that everything for them was not firmly under control—was "Oh, those loud Black girls! ...The words were usually uttered in response to a confrontation in which the teacher's sense of authority had been threatened by an attitude of defiance on the part of a group of Black

girls in a classroom or corridor. The girls' use of patois and their stubborn refusal to conform to standards of "good behavior," without entering the realm of "bad behavior" by breaking any school rules was exasperating for many teachers. The behavior of the girls could be located in the outer limits of tolerable behavior, and they patrolled this territory with much skill, sending out a distinct message of being in and for themselves (Evans, 1988, p. 193).

The complexity of the navigational skills employed by African American girls within school settings requires routine border crossing and manipulation of rules and standards of the system. They successfully flirt with rules and maintain an image as both bad and good with teachers and administrators.

Gender borders manifest when the school context endorses passivity and silence for girls and a lack of tolerance of girls who do not conform to societal expectations of femininity (Harrison, 1997). Several studies have shown that schools impose mainstream notions of femininity by mislabeling cultural expressions of Black womanhood as anti-social behavior (Lei, 2003; Fordham, 1993; Taylor, Gilligan & Sullivan, 1995). African American girls must then negotiate the incongruence of socialized ideals of being strong, assertive, independent, and nurturance taught to them by female family members (Collin, 2000). Within the African American familial context, assertiveness is cultivated and valued but is strongly discouraged within school settings. Several studies have shown that African American girls are more often reprimanded by teachers for being unladylike more often than their non-black counterparts (Blake, Butler, Lewis & Darenshourg, 2011; Henry, 1998; Horvat & Antonio, 1999; Morris, 2007).). The "loud and confrontational" behaviors of African American girls are judged as threatening and evidence of low academic ability (Morris, 2007) rather than being recognized as skills that are used to cross sociocultural and gender borders.

Being outspoken and visible creates difficulty in crossing gender borders. Lei (2003) described how voice is used by African American girls in schools. Many girls know the academic and social consequences, but do not transition gender borders because they value how they were raised, "loud like their mothers" (Lei, 2003). Lindsay-Dennis (2010) reported that early adolescent African American girls recognized that their teachers viewed them as loud, "ghetto." *Ghetto* is defined as a derogatory term referring individuals who lack knowledge and behaviors associated with appropriate mainstream social interactions and values. So these girls are viewed as lacking social decorum. A fear of confirming to negative stereotypes perpetuated by society forces these young girls to protect their cultural, gender, and academic identities. In order to cope with this oppressive environment, some girls use a façade of toughness to protect their identities (Robinson & Ward, 1991; Stevens, 1997). Other girls cope with this stereotype threat by endorsing the mainstream ideals of femininity by being submissive and silent (Taylor et al., 1995).

African American girls' perceived strength, independence and aggressiveness are not always reprimanded in educational settings. An extensive review of the literature shows that pro-social behavior for African American girls focuses on caretaking, independence, and strength. Many African American girls succumb to the majority culture's standards of 'proper' femininity by becoming passive, quiet, raceless caregivers. Pro-social behaviors for this population were routinely focused on caretaking and high levels of maturity (Grant, 1984).These pro-social behaviors manifest in a shared responsibility for classroom management. Studies have also shown that teachers' emphasis on the maturity of their African American female students may pose a significant threat to girls' immediate and future achievement (Grant, 1984, Evans-Winters, 2005). For example, Grant (1984) examined African American girls' role in elementary classrooms. Teachers within this study described African American girls as mature, nurturing, independent and self-sufficient (Grant, 1984). Many teachers utilized these non-cognitive skills for their advantage. Grant's (1984) classroom observations revealed that teachers relied on African American girls to play caretaker roles by serving as tutors, rule enforcers, and classroom messengers. Expecting African American girls to be caretakers (little Mammies) often puts them at-risk for underachievement by limiting the amount of time to engage in instructional activities. Scantlebury (2005) argues that African American girls acting as caretakers within classroom settings, takes the focus away from their own academic learning.

For one of the researchers and many other African American girls and women, the caretaker demands made by teachers create problems amongst peer groups. One researcher reflects on this saying:

> When I was in the 3rd grade, my teacher used to ask me to write down names of students who talked when she left the room. I remember going to the front and standing by her desk with a pencil ready to write down my classmates' names for any infraction. It was strangely an honor and a punishment. I had been chosen by the teacher to 'help' but my classmates disliked me because I had to tattle on them. Now, I remember how costly it was to my connections within my peer group. (L. Cummings, personal communication, December 5, 2012).

For this researcher and many African American girls, navigating school and peer networks requires the development of advanced borders crossing skills and bi-cultural competencies. The lack development of these skills may result in social isolation. There is a need to closely examine the realities of African American girls that face may social isolation and/or academic disengagement due narrow views about their anti-social and pro-social behaviors.

Achievement motivation

Achievement motivation represents the ubiquitous factor that indirectly and directly affects all three of the preceding non-cognitive factors (academic self-concept/identity, effort and antisocial/pro-social behavior). A review of relevant literature shows that achievement motivation for African American girls involves cognitive and non-cognitive processes. The cognitive aspect of achievement motivation includes instrumental judgments and beliefs about the value of accomplishing a task, while the non-cognitive aspect reflects the emotional attitudes and reactions to a task (Rosen et al, 2010). Based on this concept, students who endorse as stronger connection with academics are motivated to succeed because their sense of self is directly linked to their academic performance. The incongruence between students' academic performance and sense of self is defined as academic disidentification. Negative school experiences are strongly associated with academic disindentification and decreased levels of achievement motivation (Osborne, 1997; Steele, 1992)

African American girls experience multiple threats such as teachers' beliefs about their inferior intellectual ability, devaluation of their home worlds, and expectations for early pregnancy. These threats often influence African American girls' beliefs about their academic success and create negative attitudes toward school. Pejorative attitudes toward school contribute to lowered achievement motivation and contribute to "not learning." Some African American girls rebel in the learning context (i.e. refusing to complete class work, disobeying class rules and violating school policies). One researcher reflects on an experience that inspired her to refuse to learn in her class.

> I was in a magnet program for gifted students, established to fulfill the Georgia desegregation requirements for federal funding. In eighth grade, I started algebra with a highly diverse cohort. My best friend, a soft spoken African American girl, was in my class and from the beginning of the course my teacher would always make comparisons between us. She would applaud her work, describe her as the ideal student (quiet, submissive), and encourage me to emulate her. I on the other hand was prone to ask questions and speak out in class. I began to hate that class and her as my teacher. I told her that I was not going to do any more homework, class work, or participate in class. I felt that failed to recognize what I added to the class. She would ask me daily for my work and I would remind her that I told her I was not going to do anymore of her work. She would walk away saying that I was only hurting myself and that I would fail the class. I stubbornly held to my resolve and failed that class even though I typically excelled at math. I failed her course because I had lost the motivation to perform even though I had never gotten less than a B in any prior math course. I was required to attend summer school with the 'bad kids' where I ended up teaching most of my classmates how to do algebra. (L. Cummings, personal communication, January 18, 2013).

Peer accusations of "acting white" and stress resulting from straddling their peer, home, and schools worlds also affects African American girls' achievement motivation. For instance, Ford's (1995) research shows that some African American girlsintentionally underachieve to protect their peers' academic self-concept. In essence, some African American girls self-sabotage their academic performance to not only maintain their sense of self but to sustain a sense of connectedness to their peers and families (Ford, 1995); while other girls work hard to succeed as a means to uplift their cultural community (Hamilton, 1996).

African American girls who maintain high achievement motivation learn to navigate successfully through multiple borders. Many of these girls have been taught by their families that school is an integral part their family's success and a means to overcome racial, gender, and class barriers (Hamilton, 1996). Hamilton (1996) examined young African American women's motivation for educational success and attainment. Findings from this study revealed two motivational frameworks stressing that a college education is necessary for personal independence and to uplifting the African American community. The motivation to perform academically is believed to be a result of socialization regarding embedded achievement. This concept refers to the belief that African American girls are taught that their identity and connection to their racial/ethnic group is characterized and enhanced by personal academic attainment. Oyserman, Terry and Bybee (2001) suggest that embedded achievement is an important factor relating to girls' achievement motivation. African American girls' sense of personal responsibility for obtaining success helps them sustain high levels of achievement motivation when faced with sociocultural and psychosocial barriers. For many African American girls, schools serve as the gateway for a better life (Harrison, 1997).

In contrast, other African American girls view schools as places where their culture is discounted, devalued, and misunderstood (Ford, 1995). Many of these African American girls experience difficulty navigating between their home, school and social worlds and often suffer academically (Phelan, Cao Yu, & Davidson, 1998). Harrison (1997) argues that African American girls experiences problems adjusting in school because educators devalue their home worlds. Thus, many girls have trouble dealing with their teachers' perceptions of who they are, where they come from, and how they are taught to speak, dress and behave. For these young women, school is a hostile environment evokes negative feelings about school and lessens overall motivation to succeed. In order to navigate psychosocial, sociocultural, and gender borders, some African American girls respond by exhibiting anti-social behaviors (i.e. becoming the loud black girl). The manifestation of these anti-social behavior increases the likelihood structural border will be erected limiting their capacity to sustain engagement in school.

Conclusion

Based on this review, it is clear that there is a need to use a cultural and contextualized lens to examine the non-cognitive skills and behaviors of African American girls. Situating this population within the multiple worlds framework helps researchers and practitioners to understand the dichotomous roles assigned to African American girls within the school settings. Educational researchers and practitioners rarely consider how non-cognitive factors impact African American girls' experiences in school. Most often these girls are viewed through a bilateral lens that portrays them as 'at-risk' or academic superstars. These dichotomous roles directly and indirectly impact how their non-cognitive skills are perceived. Environments that focus on non-cognitive factors as performance indicators as well as environments that alienate and dehumanize African American female students inadvertently puts them at academic risk and marginalizes them in schools.

When looking at African American girls within schools, a sobering trend emerges where teacher perceptions and interpretations of non-cognitive behaviors dictate their academic success or failure. For this population their academic self-concept/identity, effort, anti-social/pro-social behaviors and achievement motivation often create difficulties when attempting to move between school, peer, and family worlds. This conflict often results in teachers categorizing cognitively capable students as nonperformers. This misjudgment of African American female students' capacity may have long-term effects on their educational outcomes and occupational trajectories. These perceptions often result in unfair administrative practices such as disproportionate referrals for minor infractions and dress code violations (Archer-Banks & Behar-Horenstein, 2012).

A positive academic self-concept/identity for African American girls is influenced by their capacity to navigate across psychosocial, sociocultural, gender, and linguistic borders. Within this review, effort emerged as an important non-cognitive factor that influences African American girls' academic experiences. For some girls, engaging in school is difficult when they feel devalued by teachers and administrators. Both antisocial and pro-social behavior surfaced as the culturally situated non-cognitive factors that both impede and facilitate navigation across school, family, and peer worlds. Anti-social behaviors within the literature that are attributed to African American girls include confrontation, aggressiveness, and lack of respect for authority figures (Evans, 1988; Fordham, 1993). Pro-social behaviors manifest in classroom teachers' assessments of maturity and shared responsibility for classroom management. Achievement motivation provides an overarching basis for understanding the role of cognitive and non-cognitive processes on African American girls' experiences in school. Contextualizing achievement motivation as a multidimensional factor helps to understand the interconnectedness of academic self-concept/identity, effort, and anti-social/pro-social behaviors for this population. In general, the devaluation of the culturally situated non-cognitive skills of African American girls often creates difficulty when attempting to cross psychosocial, sociocultural, gender, linguistic and structural borders in school contexts. More specifically, academic success and failure may come at a significant cost to African American girls because of its implicit challenges to their cultural identity. Thus, *it is clear that non-cognitive factors are not devoid of cultural interpretations.*

Recommendations for Research and Practice

In order to further understand processes and develop effective ways to accurately assess African American girls' non-cognitive skill set, there is a need for continued research in this area. More specifically, this review reveals a need for in-depth empirical studies that explicate the relationship between culture and non-cognitive factors. Examining this topic will help researchers and practitioners to understand the inconsistencies in the evaluation of African American girls' cognitive and non-cognitive skills. To further understand the non-cognitive skills exhibited by African American girls, there is a need to also examine parental socialization processes. Systematic research that examines the frequency and content of socialization messages regarding navigating hostile environments (i.e., school domains) can advance our knowledge about the development of non-cognitive skills. Lastly, researchers need to use a strength-based perspective that acknowledges the inherent value of African American girls' cultural grounding and its impact on their classroom experiences. This strength based research is needed to further examine the interconnectedness of academic motivation, academic self-concept/identity, effort, and anti-social/pro-social behavior.

The implications from this proposed area of research may encourage practitioners to examine personal truths, hidden values, and experiences about student's cognitive and non-cognitive abilities. Clarity about personal bias may facilitate more appropriate interactions with African American girls. This process requires that service providers learn about and consider how societal beliefs about African American girls affect their ability to provide supportive environments for optimal growth and development. For educators, this reflective practice allows them to continuously examine the underlying meaning behind how and why they reprimand and discipline African American girls. It is especially important for educators from different worlds. Purposefully acknowledging how differing worlds may create barriers for students can help practitioners to bring the gaps between youth's multiple worlds. .

Practitioner focused programs (teacher education, social work, nursing, and public health) should expose future human service professionals to contextual theories such as the multiple-worlds framework to better prepare them to work with increasingly diverse youth populations. By employing a culturally responsive approach, human service professionals can create a safe, transformative space for youth to be their authentic selves. For African American girls, this would involve creating less hostile experience that encourages various modes of expression. Such an environment would aid in the establishment of positive teacher-student or client-provider relationships. Lastly, educators, service providers, and parents should work collaboratively to help African American develop important non-cognitive skills. Building effective border crossing strategies will increase this population's success in multiple domains (Robinson & Ward, 1991), promote long-term goal orientation, and decrease short term solutions (i.e., acting out in class, not learning, and engaging in risky behaviors).

From this analysis we conclude that non-cognitive factors and behaviors play a critical role in the academic experiences and capacity to cross borders. While some African American girls may experience difficulty crossing psychological, gender, linguistic and structural borders, others can smoothly transition into multiple worlds. Many African American girls, especially those who do not have familial and social support, need safe spaces where they can develop appropriate non-cognitive skills that increases their capacity to manage multiple worlds (Bemak, Chi-Ying, & Siroskey-Sabdo, 2005; Holcomb-McCoy, 2004; Lindsay-Dennis, Cummings, & McClendon, 2011). These safe spaces can be created through group counseling sessions, school-based mentoring programs, and community based interventions. The use of culturally appropriate methods that draws on African American girls' cultural characteristics may help them develop better navigational skills for future success (Corneille, Ashcraft, & Belgrave, 2005).

References

Archer-Banks, D. A. & Behar-Horenstein, L. S. (2012). Ogbu revisited: unpacking high achieving African American girls' high school experiences. *Urban Education* 47(1), 198-223.

Bandura, A. (1973). *Aggressiveness: A social learning analysis.* New York: Prentice Hall.

Bemak, F., Chi-Ying, R., Siroskey-Sabdo, L. A. (2005). Empowerment groups for academic success: An innovative approach to present high school failure for at risk, urban African American girls. *Professional School Counseling,* 8(5), 377-390.

Blake, J. J., Butler, B. R., Lewis, C. W., & Darensbourg, A. (2011). Unmasking the inequitable discipline experiences of urban black girls: Implication for urban educational stakeholders. *Urban Review,* 43, 90-106.

Blum, R. W., & Libbey, H. (2004). School connectedness—Strengthening health and education outcomes for teenagers. R.W. Blum, H. Libbey (Eds.). Journal of School Health, 74(7), 229-299.

Chavous, T. & Cogburn, C. D. (2007). Superinvisible women: Black girls and women in education. *Black Women, Gender and Families,* 1(2), 24-51.

Collins, P. (2000). *Black Feminist thought: Knowledge, consciousness, and the politics of empowerment* (2nd ed). New York; Routledge.

Corneille, M. A., Ashcraft, A. M., & Belgrave, F. Z. (2005). What's culture gotto do with it? Prevention programs for African American adolescent girls. *Journal of Health Care for Poor and Underserved,* 16, 38-47.

Cuasay, P. (1992). Cognitive factors in academic achievement. *Higher Education Extension Service Review,* 3(3), 1-10.

Evans, G. (1988). Those loud black girls. In D. Spender & E. Sarah (Eds.), *Learning to lose: Sexism and education* (2nd ed., pp. 183-190). London: Women's Press.

Evans-Winters, Venus E. (2005). *Teaching Black Girls: Resiliency in Urban Classrooms.* New York: Peter Lang Publishing, Inc.

Farkas, G. (2003). Cognitive skills and non-cognitive traits and behaviors in stratification processes. *Annual Review of Sociology,* 29, 541–562.

Ford, D. (1995). Underachievement among gifted and non-gifted Black females: A study of perceptions. *The Journal of Secondary Gifted Education,* 6 (2), 165-175.

Fordham, S. (1993). Those loud black girls: (Black) women, silence, and gender passing in the academy. *Anthropology and Education.* 24(1), 3-24.

Gilmore, P. (1991). "Gimme Room": School Resistance, Attitude, and Access to Literacy. In C. Mitchell & K. Weiler (Eds.), *Rewriting Literacy: Culture and the Discourse of Other* (pp. 57-76). New York: Bergin & Garvey.

Grant, L. (1984). Black females "place" in desegregated classrooms. *Sociology of Education,* 5, 98-11.

Hamilton, C. W. (1996). Nature of motivation for educational achievement among African American female college students. *Urban Education,* 31(1), 72-90.

Harrison, J. (1997). Lisa's quiet fight: School structure and African American adolescent females. In K. Lomotey (Ed.), Sailing against the wind: African-Americans and women in U.S. education (pp. 45-54). New York: State University of New York Press.

Heckman, J. J., & Rubinstein, Y. (2001). The importance of non-cognitive skills: Lessons from the GED testing program. *American Economic Review,* 91(2), 145–149.

Henry, A. (1998). Invisible and womanish: Black girls negotiating their lives in an African centered school in the USA. *Race, Ethnicity, & Education,* 1(2), 151-170.

Holcomb-McCoy, C. (2004). Group mentoring with urban African American female adolescents. *Journal of Teaching and Learning in Diverse Setting, 2,* 161-176.

Horvat, E. M. & Antonio, A. L. (1999). Hey those shoes are out of uniform: African American girls in an elite high school and the importance of habitus. *Anthropology and Education & Quarterly,* 30(3), 317-342.

Jones, C., & Shorter-Gooden, K. (2003). *Shifting: The Double Lives of Black Women in America.* New York: HarperCollins.

Kerckhoff, A., & Glennie, E. (1999). The Matthew effect in American education. Research in the *Sociology of Education,* 12, 35–66.

Kindermann, T. A. (2007). Effects of naturally existing peer groups on changes in academic engagement in a cohort of sixth graders. *Child Development,* 78(4), 1186–1203.

Kohl, H. (1994). "I won't learn from you": Confronting student resistance. In *Rethinking our classrooms: Teaching for equity and social justice* (pp. 134-135). Milwaukee, WI: Rethinking Schools.

Lei, J. I. (2003). (Un)necessary toughness: Those loud black girls and those quiet Asian boys. *Anthropology & Education Quarterly,* 34(2), 158-181.

Lindsay-Dennis, L. A. (2010). *The influence of familial socialization and involvement on the multiple identities and the academic performance of African American adolescent girls.* Unpublished dissertation manuscript.

Lindsay-Dennis, L.A., Cummings, L. & McClendon, S.C. (2011). Toward a culturally responsive mentoring paradigm for urban African American girls. *Black Women, Gender, & Families: A Black Women's Studies Journal,* 5(2), 66-99.

Morris, E. W. (2007). Ladies or loudies: Perceptions and experiences of Black girls in classrooms. *Youth & Society,* 38, 490-515.

Ogbu, J. U. (2003). *Black American students in an affluent suburb: A study of academic disengagement.* New Jersey: Lawrence Erlbaum.

Osborne, J, W. (1997). Race and academic dis-identification. *Journal of Educational Psychology,* 89(4), 729-735.

Oyserman, D., Harrison, K., & Bybee, D. (2001) Can racial identity be promotive of academic efficacy? *International Journal of Behavioral Development,* 25(4), 379 385.

Phelan, P., Cao Yu, H., Davidson, A. L. (1994). Navigating the psychosocial pressures of adolescents: The voices and experiences of high school youth. *American Educational Research Association Journal,* 31 (2), 415-447.

Robinson, T. & Ward, J. V. (1991). A Belief in Self Far Greater Than Anyone's Disbelief: Cultivating Resistance Among African American Female Adolescents. *Women & Therapy* 11(3-4), 87-103.

Rosen, J. A., Glennie, E. J., Dalton B. W., Lennon, J. M., and Bozick, R. N. (2010). *Non-cognitive Skills in the Classroom: New Perspectives on Educational Research.* Research Triangle Park, NC: RTI International.

Saunders, J., Davis, L., Williams, T., & Williams, J. H. (2004). Gender differences in self-perceptions and academic outcomes: A study of African American high school students. *Journal of Youth and Adolescence,* 33(1), 81-90.

Chapter Six
Learning Black Womanhood: An Autoethnography
Denise Davis-Maye

Introduction

Womanhood is a concept that is societally constructed. There are certainly ascribed roles, skill sets, and characteristics which females are supposed to possess and exhibit. In the narrative analysis that follows, I will present the multiple messages and gender role expectations which were transmitted throughout my life. Further, I will discuss how the social context was written for Black girls and later young black women's emerging womanhood. Using a temporal application of narrative analysis, I will offer a depiction of the messages related to womanhood, and the methods and means through which they were transmitted. Additionally, sharing this narrative will enable us to discuss how these narratives, because of the marginal status of the actors, is minimized and in fact excluded from the broader narrative of womanhood. We will discover a set of underlying values and expectations for African American girls and women as they/we do gender.

The Framework

Using Autoethnography to Access a View of Womanhood through Hip Hop

Individuals actively construct and attribute meaning and significance to the aspects of their lives and the related experiences. So to, has the author in relationship to her understanding and enacting of womanhood. The discussion of this "coming to womanhood" process and its outcome is grounded in Womanism, filtered through a Hip Hop lens and a Narrative Analysis method, specifically Autoethnographic Narrative Inquiry. The author "gazes inward" for her story and in so doing hopes to describe that experience for others while seeking to illuminate the factors which brought meaning to her experiences with and understanding of womanhood (Ellis &Bochner, 2000).

Theoretical Centering

Womanism

Womanism is the organizing epistemological framework that supports this journey. Appreciating and legitimizing women's lives and experiences is consistent with the Womanism described by Collins (1998) when she attempts to center the womanist ideology in the moral and ethical principles of the political struggles of African Americans as a group. Smitherman (1996, p. 104) goes on to describe a womanist as an African American woman who "is rooted in the Black community and committed to the development of herself and the entire community." The most relevant descriptions of Womanism come from Alice Walker (1983, p. xi), who's co-opting of the southern black vernacular expression, "You acting womanish," results in a characterization of a womanist as a woman of color who is "traditionally universalist" and is courageous, bold, responsible, and focused, while being committed to [the] survival and wholeness of entire people, male and female. Attending to and valuing Black women's experiences are at the core of Womanism. In her summation of Walker's (1983) definition of a womanist, Collins (1998, pp. 61) suggested that womanists acted in outrageous, courageous, and willful ways, using attributes that freed them from the conventions long limiting White women. Womanish girls wanted to know more and in greater depth than what were considered good for them. They were responsible, in charge and serious. Given this exploration of the etiology of the authors knowledge of womanhood and the ways she currently understands what it means to be Black and grown, and a woman, Womanism just fits.

The meanings that Black girls and women attach to their place, roles, and possibility both within the context of their communities and families of origin can be uniquely garnered through a Womanist-framed epistemology which genuinely underscores the import of valuing the distinct aspects of these women's lives. It is through the subjective experiences of women that we are able to explore the varied influences which impact women's lives. The present inquiry, which explores the narratives of the author who belongs to and holds membership in a group which is marginalized—Black women, neatly fits within the framework of Womanist epistemology.

The Method

Autoethnography

Qualitative methods have a history of honoring the voices of marginalized populations and therefore render them worthy of study (Padgett, 1998). In the case of this inquiry, the author employs an autoethnographic narrative inquiry. Autoethnography is a method which allows the actor to "gaze inward" to describe an experience. The overarching goal is not to make a claim about any specific phenomenon, but is simply illustrative in nature with the intention of inviting outsiders into the world of the actor—in this case, the author. The application of narrative inquiry in this case, allows for the analysis of this authors personal narrative in order to glean the core messages that were transmitted concerning womanhood.

The Worldview Hip Hop

A worldview is defined as a conceptual lens rooted in cultural wisdom. It helps us to understand and perceive society, the world and our place in it in order to synthesize the related information to make critical decisions that shape our future. For the first half of my life, Hip Hop was my worldview, and as such, this is the lens through which the author most comfortably critiques her experiences. In order to conceive Hip Hop as a world view, one must understand Hip Hop as a fold in the fabric of the Black aesthetic and African diasporic cultures. Drumming, call and response, layered intertextuality, and social relevance form a powerful aesthetic that has moved from the African continent to the U.S.— across time periods, genres, and gender, which shows up in different ways throughout Hip Hop. Central to this worldview is the valuing of emotional and physical strength in the face of systemic challenges. This message of strength and perseverance which shows up in a multitude of diasporic presentations over time is certainly transmitted in most forms of Hip Hop. Whether these messages are passed orally as in ancient history; through the call and response of Harriet Tubman's self-emancipation songs; the chanting, marching, picketing of Black children in Birmingham; through the piecing of quilts; or the politics of Yasiin Bey or Sister Souljah, the ability to infuse the legacy of one's ancestors into that which you now believe to be familiar is a coveted opportunity. Hip Hop represents a verbal legacy that has existed within many cultures for millennia. Hip Hop was the second form of African American music which was initially created and controlled by Blacks. The Hip Hop Worldview demonstrates the creativity, spirit, oneness/interdependence and connection that I was socialized to believe were core aspects of Black womanhood.

Where We Start—The Question

"You on some grown-a** woman *%#+," a childhood friend says to me as we get caught up on each other's life path, achievements and movements. In response, I glowed, and felt a sense of pride that this friend had lauded upon me the esteemed status of womanhood. Now granted, I had been legally a "woman" for over two decades prior to the adulation. As such, I pondered my emotional response to this accolade. What about the latter perceived positive acknowledgement from this brother, representative of the men in my community, and in fact, my community itself, lifted my head a little higher, and added some spring into my "grown-woman" step? This wonder sparked the exploration of what I understand to represent womanhood; the messages I was given about womanhood, and girls and women's roles; the context in which those the messages were transmitted; and by whom. This chapter is a reflective one which uses my experiences over time growing up in a borough of an urban, Northeastern city in the midst of one of the most significant cultural movements in contemporary history—the Hip Hop Cultural movement.

Recollections
1973: I am central

I close my eyes and reflect on long, brown legs making a stark contrast against the bright, crisp white cotton sheets as they dangle on the side of the mahogany bed. She dons a white cotton nightgown and in her hair - brown paper bag rollers sticking through the leg holes of white satin panties. Yes, panties, as in women's underwear, to protect the 1-day old press and curl from the cotton strands of the sheets. This reflection, and frankly the memory, is less of the actual occurrence, and more accurately, from the old family instamatic photograph that sparks reminiscences of the many Saturday mornings which are reflected in the one photo. These were lazy mornings, in which I was usually the last to awaken. My brothers had long awakened to watch some cartoon—Fat Albert, The Jackson 5, The Harlem Globe Trotters, or the Superfriends. My mother having washed several loads of clothes at the Laundromat would be headed out, while my dad would be leaving to go to the barbershop he owned in another borough. I was not forced to awaken to participate in the Saturday cleaning rituals like so many of my peers and I didn't volunteer to do so. But as I walked down the narrow hallway, my dad with his hands on the doorknob would stop and whistle the theme to the Miss America pageant—you know the one. My mom would stop what she was doing and being to sing "Here she is, Miss America." I would grin and bear the attention as my younger brother ignored them and me, and my older brother rolled his eyes while making disparaging comments—like "She's pretty alright—pretty ugly!" Yeah, that was my cool clog and boot-leg jeans wearing brother. He, with those five words in contrast to the messages that my parents were transmitting about my worth and my beauty in the context of my family and community could have counteracted those messages. But, because they were isolated, they became irrelevant—then.

The transmission of my significance and value in my familial context was clear. I was at the center of my family. I was at the center of the discourse at the dinner table. My school exploits were fodder for uproarious laughter with adult company. If I were picked on by a bigger kid in neighborhood, by baby brother would physically engage him. He would throw down the gauntlet, (usually a Blowpop lollipop that had been previously hanging from his lips) and literally fight my battles, because even at 8, I was important to him—valuable even.

1978: Hip Hop & Being on the Periphery

"One-two-One-two, Whatchawanna do?" reverberates across 174th Street. "Mommy please can I go downstairs? I'll be up before its dark." I plead as I look out of my 10th floor bedroom window glimpsing "The Center" with quickly filling up park benches. "No, and I'm not going to tell you again;" my mother says as "matter-of-factly" as a person can say anything. You see, this is our mantra every summer since 1978 when I first discovered, by mistake, how marvelous it was to be mingling through the crowd with scents of Love's Baby Soft & Safeguard soap, Love Bug Starskii spun and AfrikaBambaataa and The Zulu Nation stood watch.

I remember my young 12-year old self wishing that Mommy wouldn't hold my hand as we crossed the street. Didn't she see the cute brothers leaning on the fence and sitting on the chain-links? They were decked out in white t-shirts, bell-bottomed Sergio Valentes, colored Lees, suede Pumas, shell-toe Adidas, and Pro-Ked 69ers. She would remark, "They are getting ready to have another "block party." She meant a "jam." My 11-year old brother's eyes would light up—see he could be there in the midst of it all—he was a boy. I could only sit on the benches and watch. But this placement still allowed the full side view of the cement state at the rear of the Bronx River Houses Community Center. These "block parties" were called "Zulu Jams" by residents and were coveted opportunities to see the newest dances, hear the latest music and to be seen. And I watched.

"One, two, One, two." They were testing the sound system. It reverberated throughout the projects. It was dusk and there were groups of girls and boys entering the River. "What ya' wanna do…" Though this, 1978, was by no means the beginning of Hip Hop, it was smack dab in the middle of the Hip-Hop's founding decade. As I watched these groups of sisters and brothers interacting with each other, flexing for and in response to one another, it became clear what the rules were for inter-sex and intra-sex interactions in my community. The men were firmly at the center of this space. They were the disc jockey (d.j.) who at this point in the trajectory of Hip Hop was still the star. The djs were overwhelmingly male. In fact, I don't recall seeing a female d.j. until maybe four years later. They were the master of ceremony (M.C.). The preponderance of M.C.s were male, though there were a few sisters at the time holding their own, once they had been legitimized by a male M.C. or crew. They, men, were disproportionately the dancers (B-boys), but women did have a larger representative contingency among this legion than any other. I observed these interactions, these placements, these margins, and got the message. I was not at the center in this space, a voyeur maybe; a supporter, and possibly even integral, but certainly on the margins.

It was at that point that I became vividly aware of my femaleness and what that meant in the context of my community that created and was Hip-Hop. Being female meant that, though you were on the periphery, you had a role. Being female meant that you had some responsibilities. You were either a b-girl (dancer), a rapper (though in very limited numbers and earned only after proving not only your verbal skills, but your physical prowess and bravado as well), or you were someone's little sister, perpetually. Whatever role you were ascribed, assigned or you accepted had related expectations and privileges.

1982: Little Sister Coming of Age within the Evolution of Hip Hop & Embracing my Role with No Limits

In the same community, as I came of age and moved into adolescence, so did Hip Hop. Hip Hop Culture came into its own. Because I spent my early adolescence being educated outside of my community at an elite preparatory school, I had to spend an inordinate amount of time integrating and then clarifying multiple messages about what it meant to be a Black woman. Within the context of my academic environment Black womanhood was not respected, and was certainly not valued. There were instances where my blackness was stigmatized. I recall a particular instance while sitting in Latin class. I received the second highest score on our first exam in a class where I was the only one on scholarship. As class was being released, my stern white-haired teacher asked me to stay behind. She called me to her desk, and inquired about my previous exposure to Latin. Perplexed, I told her I had taken no language classes before, unless she was counting the daily exposure to *Spanglish* in my community. She then asked how and with whom I had studied. I then, with my inner-city hackles raised [See, you learn to spot trouble before it gets to you in my neighborhood], I replied "The same way I study for everything else—by myself and for myself." For me that meant at the kitchen table with dishes being washed, the background noise of my father watching *Kojak* or *Good Times* and my brothers making the noise they made. It did not mean studying in a "study" in my 35th floor Park Avenue or West End apartment like many of my classmates. After scoring the highest test score on the 2nd exam, my teacher simply said "Impressive." At the end of the term, she congratulated me on working so hard and being a "credit" to my family. She actually said that. From her perspective, my race was supposed to hinder me academically. In contrast to that teachers diminished expectations for me, the JV basketball coach encouraged me to try out for the squad, though she had never seen me play. Let's be clear, had she seen me play, they would have locked every door to the gym when they saw me approach. Because I was Black, tall and from a particular neighborhood, I was expected to be a gifted player. I still don't know how I made the team. I wouldn't have made the "biddy basketball" traveling squad in my neighborhood for 5- 12 year olds.

During another incident, I received a message about skin color in the most peculiar manner. I am sitting in study hall during a free period. A group of girls are discussing their recent Spring Break jaunts to St. Barts, Costa Rica, and the South of France. They are complimenting one another on their tans. One says, *"Have you seen Heather? She went to St. Kitts and she is Nigger Black."* This was the first time I had heard this word used by anyone not in an episode of the television series *Roots*. The word was not used in my home. The derivative

"Niggah" is not yet used widely in Hip Hop or freely in my urban neighborhood. So it was not a word I was used to hearing, and certainly not by peers. So with my back turned toward the offender, I froze. I began to process my 15 year old response. I thought *"What should I say? What should I do?"* Within three seconds, the girl approaches me and places her arm around my shoulders as she asks;*"Did you hear what I just said?"* I cowardly responded, *"No,"* and proceeded to pack my books to depart. That incident colored, no pun intended, my notions of how people perceived Black people and their skin. Actually, it was the first time in my life that I thought about my *Hershey's* Milk Chocolate colored skin and its beauty or value.

In contest, I actively sought substantive connections to my community. During this time, Hip Hop is clearly defining the roles of Black and Latina girls in my neighborhood. No matter how diligent I was about trying to fit, to dress, to talk, to be who my home culture acculturated girls to be, alternate expectations were clearly communicated to and for me. When I would appear in the park where others my age were engaged in smoking varied forms of tobacco (legal and illegal), as the "joints' were being passed liberally, someone would inadvertently intervene before it would get to me. If I lingered too long on a street corner trying to see and be seen, some boy from my community would offer to walk me home or employ some other diversionary tactic like asking me out on a date with the clear knowledge that I was too immature to even know what to say and as a result I would literally flee to a more comfortable space. At the time, I thought it was a nuisance. In hindsight, I was being corralled onto a path that my community had for me.

It became clear from brothers hurrying my "grown behind" away from the fray that my role was different. I was expected to represent my neighborhood differently. So like Hip Hop, womanhood represented possibility. Like Hip Hop, women resuscitate the vernacular of a culture—the cultural voice. Like Hip Hop, Black womanhood means to give to voice to the possibilities and deferred dreams of our foremothers. I was taught that I had a role to fulfill, in and for my community. I learned that there were no boundaries—that my place, though reinforced by community, was not restricted by my community. There were clearly object lessons transmitted that women were supposed to emotionally, sexually, spiritually hold up the men in my community. Women were expected to be the moral compass as mothers (always mothers), wives, girlfriends, and sisters. But simultaneously, almost in contrast to former messages, the community was telling one girl to go hard in the paint with male ballers in the park or to keep reading or dancing or singing or rapping into her possibility. Some might not understand the relevance of a community which told its girls that your possibilities were limitless. But if the reader considers that this community was the same community context often depicted by outsiders as barrier-laden, destructive, dangerous, resource poor, and a shell of humanity—then, only then, would the former discussion be impactful.

So, my community was burdened with so many damaging depictions that would suggest that this very community was not conducive to women's development. However, it is from this place that my and many other women's strength, persistence, and vision was birthed. It is from this space that I was told *"Girl, you are smart little thing."* It was in this context, that when I told my neighbor I wanted to be a doctor, she responded, *"Of course you do, and of course you can."*

Memes of Womanhood

Working, Communicating with Verve & Keeping your Hair Right

In addition to the major passages in my development previously discussed, my ideas regarding womanhood were also framed by regular communications regarding women and work, women and communication and women and their hair.

Womanhood & Work

My community of origin boasted poor and working-class, single, married, and cohabitating women. My extended family was laden with women—in fact we were woman-deep and woman-centered. My aunts, adult cousins, fictive aunties all represented the characteristics that were transmitted familially. Though there were women who were housewives in my community, I can only recall one of my female relatives who was not gainfully employed outside her home. Though she was a homemaker with several children, she was always perceived by the extended family as someone who lounged all day and even lazy. Probably because, in contrast, the other women were always moving, working, coming to and from work. They were making moves, going back to college as adults, while holding down full-time jobs. They were independent, though there were husbands, ex-husbands, paramours, and non-custodial parents—the women never seemed to rely on their partners to manage, or in fact, even to provide resources. They were central and their relationships were central. They were all working toward some invisible, never discussed end other than to retire with a pension. There was little focused discussion on working for peace or enjoyment. As a result of these messages, I began working at 15. And early on, work was more about "the work" and working and to no real end. At the very least, work and working hard was a vitally important social expectation.

Womanhood & Communication

There were multiple opportunities to observe and receive indirect messages about communicative styles. It took me a while to integrate those messages. Of course all environmental factors are mediated by individual personality. My innate response to conflict, for instance, had always been to avoid it—as illustrated by my earlier recounting of the "N-word" encounter. When I would encounter uncomfortable situations, I would emotionally and physically extract myself—leaving the situation and the politics intact. The women in my family circle had to be pushed to act or speak up, so my responses were not atypical. The women in my community, however, were another matter entirely. If they had been wronged, disrespected or challenged, their responses were immediate and exacting. I learned that you needed to be able to clearly articulate your feelings about the situations you faced, while placing the recipient of the missive on notice about impending outcome. For example, say a girl had issued an indirect threat or insult toward another. The threatened individual might proactively seek out the subject and address her in private with *"Don't let your mouth issue a check you're a** can't cash."* In other words *"You are engaging in a fight that you could not win. As the bigger woman, I will allow this to pass—this time."* In the code of communication, threats and insults to one's womanhood had to be managed. Allowing situations to fester without response is considered immature and cowardly. Further, managing situations with the passive aggressive, devious ways that one might observe in other contexts are viewed with disdain. We learned to say what we meant and to mean what we said. A supporting idea to this management of conflict was that you shouldn't communicate anything you are unable to support. In other words communication should be authentic or shouldn't happen at all.

Like Hip Hop provides for the space to express the anguish, pain, joy and love in innovative ways, the significant women in my life modeled creative communication with verve. Their "speak" was nuanced in the ways that they communicated rife with catch phrases, signature facial expressions, and duality. So there was a kind of vernacular was important. They crafted nuanced speech into loving, engaged communication that we participated in. We were socialized to verbally negotiate our space—to speak up at all costs. The women in my maternal family—we spoke to one another differently. It was a loving, supportive, nurturing "speak" In fact almost everyone had an endearing nickname. All our elder female relatives were referred to and treated with the respects of "Aunties." The generational boundaries, though, were flexible. Elder adult cousins played the roles of aunts, sisters and other-mothers. Around the *Pokeno* table everyone was equal—age was insignificant. It is where you got introduced to how you spoke to and handled your relationships with men and other women. It is where your significant other was assessed and discussed often in code, so that he or she were sitting at the table, they would never know they were subject of the discourse. This place is also where entre to womanhood was evaluated—how you handled a win or a loss. It was where we saw the adult women share their winnings with sisters. It was where they communicated the interdependence that was us.

In contrast, my paternal family boasted no nuance and subtlety was not valued. My uncle would say, better out than in. All of the communication was traced with humor. Whether the message was hurtful, helpful, loving or hateful—it was always couched in a joke. These communications served to create boundaries and belonging. You only used individuals as the butt of the joke when they were a part of the joke. So, if you were not a family member, your feelings were spared. One exemplar involves an uncle's attempt to help a niece manage a particularly painful ending of a relationship. As other family members attempted to sooth her pain, this uncle interjects *"Well it could happen to anyone, and so it could sure happened to you."* In other words, ending relationships happen to everyone at some point—get over it. In another incident, a relative was complaining that her feet were aching after having walked a long distance. Another relative responded by suggesting that her shoes were ill-fitting by saying, *"You should know you can't stuff California into New York, No matter how hard you try, it won't fit."*

Language was more than a means of communication. It was a means of identification with your family and community. It was the means to claim your power in and over your space. It was clear in the message that I could speak power into my space. In fact, I was able to exercise this power as I graduated secondary school. Of the seven universities which accepted me, there were three Historically Black Colleges and Universities. My guidance counselor warned me that by selecting an HBCU over two elite universities I would be *"severely limiting"* myself. I vividly remember responding, "Maybe, but not as much as I would be limiting myself if I chose [University A or B]." Communication was a tool used to negotiate and secure your peace while clarifying the boundaries related to others powers over and within your space.

Womanhood, Connection & Hair

Another childhood memory is the cumulative hair grooming rituals. It was clear fairly early that this was important for women in my community and frankly within my family. Women were supposed to care about their hair. You would see teens on park benches or on stoops braiding the hair of their peers or younger girls. Those girls who possessed braiding or hair maintenance skills were valued in the community. Mothers whose daughters' hair were well-groomed were praised. Women whose crowns were well maintained were prized. Girls and young women were expected to see one's hair grooming as important.

My earliest memory of this process is being seated in front of a small white, gas-fueled stove with blue flame leaping from one of the eyes, a jar of Ultra Sheen Pressing oil on the counter, and a black straightening comb dangling precariously off of the stove. The smell was that smell, that even as a child you knew wasn't right, but you loved it…it was ritualistic and you knew it "had" to be. By time I turned 10, I had a standing bi-weekly, Friday afternoon appointments with Ms. Lucille at Bachman's salon—shampoo, press and curl. In that space, the ritual of conferring beauty among the dozens of women who would be seated in "the chair," under the dryer, in the waiting seats as they shared their lives. We all left there curled, oiled and sleek. The women talked about how beautiful the girls were becoming, as the girls eavesdropped on conversations that they were not privy to in our generational-boundary laden homes. In addition to clearly articulating the expectations related to appearance, we also were able to share in the reality of dating, "shacking," marriage, divorce, and women's place and power in those linkages.

Grooming rituals were rife with opportunities to understand the layered nature of our community. We watched the economy of the neighborhood operate right before our eyes. On Friday evenings there would be multiple merchants selling wares ranging from basic as underwear to as far-reaching as jewelry to fish dinners. In a community where more traditional retailers were sparingly present, we were clear that we had to get what we wanted or needed the best way we knew how. We saw the women, like Miss Lucille, giving back to the community by hiring and training girls to shampoo hair and more that wasn't always in line with the licensing authority. But they lived here and knew that there was a need to give, contribute and reinvest.

Reflections on Reflections of Womanhood in Conversation with Womanism

Through the method of autoethnography, I have sought to parse out the underlying values, behavioral codes and expectations for African American girls and women as they/we do gender. For me, those memes or units which carried cultural ideas or practices (Graham, 2002), were: (1) knowing and being valued, which often meant being protected; (2) having and being a voice; (3) having no limits (or defying the odds); (4) working hard; (5) speaking up and speaking out; and (6) nurturing connections.

The memes that emerged from my analysis are consistent with a womanist perspective. *Knowing ones value* is a feature which in direct alignment with Womanism's support of women appreciating themselves and their experiences. In the context of my home community, though there were in fact conflicting messages about the worth of Black girls. The messages about my worth were consistent and potent enough that they countered the existing damaging messages. The message to value oneself was reinforced by other mothers, community members and extended family.

Being and having a voice is another idea which comports with Womanism. Knowing oneself well enough to speak for oneself and one's community is a courageous act. Speaking for oneself in circumstances which you are not value requires a boldness that was fortified by and modeled in many urban marginalized communities. Watching women and men stand up to institutions, like public housing administrations, law enforcement, and non-allied educators, as advocates for who may not have had the capacity bolstered my voice and gave me, still give me, the strength to speak up and out.

No limitations were imposed on my possibilities. We were taught that our lives had meaning and did not reflect the shell-shocked neighborhoods that were often depicted on television as a militarized zone. But that there were possibilities that were endless, limitless. At the same time we were taught to recognize the factors which could dim our stars quickly. The murk was always portrayed as purposeful and the work of some entity represented as the power structure. So the possibilities were seen as a birthright that we had to work through and in spite of the created barriers. Our possibilities were often outlined amid imagery of "us" as children of God, who, as such, only needed to step into our legacy of possibility.

The hard work that was demonstrated by the Black women in my family and community, though configured differently, was clearly hard work. These displays follow the commitment, focus and responsibility of Womanism. The practice of working hard can serve as a blessing or a curse. The drive to move, to work, can make you question the value in being still. Sometimes you have to be still before you can fully view your magnificence. Conversely, the work ethic, when focused, directly influenced my ability to see beyond imposed limits into my possibilities.

The familial communication style in which I was socialized developed into a full repertoire of language. I am as comfortable conversing using Black Vernacular English as I am when using Standard Conversational English and it is all genuinely me. I bring my authentic self to every exchange with not confusion about the message.

Finally, Womanism's endorsement of being rooted to the one's center is reflected in the meaning placed on community, interdependence and connectivity among Black women. In my community setting this connection was strengthened in settings like the beauty shop and was experienced amid grooming rituals. The rituals were practiced in a respectful, but never polite space which allowed for loving, supportive, convicted wisdom about who we were as Black women. It was in this space that women were linked. They shared intimate connection where hair could literally be let down and souls laid bare.

Attributes of Black womanhood which were conveyed throughout my childhood and adolescence blended to create my understanding of womanhood. The ways I understand these received messages influences the ways I understand my role and place as a woman. Further, these understandings definitively shape the messages I transmit to my daughter. Though the values and expectations likely vary and are dependent on community and familial context, the preceding narrative reinforces the import of sharing experiences of marginalized groups so that we can frame a full picture of what the messages are and how the messages are experienced and how they are then acted upon. Such messages create a legacy, for good or bad, of doing womanhood.

References

Collins, P. H. (1998). *Fighting Words: Black Women and the Search for Justice.* Minneapolis: University of Minnesota Press.

Ellis, C. & Bochner, A. P. (2000). Autoethnography, Personal Narrative, Reflexivity: Researcher as Subject. In N. K. Denzin & Y. S. Lincoln (eds.) *Handbook of Qualitative Research* (2nd ed.). Thousand Oaks, CA: Sage.

Graham, G. (2002). *Genes: A Philosophical Inquiry.* New York: Routledge.

Padgett, D. K. (1998). *Qualitative Methods in Social Work Research: Challenges and Rewards.* Thousand Oaks, CA: Sage.

Smitherman, G. (1996). A womanist looks at the Million Man March. In Hr. Madhubut & M. Karenga (eds.) *Million Man March Day of Absence* (pp. 104-107). Chicago: Third World Press.

Walker, A. (1983). *In Search of Our Mothers' Gardens.* New York: Harcourt Brace Jovanovich.

Section Three

Turpentine, Sugar, and Pot Liquor: Black Women and Everyday Health

> *Lord, I'm going to hold steady on to you and you've got to see me through.*
>
> Harriet Tubman, Date Unknown

Chapter Seven
Growing up Black and Female: Life Course Transitions and Depressive Symptoms
Claire Norris
Paige Miller

The two authors of this paper seem to have, in many respects, followed similar life trajectories. Both of us, for as long as we can remember, have been worriers. As young children, our worries ranged from relatively minor concerns over what we wore to school and whether our parents would allow sleepovers, to more serious concerns over getting cancer or some other dreaded disease. By adolescence, we noticed the worries changed and took on a different tenor. Those around us suggested these changes were due to hormones; puberty causing our anxieties to escalate. Like many teenage girls we became very aware of our appearances, of our parent's social position, and our status in relation to our peers.

During our early college years (emerging young adulthood), both of our anxiety levels seemed to stabilize, our friendships felt more supportive, and our economic status was mostly unnoticeable. Everyone was "broke" in college. Although race, class, and gender were topics discussed in college courses we were just becoming aware of these identities and how they positioned us within the social structure. Our consciousness was just awakening so we never fully considered the social consequences of these statuses. Not only did we experience seemingly similar transitions through the emotional landscape of adolescence and into emerging adulthood, we went through them at the same time; graduating from high school in the late nineties and completing our doctorate in sociology in 2009 as we entered our mid-twenties. We were both incredibly fortunate to get jobs right out of school (amidst the deepest recession our country has seen in some time): one of us at a small, historically black, Catholic institution in the south and the other at a small to medium sized public liberal arts college in the mid-west. From here the divergence in our perceptions and experiences began to be more noticeable.

After entering the professorate, while both of us experienced the standard stress of being non-tenured faculty members, distinctive qualitative differences in our experiences emerged. For me, being a black married woman with two sons and living in the South created a very different set of anxieties. My worries as a young adult shifted from how my own personal actions and behaviors impacted my failures or successes to how my social position—my race, class, and gender—affected my life experiences. I began to fear and resent racism and sexism in a new way. Although I was aware of these barriers prior to this time in my life (young adulthood), this was the first time I had a true stake in society. No longer under my parent's wings of protection, the cost of race and sex discrimination felt more permanent and damaging in young adulthood. The structural barriers associated with race and gender now had potential consequences for my career, my home, and my ability to care for my family. These barriers could dictate not only my life chances but also that of my husband and children.

As a white, single woman living in the Midwest considerations on the consequences of race have been more academic in nature, not a potentially anxiety inducing daily experience. Although, as a sociologist, I try to be aware of the privileges that often accompany having fair skin in a racialized society, I rarely, if ever, worry about the negative ramifications that my racial identity might have for my life chances and career. Additionally, without the added pressure of children, there is a palpable sense, one that emerges time and again in our conversations with each other, that I have less to lose. My fears stem less from concern over racial discrimination and more from awareness that, being from a working poor background, I lack the cultural capital that many of my fellow academics are able to employ so naturally. Our discussions of our separate but seemingly similar journeys through adolescence into emerging young adulthood and finally into young adulthood led to this paper. We realized the seemingly similar paths we followed masked (much like a statistical model might) the reality of race and class differences and its impact on our experiences. Because we focus on black women's experiences with depressive symptoms as they age, this paper, in a many respects, creates more questions than answers; questions related to racial, class, geographic, and gender differences, an issue we return to in the discussion.

Introduction

Mental health disparities rooted in race, gender, and age differences create and shape social groups' quality of life, life chances, and in turn, depressive symptoms and mortality and morbidity rates. The gender gap in depression remains one of the most consistent and robust findings in the mental health literature (Nolen-Hoeksema, 1987; Mirowsky & Ross, 1986; Aneshensel,

1992). That is, women average higher levels of depression than their male counterparts. While scholars note a significantly greater prevalence of depression in women, the life course perspective suggests that identifying age effects is critical to understanding mental health for women. For example, Mirowsky's (1996) work suggests that a parabolic relationship exists between age and depression for women. That is, young adults and the elderly tend to report higher levels of psychological distress than their middle-aged counterparts (Mirowsky & Ross, 1992). Despite the fact that there are sociological theories (i.e., age increment hypothesis) that predict the relationship between age and depression for women (Mirowsky, 1996), the age patterns of black women's mental health across their life trajectory remains relatively unclear in the mental health literature.

This work contributes to the health literature in three distinct ways: *First,* our work operates within a framework that seeks to understand the affects of the social context(s) of mental illness. Pearlin's (1989; 1999) work calls researchers to consider how the systems of stratification can influence social groups' well-being. He argues that, "... the most encompassing of these structures are the various systems of stratification that cut across societies, such as those based on socio-economic class, race and ethnicity, gender, and age. To the extent that these systems embody the unequal distributions of resources, opportunities ... may itself be a source of stressful life conditions" (Pearlin, 1989: 242). This work responds to Pearlin's call by examining the relationship between age patterns and mental health for black women. Although women and blacks' mental health has been extensively explored in the mental health literature, the intersections of gender, race, and age remain unclear. This work takes a step in that direction by exploring whether black women's mental health trajectory changes as they age from adolescence, into emerging young adulthood, and finally into adulthood.

Second, this research utilizes panel data to quantitatively track patterns of mental health for black women. By employing panel data, our study allows for the measurement of variation in depressive symptoms from one period to another. This work, then, provides insight into psychological distress and contributes to scholarly discourse about black women's mental health throughout womanhood.

Finally, this work serves to inform practitioners, clinicians, psychologists, and policy makers as they seek to understand and mitigate depression and other chronic diseases associated with depression (e.g., obesity, diabetes, and hypertension) for black women.

In the following pages, we discuss the framework within which this study was conceived focusing on the literature regarding black women's mental health. Most importantly for our purposes, we examine the extant literature in terms of women's mental health trajectory as they age from adolescence, to emerging young adulthood, and finally to young adulthood. We highlight the importance of focusing on black women's experiences, regardless of differences in class, geography and gender. Following a description of the methods, the sample from which our results are generated, and the variables, we seek to determine the nature of black women's depressive symptoms over time. We conclude with a discussion of the implications of our research for future studies and policy-makers.

Contextualizing Black Women's Health

In considering mental health for black women in American society, it is essential to consider Pearlin's work (1989, 1999), which highlights the systems of stratification and its impacts on resources, opportunities, and stressful experiences. With this in mind, we draw on Wilson's (1987; 1992) and Mullings (2005) works, which emphasize the psychological implications of the less structurally empowered—including black women. Wilson (1987; 1992) contends that the social conditions facing poor urban blacks have deteriorated to the extent that rates of unemployment, out-of-wedlock births, households headed by females, and dependency on welfare have dramatically increased. Additionally, the growth of the surge of imprisonment of black men has created a shortage of "marriageable men." The consequences of poverty for blacks increase their exposure to stressful experiences (i.e., poverty, joblessness, welfare dependency, and poor health) that make the negotiations of day-to-day interactions a stressful and demoralizing experience.

While Wilson focuses on race, there are a variety of arguments regarding why his claims about blacks experiences might also be gendered. Mullings (2005) "Sojourner Syndrome," for instance, expands Wilson's piece by exploring how the social and economic positions of black women make them more vulnerable to poorer mental health outcomes. Starting with social implications, women disproportionately shoulder the burden of total housework and pay greater "cost of caring" within their social circles—regardless of race or class. However since slavery, black women often construct households, friendships and social support systems that offer psychosocial resources that buffer the negative psychological impact of life's stressors (Stack, 1974; Martineau, 1977; McAdoo, 1982; Lincoln et al., 2003). In fact, Stack (1974) describes an elaborate system of supportive kinship transactions for black families in lieu of personal coping resources. Although this seems to suggest that black women's networks are well-suited to offset the burden's of poverty, researchers contend that drawing on supportive resources to combat frequent occurrences of stress might further aggravate an already resource poor support system (Stack 1974; Lincoln, Taylor & Chatters, 2003) These types of network structures for poor black women, then, can be a source of psychological distress.

While middle-class black women tend to have wider ranging network structures that offer greater access to material resources, they also tend to report less support from family. Because family members often have conflicting obligations and tend to be more spatially distant, middle-class black women tend to report restricted access to supportive resources. Additionally, educated black women with greater incomes tend to be the only ones in their families to attain a middle-class status. Therefore, the direction of material support is often uni-directional with middle-class black women primarily providing the support (Mullings, 2005). For Mullings, then, while social support systems are a critical "resistance resource," they may concurrently operate as a protective barrier and a source of stress and, thus, increase psychological distress for black women.

Another source of stress is the economic conditions of black women (e.g., low incomes, unemployment, and limited job opportunities). Black women are significantly more likely to live below the poverty line compared to their white counterparts—even after controlling for marital status (Brown, Brody & Stoneman, 2000). Mullings (2005) echoes this finding by suggesting that black women tend to occupy lower status positions in the workplace (i.e., service, technical, clerical, and laborer occupations). Furthermore, the economic return for the same levels of education is lower for blacks than whites; black women find themselves in marginal occupations that are menial, low-paying, and insecure and physical working environments lacking in basic resources. These conditions contribute to poor black women's stressful experiences and poor mental health outcomes. These outcomes, while differing in certain respects across class groups, *do* tend to cross social class lines (Pamela Jackson & Quincy Stewart, 2003 & Mullings, 2005). Of note, is that despite black middle-class women's higher status in the social structure, compared to their lower-class, black counterparts, middle-class black women also face income and employment insecurity; lack of adequate job resources; and dual discriminatory conditions based on race and gender.

Understanding Age Patterns and Depression

As previously noted, structural and economic factors influence black women's mental health outcomes. However, we argue that individual's perceptions of how economic and structural factors impact their cultural goals and expectations change over their life course. Moreover, as perceptions of social and economic factors change over time the psychological impact varies across age. That is, psychological distress for black women should not be theorized as a static concept but rather a fluid concept that fluctuates with age and changing life circumstances. Thus, this project seeks to understand whether and how depression is affected by age.

Adolescent Black Girls

According to the health literature, the adolescent years can be a stressful period (Wight, Sepulveda, & Aneshensel, 2004). In fact, researchers argue that teenagers tend to report higher rates of depressive symptoms than do young adults (Adkins et al., 2009). To understand adolescent mental health, researchers argue that it should be studied within the context of family stress. That is, when stressors occur, family members are impacted. We further that argument by maintaining that the adolescent stage is a period in which personal and social coping strategies are being cultivated and developed. Adolescents, then, tend to have strong reliance on family members for psychosocial and material support. Consequently, adolescents who are embedded in family structures possessing inadequate coping strategies will be more vulnerable to the pernicious psychological effects of stress. Therefore, some adolescent groups will report greater levels of psychological distress than do others. For example, studies show that minority adolescents exhibit greater levels of depression that their white counterparts (Adkins et al., 2009) because their families are exposed to increased stressors and often lack the adequate resources to combat such stressors.

Because black adolescent girls tend to be embedded in family structures that have increased stress exposure (i.e., poverty, single headed household structures) and are more vulnerable to the psychological effects of stress, we expect them to exhibit high levels of psychological distress during this period of their lives. Coupled with their exposure and vulnerability to stressful encounters, they often have not developed personal coping strategies that can alleviate the psychological effects of stress. Additionally, scholars acknowledge the impacts of hormonal changes among adolescent girls during puberty on psychological distress (Nolen-Hoeksema, 1990). Thus, we expect adolescent black's levels of psychological distress to be greater during their teen years than during their emerging young adult and young adult years.

Black Women and Emerging Young Adulthood

After high school, young people typically transition from a stage of dependency on families to partial, if not complete, independence as they enter emerging young adulthood. Research shows a decline in depressive symptoms from the adolescent period to emerging young adulthood. Factors such as achieving independence, establishing stable relationships, and a more developed sense of personal and social coping strategies are associated with declining rates of psychological distress for emerging adults (Ge et al., 2006; Adkins, 2009). Additionally because Western society has delayed age of marriage and childbearing, and placed emphasis on schooling and careers, we argue that emerging adulthood is a period in which expectations to achieve cultural goals (e.g., careers, marriage, homeownership) are not yet placing high demands on young people.

Despite the fact that young, black women face discrimination in social and economic institutions, little economic (i.e., lack of job experience) and social (i.e., single with no children) investments have been established during the early to mid- twenties. We contend that because groups have few economic and social assets the perception, and in turn the deleterious psychological effect of loss, is minimal during early adulthood. Therefore, we expect young black women to report a decline in stress as they transition from adolescence to emerging young adulthood.

Black Women and Young Adulthood

Young adulthood is a period in which individuals expect to achieve certain milestones, largely because of cultural notions regarding the appropriate age at which one should transition through educational and career events, and to be socially and economically more stable than at earlier points in their lives. Additionally, according to National Health Statistics Report (2012), during this period many individuals are searching and finding marriage partners (i.e., the average age of marriage for men is 28.4 and for women, 26.5).

Merton's (1986) classic work suggests that when there is a breakdown in the cultural goals (e.g., adequate levels of education, good jobs, evidence of material success) and the socially structured capacities for individuals to obtain those goals, individuals undergo strain. Given young black women's structural position, they have less access to employment opportunities and often experience slow upward mobility in the labor market. Consequently, they may not be able to display thesocially-expected outcomes of employment status. Additionally, young black women, tend to be embedded in squeezed marriage markets and the size and other dynamics of these markets (socioeconomic and ethnic concordance, local availability of marriageable partners) may be a cause of psychological distress. For young, black, adult women, then, we argue that the disjunction between culturally prescribed goals and access to those desired goals creates a sense of strain and, in turn, elevate levels of psychological distress.

As previously mentioned, we argue that because of hormonal shifts and heavy reliance on family structures (that tend to have high exposure and vulnerability to stressful encounters), black adolescent girls will have elevated levels of psychological distress. Emerging adulthood, however, is a period that allows for black women to develop their personal and social independence that is free parental and family pressures. Additionally, because emerging adulthood is a period in which expectations to achieve cultural goals (e.g., careers, marriage, and homeownership) are not yet placing high strain on young people, we expect levels of psychological distress to decline during this period. Finally, young adulthood may produce high levels of strain because young black women are often faced with the reality that there is an imbalance between their cultural goals (i.e., marriage) and their access to the means (i.e., suitable marriage partners) to achieve those prescribed goals. We argue that this disjunction creates strain for young black women and, in turn, increase levels of psychological distress. Thus we expect levels of psychological distress to peak during adolescence, decline during emerging adulthood, and increase during young adulthood.

Methods

Data

Data for this project come from the National Longitudinal Study of Adolescent Health (Add Health), a representative sample of adolescents living in the United States and who were in grades 7-12 in 1994 and 1995 (Harris et al., 2009). The primary sampling technique used for the Add Health study was a clustered school based design in which students were selected for inclusion from a sample of 80 high schools. High schools without a 7th or 8th grade helped to identify a total of 52 feeder schools—that is schools that included a 7th grade and contributed at least five students to the high school—resulting in a core sample of 132 schools.

Four waves of data were gathered beginning in 1994 and ending in 2008. Our analysis is based on the 1st (1994-1995), 3rd (2001-2002), and 4th (2007-2009) waves, with wave two being excluded due to the short interval between it and the first wave. Over 90,000 students completed an in-school survey in wave one (Harris et al. 2009). From each school a random sample of approximately 200 students was selected for an in-home interview for a total of 20,745 in-home interviews completed. In waves three and four, 15,170 and 15,701 original wave one respondents were re- interviewed. For the purposes of this paper, we employ a smaller subset of the total sample representing panel members interviewed in waves one, three, and four (approximately 4,118 respondents). Of these, our analysis is based on the 566 black girls and women who were interviewed in all three waves.

Measures

Dependent Variable: Depression

The primary purpose of the Add Health study is to understand the factors influencing health taking into account the multiple contexts in which people live as they age. Within this framework, we examine fluctuations in black girls and women's depressive symptoms as they transition from adolescence, to emerging young adulthood and finally into young adulthood. To analyze change in depressive symptoms over time, we employ an additive depression scale comprised of eight items. Our scale is a modified version of the Center for Epidemiological Studies (CES-D) depression scale. Respondents were asked to think about the past seven days and report how frequently (rarely, sometimes, occasionally, most) they experienced a variety of symptoms. Specifically, respondents were asked how frequently they felt 1.) bothered by things that usually did not bother them; 2.) that they could not shake the blues; 3.) that they were not just as good as other people; 4.) trouble focusing on what they were doing; 5.) depressed; 6.) that they did not enjoy life; 7.) sad; 8.) that people disliked them. The depression scale for each wave is internally consistent, with a Cronbach's Alpha coefficient of .78, .80, and .81 for waves one, three, and four respectively.

Independent Variable: Wave

Our primary interest in this study is to examine the shifts in depressive symptoms as young black girls age into womanhood. As such, after controlling for race and gender, our independent variable of interest is the average age of the respondents. In the first wave of the study, respondents were on average 16 years old, by the third wave they were on average 22 years old, and by the fourth and final wave of the study they had aged into young adulthood reporting a mean age of 29 years.

Control Variables: Racial Identity and Gender

In addition to changes taking place over time, we are also seeking to isolate the impact of being black and female on a person's experience with depressive symptoms. Gender is a 0, 1 variable where 0 equals female and 1 male. The intention of this paper is *not* to examine gender differences but to focus on transitions women as a group experience. As such, we select for analysis only females. Race is assessed in much the same way, as a dummy variable where 0 equals respondents of all other races and 1 equals black respondents.

The Add Health survey provides a number of means for assessing the racial identity of respondents. One, a self-identified measure in which respondents are asked to report the racial group that best characterizes them, was used in waves one and three. The second measure, used in all three waves, is based on the interviewers' assessment of a respondent's racial group. In spite of the fact that one may have more consistency using the self-identified measure of race, we argue that the way others identify a person racially has a significant impact on his/her social status. A person's treatment and position within small groups, the education system, and paid employment, just to name a few, is largely based on others perceptions of a person's significant social statuses. Hence, the degree to which there is a connection between one's experience with depressive symptoms and one's membership in a variety of social structures, is likely to be impacted by other's perception of one's racial identity. As such, we employ the interviewer's assessment of race.

Analysis

We utilize repeated-measures analysis of variance (also known as a within- subjects design) to examine changes in depression over time. In a repeated-measures ANOVA the total variance is explained by the between subject variance (or the difference between respondents' depression scores averaged over all time periods) and the within subject variance (or the change in depression scores for each respondent over time). The effect of the experimental effect or independent variable, in this instance average age at wave one, three, and four, is noticed in the within- subject variance (Field, 2005). The within subject variance, furthermore, is comprised of two things: one the effect of the experiment or independent variable and two the effect of individual differences or random factors beyond the control of the study. Repeated-measures ANOVA offer several advantages. First, by using the same subjects over time, this procedure essentially 'controls' for the subject so that one can more accurately assess the effects of time on the outcome being measured. Second, repeated-measures ANOVA offers greater statistical power relative to sample size (Minke, 1997).

Results

In order to provide a more accurate portrayal of black girls and women's shifting depressive symptoms as they age, table 7.1 presents the results of the frequency distribution for each of the eight items in the depression scale. The middle two categories, sometimes and occasionally, were merged for purposes of presentation. Regardless of age, a small percentage of respondents report feeling any of the eight items most of the days of the week. In other words, depressive symptoms are not common for the majority of the girls and women in our sample and over time. Instead, the majority of respondents report either rarely or sometimes/occasionally dealing with these issues. Indeed, most of the respondents in adolescence, emerging young adulthood, and young adulthood, responded rarely to feeling unable to shake the blues, depressed, and feeling that people disliked them (rows 2, 5, and 8), while an approximately equal percentage of respondents across all ages reported sometimes/occasionally and rarely feeling that unusual things bothered them, they had trouble focusing on what they were doing, they did not enjoy life, that they were not just as good as others, and sad (rows 1, 3, 4, 6, and 7).

Table 7.1 Response Percentages for Black Women on the Depression Scale across the Life Course

	Rarely & Sometimes/Occasionally %			Most %		
Items in Scale	Adolescent	Emerging Young Adult	Young Adult	Adolescent	Emerging Young Adult	Young Adult

Depression Scale						
1.) Bothered by things...	96.8	97.9	94.7	3.2	2.1	5.3
2.) Could not shake the blues	96.3	96.1	95.2	3.7	3.9	4.8
	83.7	90.2	93.3	16.3	9.8	6.7
3.) Felt not as good as others	94.9	96.3	93.8	5.1	3.7	6.2
4.) Trouble focusing	94.1	96.6	96.6	5.9	3.4	3.4
5.) Felt depressed	95.0	97.5	97.9	5.0	2.5	2.1
6.) Did not enjoy life	96.3	97.2	97.2	3.7	2.8	2.8
7.) Felt sad	97.3	97.5	97.0	2.7	2.5	3.0

However, the general pattern that emerges from this table is that for the majority of the eight items included in the scale, the results go from a high percentage reporting rarely in adolescence, to an even higher percentage as they age into emerging young adulthood, before dropping again in young adulthood, suggesting that almost without exception black girls and women's feelings of depression do not follow a linear pattern as they age, but instead follow a curvilinear pattern, with levels of depression bottoming in emerging young adulthood before rising again in young adulthood. These results, however, do not tell us if these changes are significant overtime. For this, we turn to table 7.2.

As a reminder, the depression scale used here ranges from 0 to 24 with 0 being no depressive symptoms during a typical week and 24 being someone who experiences depressive symptoms frequently during a typical week. Based on the results reported in table 7.2, black women's depression levels follow a u shaped pattern. As adolescents, women report a mean depression score of 5.82 (4.35). The average value drops as women enter emerging young adulthood to 4.53 (4.11) and then rises again as they enter young adulthood to 5.06 (4.21). The results, furthermore, show that depression levels undergo a significant change over time.

Table 7.2. Descriptive Statistics for Repeated Measures ANOVA on Depression

	Mean	Std. Deviation	N
Depression Scale Wave 1***	5.82	4.35	560
Depression Scale Wave 2	4.53	4.11	560
Depression Scale Wave 3	5.06	4.21	560

*p<.05, **p<.01, ***p<.001 Significance was determined using Wilkes' Lambda (.931)

Discussion

Although there is an abundance of sociological theories that predict mental health for blacks in the health literature, the majority of the research (Thoits, 1995; Lincoln et al., 2003) treats blacks as a monolithic group and, thus, fails to account for age and gender differences on the levels of psychological distress. We fill that gap by isolating the impact of being black and female upon depressive symptoms over time. Our findings supported our hypotheses, which suggest a u-curved relationship in depression for black females. That is, black adolescents and young adults report higher levels of psychological distress than those who are in emerging adulthood. We contend that changes in social and economic factors influence variations in levels of psychological distress throughout black women's life course.

Considering our suppositions, we believe that this work lays preliminary conceptual and theoretical groundwork for understanding mental health trajectories for black women across age. *First*, given the strong correlation between depression and physical illnesses (e.g., infant mortality, cardiac disease, and obesity) and unhealthy behaviors (i.e., smoking, drug abuse, and unhealthy sexual behaviors), we believe that our findings give health professionals critical age points to target in terms of depression for black women. For example, our findings suggest that depression increases from early adulthood to young adulthood for black women. It is important to note that young adulthood (ages 25-34) is also a time in which women are in childbearing years. Thus, the implications of depression on maternal health outcomes are worthy of noting during this stage for black women. Informing obstetricians/gynecologists of young, adult, black women's vulnerability to depression might serve to reduce the high rates of infant mortality and low birth weights within black communities.

Second, our findings can empower black girls and women by informing them of the age stages in which they are most vulnerable to psychological distress. Adolescence and young adulthood seem to be critical periods in terms of mental health. For example, informing adolescents of the strong correlations between depression and unhealthy behaviors, such as smoking, risky sexual behaviors, and drug and alcohol abuse can reduce poor health outcomes such as teenage pregnancy, rates of STD's, and drug and alcohol dependency. Additionally, family members can work to create strong support systems in which expressive resources such as mentorship and guidance flow freely.

Finally, although informal networks (i.e., family and friends) often serve to mitigate the deleterious effects of stress on depressive symptoms, these ties and the resources possessed by them are often an unreliable source of support in minority communities. Thus, we argue that a comprehensive, community-based health programs that promote health education and mobilize community leaders can have positive effects on social systems by influencing cultural norms within a community. These approaches can be more successful at achieving long-term behavioral changes because they affect the culture in which people live, work, and socialize. We acknowledge that for minority populations, trusting and relying on medical or governmental agencies for formalized support may be challenging. Thus, we encourage the usage of community based health centers (CBHC) that tend to be more aware of community members needs and, in turn, promote culturally, effective health strategies that can reduce poor mental health outcomes for black girls and women.

While this study represents an initial attempt to understand the relationship between age and depression for black women, we realize it raises more questions than it answers, highlighting the need for future research. Among the questions this research raises are: What happens to black women's mental health as they continue to age? Given that our data only allowed for an analysis of black women's depression at adolescence, emerging young adulthood, and young adulthood, future work should stretch this timeline to investigate mental health as black women age beyond young adulthood. We suspect that moments of transition will be linked with depression levels as black women age so that, much like during emerging young adulthood, depressive symptoms stabilize before rising again as black women reach other life transitions (retirement, for instance).

Secondly, and perhaps more importantly, we must ask whether or not the pattern noted here is unique to black women? Do women from other racial or ethnic backgrounds follow a similar u-shaped pattern? And if so, what does this suggest about the role of racial and ethnic identity in one's experiences with emotional distress? As noted in the introduction to this paper, our experiences seem quite similar at least on the surface. Might the pattern belie, much like our personal life stories, deeper differences connected to a racial experience? Preliminary analyses (data not shown) suggest that, indeed, white women also follow the u-shaped pattern noted here but the *magnitude* of their depressive symptoms is consistently smaller than that for black women at each time point. In other words, the shape of the relationship between age and depressive symptoms is quite similar between white and black women, but there are clearly quantitative and qualitative differences that bare further exploration.

Moving beyond the role of race and ethnicity, social class is a hugely important factor contributing to one's place within the social structure. Not only do the authors of this paper differ racially, we also come from dramatically different social class backgrounds. In what way might growing up in a poor, white home influence the experiences of the second author, compared with the first author who grew up in an middle class, black home? While we are not making an argument for socioeconomic status being more or less important in regards to depressive symptoms than racial or ethnic identity, we do argue that we cannot examine our experiences with depression or anxiety without regard for our positions within a variety of intersecting social structures. Future research into this area should account for the interaction of socio- economic status with race, gender, and age to provide academics and health professionals alike with a more nuanced understanding of black women's risks of experiencing the negative consequences of depressive symptoms.

References

Adkins, D. E., Wang, V., Dupre, M. E., Edwin, J.C.G., & Elder, G.H. (2009). Structure and Stress: Trajectories of Depressive Symptoms across Adolescence and Young Adulthood. *Social Forces,* 88(1), 31-60.

Aneshensel, C. S. (1992). Social Stress: Theory and Research. *Annual Review of Sociology,* 18, 15-38.

Brown, A. C., Brody, G. H., & Stoneman, Z. (2000). Rural Black Women and Depression: A Contextual Analysis. *Journal of Marriage and Family,* 62(1), 187-198.

Copen, C. E., Daniels, K., Vespa, J., & Mosher, W. D. First Marriages in the United States: Data from 2006-2010. National Survey of Family Growth. *National Health Statistics Report,* vol. 49 Hyattsville, MD: National Center for Health Statistics.

Field, A. (2005). *Discovering Statistics Using SPSS (2nd edition).* London: Sage Publications.

Ge, X., Natsuaki, M., & Conger, R. (2006). Trajectories of Depressive Symptoms and Stressful Life Events among Male and Female Adolescents in Divorced and Non Divorced Families. *Development & Psychopathology,* 18(1), 253-273.

Harris, K.M., Halpern, C.T., Whitsel, E., Hussey, J., Tabor, J., Entzel, P., & Udry, J.R. (2009). The National Longitudinal Study of Adolescent Health: Research Design.

Martineau, W. H. (1977). Informal Social Ties Among Urban Black Americans: Some New Data and Review of the Problem. *Journal of Black Studies,* 8(6), 83-104.

McAdoo, H. P. (1982). Stress Absorbing Systems in Black Families. *Family Relations,* 31(4), 479-488.

McLeod, J. D. & Owens, T. J. (2004). Psychological Well-Being in Early Life Course: Variation by Socioeconomic Status, Gender and Race/Ethnicity. *Social Psychology Quarterly,* 67(3), 257-78.

Merton, R. (1938). Social Structure and Anomie. *American Sociological Review,* 3, 672-82.

Minke, A. (1997). *Conducting Repeated Measures Analyses: Experimental Design Considerations.* Paper presented at the Annual Meeting of the Southwest Educational Research Association, Austin, TX. (ERIC Document Reproduction Service No. ED407415)

Mirowsky, J. (1996). Age and the Gender Gap in Depression. *Journal of Health and Social Behavior,* 37(4), 362-380.

Mirowsky, J & Ross, C. E. (1986). Social Patterns of Distress. *Annual Review of Sociology,* 12: 23-45.

———. (1992). Age and Depression. *Journal of Health and Social Behavior,* 33, 187-205.

Mullings, L. (2005). Resistance and Resislence: The Sojourner Syndrome and the Social Context of Reproduction in Central Harlem. *Transforming Anthropology,* 13(2), 75-91.

Lincoln, K,D., Chatters L. M., & Taylor, R. J. (2003). Psychological distress among black and white American: Differential effects of social support, negative interaction and personal control. *Journal of Health and Social Behavior,* 44, 390-407.

Nolen-Hoeksema, S. (1987). Sex Differences in Unipolar Depression: Evidence and Theory. *Psychological Bulletin,* 101, 259-82.

Pearlin, L. I. (1989). The Sociological Study of Stress. *Journal of Health and Social Behavior,* 30(3), 241-256.

Pearlin, L. I. (1999). The Stress Process Revisited: Reflections on concepts and their

Interrelationships. Pp. 395-416. In *Handbook of Sociology of Mental Health*, edited by Carol S. Aneshensel and Jo C. Phenlan. New York: Springer.

Stack, C. B. (1974). *All our Kin: Strategies for Survival in the Black Community*. New York: Harper & Row.

Wight, R. G., Sepulveda, J. E., & Aneshensel, C. S. (2004). Depressive symptoms: How do adolescents compare with adults? *Journal of Adolescent Health (34)*, 314–323.

Wilson, J. W. (1987). *The Truly Disadvantaged*. Chicago: University of Chicago Press.

———. (1992). Another look at the truly disadvantaged. *Political Science Quarterly*.

Chapter Eight
Saving My Soul and Making Me Fat?: Black Mothers and the Church
Annice Dale Yarber

It's Personal

I hear the voices of the church women who helped teach me about life, womanhood, and living—"Your body is the temple of God so you must take good care of it. If you take care of it, you will have long life." As a medical sociologist, I am keenly aware of the health disparities that exist in our community, more pointedly, that African American women have a higher rate of obesity than other racial and ethnic groups. I vowed not to become *that* statistic.

It was October 2010 that I began to be increasingly concerned about my weight. Although I wore a size 8, I weighed 170 pounds! To make matters worse, at my annual check-up that month, my Latina doctor saw me and exclaimed, "Wow, you look fabulous"! During the examination, I expressed concern that I was putting on weight and was only 30 pounds shy of 200. That is, according to the body mass index (BMI) I was overweight. She said not to worry, that my tests results consistently looked good and that the BMI is only one of several tools used to gauge healthy versus unhealthy weight. Her comment about the BMI inspired me to research this tool. I found that while the term was coined and popularized by Ancel Keys in 1972, its origins actually date back to the work of the Belgian scientist Adolphe Quetelet who calculated the best predictor of body fat percentage as being weight divided by height squared (Keys, Fidanza, Karvonen, Kimura & Taylor, 1972). In 1980, the BMI became an international tool to measure weight, although the standard for what constituted healthy weight varied from country to country. By 1985, the National Institutes of Health (NIH) began defining obesity based on BMI and doctors were advised to warn patients not meeting the sex-based BMI thresholds that they were at risk for a variety of obesity-related conditions (NIH, 1985). Later, in 1998, NIH combined the BMI thresholds for men and women which raised the overall threshold for obesity among women and added the additional category of "overweight" (NIH, 1998). Consequently, thirty million Americans who were identified as "healthy" weight were now included in the "overweight" category. While my doctor wisely suggested that healthy weight was not measured by BMI or any singular indicator and my test results provided comfort; my BMI which indicated that I was overweight was enough to motivate me to join a gym for the long-term health benefits that exercising provides.

In January 2011, I joined the local gym. It was difficult at first, but as I began to interact with the gym staff and other patrons, I learned about various exercises that would help me achieve my goals. In the spring, I began walking with two gentlemen who frequent the gym. We walked every weekday at 5:30 a.m. for 5 – 7 miles. As my stamina increased, I began to feel a renewed sense of self and looked forward to more challenging walks. Clearly something positive was happening to my body—I was losing inches but no weight. I thought, "No problem, all is well. I am doing an excellent job of taking care of my body.

In October 2011, I went in for my annual exam. My doctor saw me and again exclaimed, "You look fabulous"! With confidence and pride, I shared with her the steps I had taken to improve my overall health and well-being. Impressed with my progress, she encouraged me to stay the course. Then came the exam—weigh in, temperature, blood drawing, blood pressure testing, checking of ears, nose, and throat, and gynecological testing. Results....shocking! While all my test results were within normal limits, I had actually gained weight, from 170 to 176 pounds! Unbelievable! However, the weight gain did not seem to trouble my doctor at all. She iterated that my test results looked good, and that I was healthy—not to worry.

The University has a health promotion program. Those who are interested can take a general heath screen and get a reduction in their monthly insurance premiums. Sign me up! November 2011, I took the health screening. Results of the screening revealed that I was overweight; that is, I had a BMI of 27.6. My head began to pound (my normal blood pressure skyrocketed) and as I continued to think about the results in light of my exercise regimen, I became extremely depressed. What's the use? I found myself slowly becoming more and more disinterested in my exercise program until I was no longer engaged in my routine. I began to wonder if my situation was somehow indicative of a larger issue: was there a correlation between obesity and depression? No matter the effort or the progress, it appeared that African American women just couldn't seem to get ahead....how depressing. I began to ask, "God, where are you?"

Introduction

This paper examines the effects of religiosity on obesity among middle and low-income African American single mothers. Four out of five African American women are either overweight or obese (Women's Health.gov) and 40% of African American children aged 2 -19 are obese (Lets Move.org). Obesity is correlated with a host of negative health outcomes, many of which disproportionately affect African American women. That is, African American women have higher rates of heart disease, diabetes, cancer, respiratory problems, and reproductive complication, all which are associated with obesity, than women in other racial and ethnic groups (Flegal et. al, 2002). Additionally, obesity is associated with a five year decrease in life expectancy for African American women.

The high rate of obesity within the African American community has drawn national attention, in part, because parental obesity is a significant predictor of child and adolescent obesity (Whitaker, et al., 1997). Speaking at the 101st National Convention of the National Association for the Advancement of Colored People (NAACP), First Lady Michelle Obama stated,

> African American children are significantly more likely to be obese than are white children. Nearly half of African American children will develop diabetes at some point in their lives. People, that's half of our children. ...We can build our kids the best schools on earth, but if they don't have the basic nutrition they need to concentrate, they're still going to have challenge learning.

Through her Lets Move! Initiative, Mrs. Obama, is rallying parents, caregivers, elected officials from all levels of government, schools, health care professionals, faith-based and community-based organizations, and private sector companies to assist in the fight against childhood obesity.

The Black Church and black religion has been and remains a cornerstone of social integration and social support for the African American community. At the center of church activities are the women of the church - mothers who cultivate and sustain a safe space for training and development of families.

Single mothers, in general, have greater levels of stress and access to fewer resources than married mothers. The intersection of race, gender and family status contribute to the vulnerability of African American single mothers. In addition, research has suggested that obesity influences mental health. For instance, obesity has been associated with depression, anxiety, body image issues, low self-esteem, and social isolation (McGee, 1998). A study by the Kaiser Family Foundation and The Washington Post earlier this year found that 66% of overweight black women had high self-esteem, while 41% of average-sized or thin white women had high self-esteem.

Despite the importance of religiosity in shaping health outcomes on the one hand and the large disparity in obesity on the other hand, little is known about the influence of religiosity on obesity among African Americans single mothers. Although there have been numerous studies examining the influence of religiosity on obesity, few have focused specifically on single mothers in the African American community (Byron and Yarber, 2011). Given that in 2008, 65% of African American children under the age of 18 resided in single parent homes, most of which were mother-headed homes (The National Children Count Program), it is important to identify factors that are related to maternal obesity so that effective programs can be developed to prevent increased rates of childhood obesity. This paper examines the effect of religiosity on obesity among middle and low-income single mothers in the African American community. Using a sample from the nationally representative 2001-2003 National Survey of American Life (NSAL), the study investigates the general hypothesis that high levels of religiosity is related to less obesity among respondents. The relationship between various aspects of religiosity and obesity will be analyzed with controls for social and demographic factors that are correlated with obesity.

Religiosity

Religiosity has many definitions; however, it is broadly referred to as the various aspects of religious expression or activity. Despite disagreement about the exact definition or nature of religiosity, several models of religiosity have been developed, such as Glock and Stark (1965) five dimensional model, Rohrbaugh and Jessor (1975) religiosity scale, Pargament's (1998) theory of religious coping, and the Fetzer Institute's 12-component model of religiosity. As mentioned earlier, Glock and Stark (1965) distinguished five dimensions of religiosity: 1) intellectual (knowledge of the basic tenets of the faith); 2) ideological (holding certain beliefs about God), 3) consequential (the effect of religion on everyday life), 4) experiential (having an emotional tie to religion), and 5) ritualistic (frequency of attendance/participation in various religious activities). Departing slightly from the Glock and Stark (1965) conceptualization of religiosity, this study uses the Rohrbaugh and Jessor (1975) scale to define the two dimensions of religiosity that are found in the literature to influence health outcomes—ritualistic and experiential religiosity. Ritualistic religiosity here is defined as how often individuals prayed and attended religions services, while experiential religiosity refers to how religious a person felt and the degree to which they found comfort and security in their religion and the significance of religious practice in their life (for instance in dealing with stressful situations).

It is well documented in the literature that African American women are significantly invested in religious and spiritual activities (Ferraro, 1998; Taylor et al., 1999), using religion to cope with and resolve adversity (Lehman and Myers, 1985; Mattis, J. S., 2002). Using national data from the 1986 Americans' Changing Lives Survey, Ferraro and Koch (1994) found that African Americans depend more on religion than do whites when there is a health crisis and that high levels of religious practice is positively linked to health. Byron and Yarber (2011) found some aspects of religious involvement and participation mitigate the effect of stress on body weight among African American women. Other studies have suggested that religiosity significantly influences wellbeing (Krause, 1998; Ellison et al., 2001), life satisfaction (Ellison and Gay, 1990), mental health (Pargament et al., 1990; Zahn et al., 1998), HIV coping strategies (Siegel and Schrimshaw, 2000), cancer survival (Hoffman-Goetz, 1999), and dietary beliefs (Holt et al., 2005) as well as provide comfort to the dying (Pevey et al., 2008).

There are several mechanisms through which religiosity may promote healthy living. Decades of research have suggested ways in which aspects of religious practices may help promote healthy living among adults (Lee-Roff *et al.*,2005, Brown and Gary, 1994, Krause, 2010, and Harding et al.,2005). First, religious teachings usually promote and encourage healthy dietary patterns (Idler et al., 2003). Therefore, attendance at religious services provides the opportunity to hear health-related messages, such as the benefits of diet and exercise. Second, members of religious groups are more likely to conform to the norms of the group (Musick, Blazer, and Hayes 2000), in this case, norms regarding healthy behavior. Third, religious groups usually provide their members with support through programs to promote health and assurance of the value and worth of their lives despite the challenges of single parenting. Furthermore, church members receive emotional support from fellow congregants and thus feel sense belongingness. Finally, a sense of belongingness promotes a strong sense of personal control and thus better physical and mental health (Krause and Bastida, 2011). For instance, Shapiro (2010) found that ritualistic religiosity increases social support and interaction among church members which leads to better health outcomes. Moreover, in a community sample of 546 Kim (2006) found that those reporting high levels of social support were more likely to diet than those reporting lower levels.

While aspects of religiosity serve to protect from negative health outcomes, does religion protect African American single mothers from obesity? The NSAL survey data include variables that can be used to measure the two dimensions of religiosity examined in this paper. The study sample includes only middle and low-income African American single mothers. We hypothesize that this subgroup of mothers who are frequent participants in church and church activities (ritualistic religiosity) or have positive and fulfilling experiences within religious communities (experiential religiosity) will be associated with healthy behavior. To the extent that ritualistic and experiential religious practices are associated with healthy outcomes among this sub-population, funding can be directed to developing programs through this social network to change what has become more the norm in their health outcomes (e.g. National Institute of Health, the Center for Disease Control, the Black Women's Health Council).

This study predicts that: (1) High levels of ritualistic religiosity decreases the likelihood of obesity among African American single mothers; (2) High levels of experiential religiosity decreases the likelihood of obesity among African American single mothers; and (3) High levels of interaction between ritualistic and experiential religiosity decreases the likelihood of obesity among African American single mothers.

Methodology

The purpose of the current study was to examine whether two dimensions of religiosity (ritualistic and experiential) were related to obesity among low- and middle-income African American mothers using data from the NSAL. The NSAL is uniquely suited for the study of African American single mothers and obesity as it is designed to measure the effects of income, family, peer group, neighborhood, religious institution, and community influences on the African-American and Afro-Caribbean population that promote good health or which may lead to unhealthy, self-destructive behaviors.

Sample

The population of the NSAL survey includes adults aged 18 years and older residing in households located in the United States in three target groups: Black Americans of African descent, Black Americans of Caribbean descent, and White Americans. The study sample includes Black American single mothers of African descent who are heads of households (n = 539). Given the focus of the present study, participants missing the body mass index (BMI) were omitted from the sample.

Outcome Variable

The BMI was used to measure obesity and was recoded as a binary variable to indicate whether the women of the sample were obese (=1 if BMI score ≥ 30) or not obese (=0 if BMI ≤ 29.9).

Explanatory Variables

There were two independent constructs essential to test the effect of religiosity on obesity: ritualistic religiosity and experiential religiosity.

Ritualistic religiosity captures the frequency of attendance at church or other religious meetings. The NSAL dataset contains numerous questions that can be used to assess attendance. Ritualistic religiosity was measured using an index made up of seven questions. Respondents were asked about the frequency of: "attendance at faith-based meetings"; "meeting with church members"; "participation in church activities"; "reading religious books"; "watching and listening to television programs"; "listening to radio programs"; and "engaging in prayer." Response categories were recoded to reflect increased frequency of the activity, that is, (1= never to a few times a year), (2= a few times to at least once a month) and (3= 1 to more than 4 times a week). Higher scores indicated more ritualistic religiosity.

Experiential religiosity reflects how religious a respondent felt and the degree to which they found comfort and security in their religion and the significance of religious practice in their life. Experiential religiosity was measured using an index made up of four questions: "satisfaction with the quality of relations with people"; "closeness to church members"; "whether church members make the individual feel loved and expressed interest in well-being"; and "whether religion and spirituality are important in the home life and in dealing with stressful situations." Response categories were recoded to reflect increased intensity so that (1= never), (2= not too often), (3=fairly often) and (4= very often). Higher scores indicated more experiential religiosity.

Control Variables

The study controlled for variables that previous researchers identified as relevant to the study of obesity: overall health, depression, cigarette use, age, education, marital status, income, religious preference, and the number of children present in the home.

Analytic Strategy

Several steps were taken to prepare data for analyses. Composite indices of ritualistic and experiential religiosity were formulated using summation. To create the indices used in this study, correlational analysis was conducted to assess the relationship between items addressing the constructs of interest (experiential and religiosity).

Because of the dichotomous nature of the dependent variable, data were analyzed using logistic regression techniques. Other researchers who examined correlates of obesity have used logistic regression (Hillemeier et al., 2010; Sparks and Bollinger, 2011; Ayers et al., 2010; and Hayatbakhsh et al., 2010). The exponent of the coefficient (odds ratio) provides the relative odds of being obesity (versus not) for each unit change in the independent variable. For ease of interpretation, the odds ratio (Exp(B)) is presented, and, in case of ordinal level variables, the odds ratio is converted to percent.

Results

Seventy percent of the women in this study were classified as obese. According to the Centers for Disease Control, in 2008 fifty-one percent of African American women aged 20 years and older were obese. Hence, the percentage of obese women in the NSAL sample was considerably greater than the national rate.

What is the relationship between ritualistic religiosity, experiential religiosity, the interaction term and obesity? Results show that the religiosity measures are statistically significant but provide mixed support for our hypotheses. For instance, we hypothesized that experiential religiosity and the interaction term would significantly decrease the likelihood obesity; yet the results suggest the opposite. That is, the likelihood of obesity ($p < 0.01$) significantly increases with religious practice being more important to the respondent's life (an increase in the experiential religiosity measure). Likewise, frequency and importance of religious practice (the multiplicative effect of ritualistic and experiential religiosity) together significantly increases the likelihood of obesity ($p < 0.05$). As hypothesized, ritualistic religiosity decreases the likelihood of obesity; but its effect on obesity was statistically insignificant.

Although 70% of the women were obese, results suggests that certain factors seem to offer protection from obesity. Results suggests that having a bachelor's degree or higher significantly decreases the likelihood of obesity by 57% ($p < .05$). This finding is interesting as Burke et al. (1992) found this same association between education and body size with white women but not in Black women. In addition to the influence of educational attainment on obesity, as self-reported health status increases, there is a 21% decrease in the likelihood of obesity ($p < .05$).

What is the combined effect of experiential and ritualistic religiosity on obesity? Results suggest that a one unit increase in the combined effect of participating and finding comfort in religious activities increases the likelihood of obesity by roughly 10 percent. This finding is surprising and does not provide support for the hypothesis that the interaction term would significantly decrease the likelihood of obesity among African American single mothers.

Disscussion

Although there have been numerous studies examining the influence of religiosity on obesity, very few have focused specifically on single mothers in the African American community. This study examined whether two dimensions of religiosity (ritualistic and experiential) were related to obesity among single mothers within the African American community and if so, what was the relationship. Based on previous research, we hypothesized the following: (1) High levels of ritualistic religiosity significantly decreases the likelihood of obesity among African American single mothers; (2) High levels of experiential religiosity significantly decreases the likelihood of obesity among African American single mothers; and (3) High levels of interaction between ritualistic and experiential religiosity significantly decreases the likelihood of obesity among African American single mothers. Hypotheses were systematically examined using several analytic strategies and data from the 2001 – 2002 NSAL.

Results from this study provide some insight into factors that may explain variation in obesity among African American single mothers. Seventy percent of the sample was obese (BMI ≥ 30). In general, the percent of obesity among African American single mothers with a bachelor's degree or higher and those who self-reported excellent physical health was less than those who had no high school diploma and reported poor physical health. We found that 52 percent of our sample rated their health as either very good or excellent. Self-reported health was the only factor that was significantly associated with a lower likelihood of obesity in all eight models.

Multivariate analysis assessed the effect of religiosity on obesity given a set of explanatory and socio-demographic variables. The multivariate models found mixed support for our hypotheses. As predicted, results indicated ritualistic religiosity decreased the likelihood of obesity, that is, frequent participation in religious activities decreased the likelihood of obesity among African American single mothers; however the effect was insignificant. Cline and Ferraro (2006) found that attendance at religious services was associated with a lower risk of the incidence of obesity for women in general, while Gillum (2006) found an inverse relationship. Our finding may support the argument that frequent attendance at religious services provides opportunity to hear health-related messages, such as the benefits of diet and exercise which may result in adherence to healthy lifestyle and thus, less obesity. Contrary to our hypotheses, in the full model we found that, while not significant, experiential religiosity—finding comfort and support in religion—as well as the interaction term increased the likelihood of obesity among African American single mothers. However, only self-reported health status maintained its significance in the full equation model.

Due to several data limitations, the findings presented in this study should be regarded with caution. First, the NSAL is a nationally representative survey that oversamples in the African American and Black population. However, the rate of obesity in our study was significantly greater than estimates from the Centers for Disease Control (70 versus 51 percent); thus our result may not be generalizable to or represent the experiences of all African American single mothers. Second, while we utilized the standard definitions for the religiosity measures examined in the study, it is possible that choosing a different set of dimensions could yield different results. Finally, the cross-sectional nature of the data precludes establishing how the religiosity effects change over time.

This study makes noteworthy contributions to the literature on religiosity and obesity. First, there are a dearth of studies that focus on the relationship between religiosity and obesity among African Americans. This study furnishes valuable information to the discussion of obesity in the African American community. Second, the approach of this study was identifying factors that are associated with a decrease in obesity; hence contributing valuable information to community-based prevention efforts. Finally, we provide an assessment of the relative importance of experiential and ritualistic religiosity on obesity for African American mothers, allowing us to draw stronger conclusions about these associations.

The findings of the present study have practical significance and add to our current knowledge of obesity among African American single mothers. Although we know risks factors for obesity, less is known about those factors that protect African American single mothers from obesity. The findings presented here clearly suggest that factors (e.g., religiosity) that protect one group may not serve to protect another and perhaps there are other confounding factors. Finally, given that our full model explained only 5% of the variation in obesity among African American single mothers; future research may focus on building a more complex explanatory model which integrates socio-environmental and structural variables as well.

Ultimately, the Black church may play a critical role in saving both the souls and the hearts of African American women. I can still hear the words of the church mothers, saying, "Your body is the temple of God so you must take good care of it." Despite continuing to have great test results and encouraging words from my physician, my BMI still places me in the category of being overweight; however, I have made peace with my weight and exercise regularly to improve my overall health and well-being and I plan to live a very long, healthy life.

References

Ayers, J. W., Hofstetter, C., Irvin, V. L., Song, Y., Park, H., Paik, H., and Hovell, M. F. (2010). Can Religion Help Prevent Obesity? Religious messages and the prevalence of being overweight or obese among Korean women in California. *Journal for the Scientific Study of Religion* 49(3): 536-549.

Brown, D. R. and Gary, L. E. (1994). Religious involvement and health status among African-American males. *Journal of the National Medical Association* 86(11): 825–831.

Burke, V., Beilin, L. J., and Dunbar, D. (2001). Family lifestyle and parental body mass index as predictors of body mass index in Australian children: a longitudinal study. *International Journal of Obesity Related Metabolic Disorders* 25(2):147-57.

Byron, S. and Yarber, A. D. (2011). Stressed, religious and obese: does religious practice influence obesity among women. Unpublished manuscript.

Casey, A. E. National Kid Count Program: data across states. Retrieved from http://datacenter.kidscount.org/data/acrossstates/Rankings.aspx?ind=107.

Centers for Disease Control. Health United States, 2009. Retrieved from http://www.cdc.gov/nchs/data/hus/hus09.pdf.

Davis M. M., McGonagle, K., Schoeni, R. F., and Stafford, F. (2008). Grandparental and parental obesity influences on childhood overweight: implications for primary care practice. *Journal of the American Board of Family Medicine* 21(6):549-54.

Burke, G. L., Savage, P. J., Manolio, T. A., Sprafka, J., Wagenknecht, L. E., Sidney, S., and Jacobs Jr., D. R. (1992). Correlates of obesity in young Black and White women: the CARDIA study. *American Journal of Public Health* 82(12): 1621-1625.

Ellison, C. G.; Boardman, J. D.; Williams, D. R. and Jackson, J. S. (2001). Religious involvement, stress, and mental health: findings from the 1995 Detroit Area Study', *Social Forces* 80(1): 215-249.

Ellison, C. G., and Gay, D. A. (1990). Region, religious commitment, and life satisfaction among Black Americans. *Sociological Quarterly* 31(1): 123-147.

Ferraro, K. F. and Koch, K. R. (1994). Religion and health among Black and White adults: examining social support and consolation. *Journal for the Scientific Study of Religion* 33 (4): 362-375.

Ferraro, K. F. (1998). Firm Believers? Religion, Body Weight, and Well-Being. *Review of Religious Research* 39(3): 224-244.

Flegal, K. M., Carroll, M. D., Ogden, C. L., and Johnson, C. L. (2002). Prevalence and trends in obesity among U. S. adults, 1999-2000. *Journal of the American Medical Association* 288(14): 17-23.

Flegal, K. M., Carroll, M. D., Kit, B. K. and C. L. Ogden (2002). Prevalence of Obesity and Trends in the Distribution of Body Mass Index among U. S. adults, 1999-2010. *Journal of the American Medical Association* 307(5): 491-97.

Gillum, R. F. (2006). Frequency of Attendance at Religious Services, Overweight, and Obesity in American Women and Men: The Third National Health and Nutrition Examination Survey. *Annals of Epidemiology* 16 (9): 655-660.

Hammond, R. and Levine, R. (2010). The economic impact of obesity in the United States. *Diabetes, Metabolic Syndrome and Obesity: Targets and Therapy* 3: 285-295.

Hawkins, B. (2007), African American Women and Obesity: From Explanations to Prevention, *Journal of African American Studies* 11: 79-93.

Hayatbakhsh, M. R., O'Callaghan, M. J., Mamun, A. A., Williams, G. M., Clavarino, A., and Najman, J. M. (2010). Cannabis use and obesity and young adults. *American Journal of Drug and Alcohol Abuse* 36(6): 350-356.

Hillemeier, M. M., Weisman, C. S., Chuang, C., Downs, D., McCall-Hosenfeld, J., and Camacho, F. (2011). Transition to overweight or obesity among women of reproductive age. *Journal of Women's Health* 20(5): 703-710.

Hoffman-Goetz L., Breen, N. L., and Meissner H. (1998). The impact of social class on the use of cancer screening within three racial/ethnic groups in the United States. *Ethnicity and Disease* 8(1):43-51.

Holt, C. L., Haire-Joshu, D. L., Lukwago, S. N. (2005). The role of religiosity in dietary beliefs and behaviors among urban African American women. November. *Cancer Control.*

Hosmer, David W. and Stanley Lemeshow. 2000. *Applied logistic regression.* Second edition. New York: John Wiley and Sons.

Huijts, T., and Kraaykamp, G. (2011). Religious involvement, religious context, and self assessed health in Europe. *Journal of Health and Social Behavior* 52(1): 91-106.

Idler, E. L., Musick, M. A., Ellison, C. G., George, L. K., Krause, N., Ory, M. G., Pargament K. I., Powell, L. H., Underwood, L. G., and Williams D. R. 2003. Measuring multiple dimensions of religion and spirituality for health research. *Research on Aging* 25 (4): 327.

Keys, A., Fidanza, F., Karvonen, M., Kimura, N. and Taylor, H. (1972). Indices of Relative Weight and Obesity. *Journal of Chronic Diseases* 25:329-343.

Krause, N. (2010). Stress, Religious-based Coping, and Physical Health. *Religion and the Social Order 19:* 207-237.

Krause, N., and Bastida, E. (2011). Church-Based Social Relationships, Belonging, and Health Among Older Mexican Americans. *Journal for the Scientific Study of Religion. 50*(2): 397-409.

Lehman, J. D. and Myers, L. G. (1995). What are they, what will they do? *Corrections Today* 57(4): 156-161.

Mattis, J. S. (2002). Religion and spirituality in the meaning–making and coping experiences of African American women: a qualitative analysis. *Psychology of Women Quarterly* 26(4): 309-321.

Musick, M. A., Blazer, D. G., and Hays, J. C. (2000). Religious activity, alcohol use, and depression in a sample of elderly Baptists. *Research on Aging* 22(2): 91-116.

National Institutes of Health (1998) The Clinical Guidelines on the Identification, Evaluation, and Treatment of Overweight and Obesity in Adults:Evidence Report. NIH Publication # 4083. Retrieved on-line on April 12, 2013 at: http://www.nhlbi.nih.gov/guidelines/obesity/prctgd_c. pdf.

National Institutes of Health (1985) Health Implications of Obesity. NIH Consensus Statement 5(9):1-7.Retrieved Online April 12, 2013 at: http://consensus.nih.gov/1985/1985Obesity049html.htm.

Ogden, C. L., Carroll, M. D., Kit, B.K., & Flegal, K. M. (2012). Prevalence of obesity and trends in body mass index among U.S. children and adolescents, 1999-2010. *Journal of the American Medical Association*, 307(5), 483-490.

Pargament, K. I., Smith, B. W., Koenig, H. G., and Perez, L. (1998). Patterns of positive and negative religious coping with major life stressors. *Journal for the Scientific Study of Religion 37*(4): 710-724.

Pargament, K. I.; Kennell, J.; Hathaway, W.; Grevengoed, N.; Newman, J. and Jones, W. (1988). Religion and the problem-solving process: three styles of coping. *Journal for the Scientific Study of Religion* 27(1): 90-104.

Pevey, C. F., Jones, T. J., and Yarber, A. D. (2008). How religion comforts the dying: a qualitative inquiry. *Journal of Death and Dying* 58(1): 41-59.

Roff, L., Klemmack, D. L., Parker, M., Koenig, H. G., Sawyer-Baker, P., and Allman, R. M. (2005). Religiosity, smoking, exercise, and obesity among southern, community-dwelling older adults. *Journal of Applied Gerontology* 24(4): 337-354.

Rohrbaugh, J., and Jessor, R. (1975). Religiosity in youth: a personal control against deviant behavior. *Journal of Personality* 43(1): 136-155.

Shapiro, E. (2010). Religious involvement and Latino immigrant health. *Religion and the Social Order 19:* 175-205.

Siegel, K., Schrimshaw, E. W., and Pretter, S. (2005). Stress-related growth among women living with HIV/AIDS: examination of an explanatory model. *Journal of Behavioral Medicine* 28(5): 403-414.

Sparks, Johnelle, P. P., and Bollinger, M. (2011). A demographic profile of obesity in the adult and veteran U. S. populations in 2008. *Population Research and Policy Review* 30(2): 211 233.

Stark, R., and Glock, C. Y. (1965). The "New Denominationalism." *Review of Religious Research* 7(1): 8-17.

Whitaker, K.L., Jarvis, M. J., Beken, R. J., Bonafice, D., and Wardle, J. (2010). Comparing maternal and paternal intergenerational transmission of obesity in a large population based sample. *American Journal of Clinical Nutrition* Jun 91 (6): 1560-67.

Whitaker, R. C., Wright, J. A., Pepe, M. S., Seidel, K. D., and Deitz, W. H. (1997). Predicting obesity in young adulthood from childhood and parental obesity.

Section Four

Speaking Change and Writing Wrongs: Representations of Activism

> *The true aim of female education should be, not a development of one or two, but all the faculties of the human soul, because no perfect womanhood is developed by perfect culture.*
>
> Frances Ellen Watkins Harper, 1859

Chapter Nine
The Art of Activist Mothering: Black Feminist Leadership &
Knowing What To Do
Denise McLane-Davison

Introduction

Black women's leadership in HIV/AIDS borrows from the efforts of the liberation and uplift work of the Black Clubwomen of the 19th century, as well as the Black communal leadership of the Civil Rights Era, to address the social injustices of HIV/AIDS. Their lived experiences at the intersection of multiple oppressions (Collins, 2000), indicates that they have a "means of knowing" how to address the issues that impact the Black community's quality of life and mortality.

The following discussion draws from a larger exploratory research study (Davison, 2010), on Black feminist leadership and HIV/AIDS community work. Interviews with African-American women leaders yielded a unique set of qualities based on the collective understanding of being both Black and female. Leadership for these women was influenced by their relationships with one another, and their power was centered in mothering characteristics that fostered mutual support, while connecting to them to the community at large. Their ability to insert humanity and love into an epidemic that is stigmatized by hatred, blaming, and victimization, also repositioned their leadership from being at the fringes to being the center component that created a space for everyone to be a part of the solution process. Their rationale for taking on the HIV/AIDS fight, can be traced through the historic leadership style of "activist mothering" (McDonald, 1997) and "community mothering" (Gilkes, 1980); "Black mothers have always known what to do."

Context of Leadership

Historical Activism

Examples of Black women's leadership appear as politicized narratives of a few women (Ida. B. Wells, Harriet Tubman, Sojourner Truth, Mary McLeod Bethune, Mary Church Terrell, Fannie Lou Hammer, and Rosa Parks) which have the core focus of community building (Nance, 1996; Abudullah, 2007). These women, although singled out for their individual contributions, acted in conjunction with their gendered and racial peers to bring about social change. Their stories reveal common themes around family, education, and religious values, as well as, commitment to community survival, cooperative relationships with Black men, supportive social networks, and shared leadership. Often excluded from participating in traditional patriarchal political processes, Black women developed their own political voice and brand of informal and formal leadership. Their style of leadership is birthed through their roles as mothers, daughters, and extended caregiving roles. Black women's leadership developed from their own strategies based on expressing their female strengths rather than denying gender traits and are rooted in their personal and social roles (Radford-Hill, 2000; Parker, 1996; Roth, 1999).

During the Progressive Era (1891-1918), the Black women's Club Movement (BWCM) was built on the self-help traditions of Africans in America, while expanding the social welfare of the Black church (Martin & Martin, 1985; Sanders, 1995; Townes, 1995; Smith, 1995). These women served as the conscience of the community and actively set the political agenda for human rights through their Club work and involvement in church women's groups and other female auxiliaries (Brice, 2005; Carlton-LaNey, 1999; Smith, 1995). Through their community mothering leadership, Smith (1995), these women "formed the backbone of the Black Health Movement and were central to the founding and maintenance of African American public health projects" (p. 1). These women implemented health reform measures at the local level, and in so doing, translated health policy into health programs. Black women served as conduits in the community because of their roles in the family as primary givers, and translated these skills into their community roles.

Black women's club activities reflect a means of institutionalizing their leadership practices. Black middle-class women, through their civic engagement, have led the way in racial uplift (Carlton-LaNey, 1999) and "Black activist mothering" (McDonald, 1997; Roth, 1999, Gilkes 1980). This practice, from the time of slavery to the early 1940's, demonstrates a legacy of "normative empathy" as a significant motivator for middle-class maternal activism. Their mothering efforts, McDonald (1997), represent a core component of "their strategy for intervention, born from a conscious, collective need to resist racist and sexist oppression is passed down from many generations by their Black activist foremothers" (p. 774). Thus, the role and function of mother, through the African women's experiences, is expanded and inclusive of "bloodmothers," "othermothers," and "community othermothers," as preferred normative behavior. In fact, these forms of community mothering are birthed out of a personal and social motivation to address the suffering of African women through solidarity, responsibility, and accountability, or "maternal activism" (Gilkes, 2001; McDonald, 1997, Ngunjiri, 2011).

Black Feminist Epistemology

Black feminist thought maintains that it is important to rearticulate how the social sciences define African-American women and for Black women to collectively identify their experiences in their own terms (Abdullah, 2007; Collins, 2007; Radford-Hill, 2000; Hamilton-Howard, 2003). Collins (1990) contends "This different view encourages African-American women to value their own subjective knowledge base, culture and traditions, rearticulate a consciousness that already exists, and provides a tool of resistance to all forms of their subordination. Black feminist thought specializes in formulating and rearticulating the distinctive, self-defined standpoint" (p. 750).

Recognizing that not all Black women's experiences are homogenous based on race and gender, Collins (2000) contends there are distinct experiences that connect Black women's ways of knowing back to their African ancestry. Despite varying histories, Black societies reflect elements of a core African value system that existed prior to and independently of colonialism, imperialism, slavery, apartheid, and other systems of racial domination (King, 2011; Martin & Martin, 1985). These familiar encounters of inhumane conditions fostered shared "ways of knowing" which are evident in the family structure, religious institutions, cultural traditions, and communal village of Black s throughout the African Diaspora. This African-centered consciousness permeates the shared history of people of African descent to give rise to a distinctive Afrocentric epistemology (Collins, 2000).

Black Women's Leadership

The re-articulation of leadership is both necessary and viable to a discussion on community building. Missing from traditional models of leadership, such as trait and transactional (Bass 1997), are the activities and experiences of Black women in community. Most recently, the literature has begun to reflect the ways in which Black women have "self-defined" and emerged as the "intellectual voice" of the community during times of societal unrest. Contemporary definitions of Black women's leadership take into account the historical presence of Black women's experiences of "racial uplift," activism, and resistance, to produce Black women's self-defined leadership which incorporates group-centered models of leadership, Black feminist leadership, and Black women's community leadership.

Black Female Community Leadership

One of the first definitions to encompass our collective group experience as women of African descent emerged out of Allen's (1995), assessment of characteristics, behaviors and values that define Black female community leadership. Female social support networks formed from "the struggle for group survival whereby group collective experience, and group socio-emotional support," encouraged "institution building, merged to form collective action for cultural maintenance and Blackcommunity empowerment" (p. 47). This definition is supported by the social and historical experiences of Black women in America, based on their race and gender. Thus, anecdotal documentation of how women developed leadership skills becomes critical to sustaining this style of leadership from generation to generation.

Black Self-Defined Leadership

Black women's leadership is rooted in traditional West African traditions and the historical response to the political tides of Africans in America. Abdullah's (2003), discussion of leadership emphasizes a communal model that emerged from the voices of grassroots efforts to address social problems in the community.

Abdullah (2003) synergizes the historical community work of Black women's political leadership and activism to arrive at an independent model of self-defined leadership that includes four tenets: "(a) it is proactive in nature (versus simply reactive), (b) it bridges theory with practice, with each constantly informing the other, (c) it embraces collective action/group-centered leadership (as opposed to a leader-centered group), and (d) it employs both traditional and nontraditional methods of political engagement" (p. 3).

Black Feminist Leadership

Abdullah (2007) further expands her definition of "self-defined leadership" to include the collective activist work of the Black women's Club Movement, the Anti-Lynching Movement, and the Civil Rights Movement, and introduces the term, "Black feminist leadership in *"Emergence of a Black Feminist Leadership Model."* Through her consideration of the communal aspect of leadership she takes into account the leadership contributions of Black feminist groups such as, the Black women's Health Project, the National Black Feminist Organization and the Combahee River Collective (Grace, 1999; Roth, 1999). Abdullah (2007) through her analysis, interprets the leadership behavior of Black women as having four key characteristics; "(a) it connects theory and practice, with each constantly informing the other, (b) it is proactive and not simply reactive, (c) it adopts a group-centered approach in which all members share the responsibility of leadership and collectively "own" the movement, and (d) it utilizes both traditional and nontraditional forms of activism" (p. 329).

Simultaneously, author Hall, et.al. (2007) published a definition of Black feminist leadership which connect the individual role to group outcome, and the Black feminist leadership with engaging in political struggles for justice and liberation. "Black women activists who, from the intersections of race and gender, develop paths, provide direction, and give voice to Black women.... Black feminist leaders lead by example and generate opportunities for change, provide encouragement and skills to others, and ignite a desire in other Black women to create conditions for success....(Black feminist leadership) is a designation that is accorded to a person-formally or informally" (p. 283).

Black women's community leadership, Black women's self-defined leadership, Black feminist leadership, and Black feminist leadership models, are all definitions of leadership, developed from a Black feminist standpoint, and were used to guide the discussion regarding Black women's community work within the fight against HIV/AIDS.

Methodology and Procedure

Research Design

The research design is inclusive of phenomenological (Creswell, 2007; Vaz, 1997) and Black feminist epistemology (Collins, 1990; Banks-Wallace, 2000; Taylor, 1999; Hamilton-Howard, 2003). The philosophical orientation most often associated with qualitative research is the interpretive research model which positions itself in understanding the process a phenomenon undergoes to exist and its link to the meanings that are entrenched in people's lived experiences. Hence, the basic guiding assumption for all types of qualitative research are that reality and truth are socially constructed, multifaceted and ever evolving (Creswell, 2007). Phenomenological research, Few, et.al. (2003), contends that reality is socially constructed through individual or collective definition of the situation" (p.207) and assures that the natural setting is the direct source of the data collected; is primarily descriptive; is concern with the research process from which theory emerges, and holds to the participants' meanings and perceptions of the phenomena (Bogdan and Biklen,1982). Thus the analysis of the phenomenon being studied is not analyzed separately from the reality as it is experienced by Black women. (p. 207) Most notably, research that is informed by Black feminist epistemology must provide a service to Black women, rather than simply a discussion about Black women (Davis, et.al, 2010; Rosser-Mims, 2005; Few, 2003; Taylor, 1998; Abdullah, 2003; Banks-Wallace, 2000; Green-Powell, 1997).

An exploratory, phenomenological (Creswell, 2007) approach was the most effective means of capturing the unique perspectives and knowledge about how Black women experience and define leadership in their HIV/AIDS community work. Specifically, the purpose of the research was to explore the nature of Black women's leadership in HIV/AIDS community work and to understand how the characteristics of this particular leadership style could be utilized to address significant community issues (Davison, 2010). The participants' experiences are both descriptors and definitions of their leadership and focused on four key factors: leadership, community mobilization, the intersection of race and gender, and how Black women's leadership in HIV/AIDS contributes to contemporary leadership models.

Study Participants

Respondents included a purposeful sample of 10 women involved in HIV/AIDS community work. The participants self-identified their racial/ethnic identity as 7 African American, 2 Black, Non-Hispanic, and 1 Bi-racial. Their ages ranged between 23 and 64, with an average age of 46. The participants consisted of an outreach worker; program manager; project manager; health education specialist; primary care Physician Assistant; director of marketing and business development; executive director/co-founder non-profit AIDS Service Organization(ASO); Chief executive officer (CEO)/ founder national and international non-profit ASO; CEO/founder national and international non-profit faith-based organization.

Approval for the study was secured through Clark Atlanta University's Institutional Review Board.

Participant Profiles

Each participant shared a unique and defining moment that led them to begin work in the field of HIV/AIDS. Written permission was obtained from each participant prior to the taping of each interview. Pseudo names are used in this document to protect the participants from potential controversial content.

Tiye is a 49 year old administrator from the Midwest, who currently works for a federally contracted private consulting firm in the area of public health. She currently serves as program director working with peer HIV/AIDS leaders at Historically Black Colleges and Universities, Hispanic Association of Colleges and Universities, and Native American Colleges and Universities. She began working in the HIV/AIDS arena in 1982 through her work with a major metropolitan department of health in the child and maternal health division. She recalls hearing a discussion around a "mystical illness."

Afiyia is a 56 year old native of a major metropolitan city in the southeast. She currently serves as a health education specialist for the federal government. She began working in HIV/AIDS in 1986 while working with the blood banks for a national health organization. She was the first health educator hired in New York to address "this new illness."

Asha is a 39 year old Physician's Assistant in a metropolitan city in the southeast, the founder of an educational support group for women infected with HIV/AIDS, and involved in expanding health care service delivery for those in

South Africa through her service as medical advisor for a national publication. In discussing her work in HIV/AIDS she recalls "No one wanted to touch it," as she took care of over 400 patients annually in a community health center in 1984. She recalls early involvement with the epidemic as being the "one and only" person of color and woman at many education seminars where she was surrounded by health providers.

Rashida is a 49 year old administrator at an urban research center at a HBCU in the southeast. She recalls hearing about HIV/AIDS in the mid 1980's while she was in the military. She indicated after returning to the United States from being overseas, her brother disclosed that he was HIV positive.

Shani is a 50 year old administrator in an urban county department of health. In 1986 or 1987 during her work in public health she recalls hearing about a "mysterious disease," but felt it was irrelevant to her. She reports subsequently discovering that her only brother was infected with HIV.

Ngozi is the 53 year co-founder and executive director of a southeastern AIDS service organization. She reported attending a workshop given by a community public health department in 1985/86 and meeting a community activist who was providing HIV/AIDS education through local barbershops and beauty salons. A community activist approached her about serving as an administrator in an existing community organization. They began to work together providing culturally specific HIV/AIDS prevention education for the youth and community at large.

Zuri a 64 year old administrator from a major metropolitan city in the northeast is the current executive director of a community based health agency in a metropolitan southeastern state. Her introduction to HIV/AIDS began by discovering that her brother, as well as, a guy she was dating had a "mysterious disease" that involved them wasting away. It is 1979-1980 and the terms HIV/AIDS have not been coined yet. She states she remembers attending seminars and doing research to find out what was happening to the men she loved.

Nia is the 23 year old daughter of Zuri and has worked under the apprenticeship of her mother. She became formally involved in HIV/AIDS education at the age of 14 as a high school peer educator. She stated, "although it started out as work, once I started seeing persons I knew become infected, and saw how thirsty people were for information, I knew I had found my '"calling."'

Thandeka is a 43 year old Chief Executive Officer (CEO) and founder of an AIDS Service Organization (ASO) designed for and by African American women in a major metropolitan southeastern state and South Africa. Her work with HIV/AIDS stems from her work with a private feminist women's health clinic. She remembers hearing about Rock Hudson dying around 1985 and how this heightened the HIV concern among women. After working collectively with other women to develop a response through a local ASO, she recalls being compelled to "pick up the gauntlet and run" after her employer decided to dissolve their HIV/AIDS prevention efforts. She worked with a group of advisors and used her severance pay and unemployment benefits to establish her current organization that addresses justice related to reproductive rights and HIV/AIDS.

Imani is a 54 year old founder and CEO of a national and international non-profit, non-governmental faith-based organization whose primary mission is to improve the health status of people of the African ancestry by building the capacity of faith communities to address life-threatening diseases, especially HIV/AIDS. . The entrée for her work in the HIV/AIDS began with her professional employment as an immunologist in Harlem, New York around 1985. She described the death of two male friends who tragically died as a result of their HIV/AIDS status. These personal experiences with the men in the community intersected with her work at Harlem Hospital. Imani states "I had no idea this would be the work I would do. God gave me an idea, for the moment, to put together a Harlem Week of Prayer. I didn't do this to create something and I had no idea this would be my life's work."

Data Collection

Each participant was contacted by phone, email, and a written letter. Preliminary review of documents included the participant's resume, agency's website, Google search, and participant demographic survey. Semi-structured interview questions were developed and revised based on the research questions and review of the literature. Oral and written consent was obtained to audio record each interview. Field notes and analytic memos were created during the interview. Two research assistants also took field notes, and their input was used to clarify the documents.

Data Analysis

The data analysis procedure described by Creswell (2007) provided the structure to analyze the data of this phenomenological research. Lists of significant statements were generated after reviewing the field notes and the transcribed text. Each taped interview was listened to immediately after the session. Follow-up phone calls to the study participants were made for additional clarification as needed. Data was compared with the research field notes, resumes, and transcribed oral interviews to ensure that the responses from the participants were appropriately lined up under each question. This method represented a cleaning of the data. The transcripts were read and reread to create codes and to form common themes. Significant statements were grouped into larger units of information, called, "meaning units" or themes. A description of "what" the participants in the study experienced with the phenomenon; also known as a "textural description" was added. A description of "how" the experience happened; also known as the "structural description" was documented. Finally, a written composite description of the phenomenon incorporating both the textural and structural description was added. This passage is the "essence" of the experience and represents the culminating aspect of a phenomenological study.

Inter-Rater and Inter-Observer Reliability

To achieve inter-rater and inter-observer reliability mind-mapping was done independently by the researcher and the researcher assistant and compared to establish similar observations of the codes. A mind map is an outline in which the major categories radiate from a central image and lesser categories are portrayed as branches of larger branches (Budd, 2004). This technique provided a visual brainstorming method for the researcher to understand the relationships between the words. To help with reliability one research assistant also went through the transcripts and used mind mapping to look at the relationship between the codes. Additionally an objective researcher not connected to the study was asked to review the transcripts for codes. This method of inter-rated reliability was used to comparatively arrive at the final codes that were used to develop the next phase of meaning units. Reliability was achieved through data cleaning, participants reviewing of the transcripts, use of independent researcher and research assistant in coding and mind mapping, and field notes and analytic memo review.

Findings

Black feminist epistemology was the guiding theoretical framework of the study which was incorporated into the development of the research questions, the implementation of the research methodology, and throughout the data analysis. Black feminist epistemology served as the filter and lens for interpreting the findings. These women in HIV/AIDS leadership were engaged in various aspects of the fight which included direct services, such as community outreach, as healthcare providers, public health officials and as Executive Directors of their own agencies. There was a strong connection between their professional and private lives. Their work involved supporting and encouraging other Black women to develop the internal and external resources to address social injustices, but especially HIV/AIDS. Each participant expressed commitment to the value of creating positive and nurturing relationships as a part of their leadership style. Their leadership experiences, as described contain a host of qualities that were based on the collective understanding of being both Black and female.

The Nature of Black Feminist Leadership

The women described leadership as situational and contextual and in part as a living entity that is utilized by the group and for the group to achieve an outcome. Their leadership with Black women was a reciprocal relationship that is interdependent based on a commitment to pull together and do collective work on behalf of the communal survival. Although the definition and the role of leadership were used interchangeably, the women described the role of leadership as one of service and non-positional, meaning that there was not necessarily a top down approach as described in more traditional forms of leadership. They described the role of leadership as less authoritative, and more supportive, empowering, motivating, and visionary, and with the purpose of bringing about change. This role was embedded in the definition, and thus the role, purpose, and definition were seen as one. The definition of leadership was embedded in the purpose to produce change. Change was both internally and externally to the person and the community. A major part of leadership was to accept the personal responsibility and investment to support change that produces an enhanced outcome.

> I think leadership is the ability to listen to all sides, work with people and facilitate a common ground. To help the group develop a process and move it forward. It's understanding that no man is an island and you can't do it all by yourself. Everybody brings to the table talent or skills and experience and background. As a leader you place yourself as someone who can facilitate a process (Tiye, a program manager, with 27 years of experience in the field of HIV/AIDS)

> I think leadership is one who acknowledges responsibility to influence others and to guide and direct both persons and maybe the way a policy or things are governed to create change. I hope someone in leadership acknowledges their position to influence and to create change and to cause a shift to occur both in people and the environment. And then with the acknowledgment of that influence has the responsibility that they can guide and advise and help stir people to do or help people change the way they do things into a better way (Asha, a primary care PA at an AIDS clinic)

Inclusive

Traditional forms of leadership locate the role of leadership within one individual, in a hierarchy, authoritatively moving towards a goal, with or without the consensus and input of those in the group(Allen, 1997; Abdullah, 2003). The leadership described by these women was inclusive and welcomed the voice of others who sought to accomplish similar goals.

> Service through demonstrating and working a vision that you have chosen to share with others. It is the willingness to be in front; the willingness to be at the side of those in the front; it is being the backdrop so others can be in front. Leadership is taking responsibility of your ideas thoughts and action. It is also about creating space for others recognizing and others to be recognized (Thandeka, a CEO of a national and international ASO).

Collective

Application of leadership as a Black woman with Black women meant being linked to their well-being, ongoing life challenges, and understanding their common bond in the fight against HIV/AIDS and other injustices. The commonality included an interdependent relationship through commitment to build the community through personal and collective investment, as they shared in the struggle of the community. Centering their leadership in community kinship helped them to remain focused on the work of the collective and struggle towards a common goal. Black women's leadership is viewed as an extended family with a collective experience and voice focused on a common goal. It is described as linked fate based on fictive kinship, that recognizes differences and diversities, but respects the finality that there is a common bond to our lives.

> Kinship—regardless of our status in life, wherever we are and wherever we are we are in charge of leading something in our lives—good/bad. The leadership I experience with for, around, Black women is a common bond. The horizontal diversity is the least and most common denominator for Black women and says we can change whatever we need. We will get it done better when we recognize all of our strengths (Thandeka).

Intentional

Many of the women associated the term feminism as being race based and one that originated in the dominate community by women whose life experiences were different and privileged from theirs. They felt the term feminism was confining and evoked perceptions of those who had the luxury of choice to not only enter the workforce, but also to be in opposition with their male counterparts. These women felt leadership included the lived experiences at multiple intersections of being a woman; a Black woman; in partnership with Black men, Black women, and other communities of color, including the African Diaspora; connected through the experience of oppression and racism and their struggle for equality.

Self-definition included terms such as strength, liberation, humanist, opportunity, education, equality, wholeness, sustainability, and spirituality and an intentional and consistent break from other communities' attempts to contain them with their "labels." Labeling their leadership as Black feminist leadership was not as important as the intent of their behavior. Leadership was not relegated to title and position. Leadership was fluid, contextual, and rooted in liberation and spiritual practices with the intent of working on behalf of the collective. So even when the term Black feminist leadership was embraced, there was a declaration that only Black women could use this label on their terms.

> I'm sure it can be called Black feminist leadership but that's something that someone needs to try and get a further understanding of. I mean how important or how dedicated I am to women, to women's health, to Black women's health, to health of women of color, to equal opportunity and rights, to access health care, and the right an opportunity to access information that leads to health and wellness for not just women but our teens and our young women and our adolescents and our women and children who we really need to be spending more

time educating. But—so this can be a definition, but I don't like to be put into a box or to put titles on (Asha).

Yes! I would call this Black feminist leadership because I think a basic differentiation from a non-theoretical standpoint, from a lived experience is how I see it, how I feel it, my perspective. Feminism, while it isn't for everybody, it has by its very definition a limited focus on what equality entails and leaves room for different identities to define equality in different ways. Most people think of feminism as broken down strictly along misogyny, gender discrimination, and inequality among sexes. I think Black feminist theory takes equality from a woman's standpoint to another level of recognizing the intersecting complications of race/class/gender/sexuality as a whole in terms of addressing equality. I think that multiple oppressions become more clearly defined by people who live the experience of being Black and female (Thandeka).

Transformative

The qualities and characteristics of Black women who provide leadership in HIV/AIDS community work are transformative. Leadership for the study participants was experienced in a variety of ways, but most importantly focused on the transformative power to change the negative impact of HIV/AIDS into a positive. Their caregiving for the community through direct care and as CEO's of national organizations helped to transfer power back to those in crisis due to HIV risks.

> A powerful, powerful, strength that they would need to be sensitive and yet transform pain to power among the women that they're influencing, not just pain but fear to faith. (Asha, Physician Assistant).

> I came from the segregated South where the focus has always been on saving the people. I sat at the table with my grandparents, aunts, uncles, mom and dad where the discussion was always centered at saving Black people. Right now the issue just happens to be saving Black people from HIV/AIDS. We have got to save the race. This is our time so that our children's children will be able to save the community for the next generation (Imani, CEO of a faith-based national and international ASO)

Mothering on Behalf of the Community's Welfare

Community mobilization to address HIV/AIDS was expressed through various roles as community and bridge builders, but centered the context of birthing and God talk. The women confidently described their leadership contributions using terms such as strength, resilience, spiritual voice, empowerment, problem solvers, gatekeepers, beauty, intellect, respect, advocacy spirit, genuine, and human rights were used to describe their views. They talked about "pulling together" and "setting the agenda." There was a sense of determination and hope that through their contributions HIV/AIDS could be resolved. The terms community builders and bridge builders are used to express their sense of worth as leaders.

Community Builders

As community builders they described how Black women create a space for developing solutions around HIV/AIDS. The activities varied. They included the creation of an agency despite not receiving government resources, recruiting other health providers to the HIV/AIDS fight, teaching HIV/AIDS positive women to peer educate, bringing an "advocacy spirit" to the decision making table, and accepting the responsibility to lead and make sure that the Black community's interest were represented. Several of them spoke about witnessing the resilience and compassion of Black women who took their personal resources and created agencies to address the epidemic of HIV/AIDS. While some of these actions can also be seen as bridge building, there was a tendency to talk about the characteristics of the women who make this type of commitment to building the community.

For the Black women in HIV/AIDS their value as leaders was grounded in historical and contemporary experiences related to race and gender. Resilience, passion, and empowerment were used to describe their position as knowing how to make things happen even at the beginning of the AIDS epidemic when no one knew what to do. Despite recounting stories of being forced outside of the power circles, they described unconditional love and caretaking for their intimate partners, families and communities. For many of them, standing up for the community meant being in harm's way and self-sacrifice to make sure that their community participated in its own survival.

> We bring resilience! We bring that compassion! We're the ones that can make a whole lot of something out of nothing! I've seen Black women from their compassion pull together agencies and now these agencies are national organizations. I've seen Sistahs start agencies in their basements and work it! Some of them were fortunate enough to get funding, others weren't, but that didn't stop them. They moved forward. So we bring "that" to this fight and in some respect we've been sent to the back room to eat when clearly at that kitchen table we felt all the problems of the world. So, I think it's the strength of the Black female, her character, her resilience, her determination that we bring to this that helps keep it moving. We can solve this thing! We could fix this and move it forward (Tiye).

> The women that I've talked to have had focused scripts about how they would prefer to be treated. Not a hundred percent of the time, but most often, in my experience, they want to be treated by a woman and a woman of color. To build their understanding and comfort level and self-definition so that HIV is something that they can see as something they are destroying. This might empower them to destroy it in their younger sisters and older sisters and mothers and community members. In this case "each one teach one" how *not* to get infected. And I believe that's possible. We really have to work with the women, and as women, we can do that work together, help the women recognize they are more than the HIV diagnosis and they have the power to change and prevent their children and their daughters in getting infected (Asha).

> I bring my presence! .... (you're) not going to talk about people, without our presence. Black women bring our intellect, our beauty, our rights as women, our knowledge and our technological skills that accompany that knowledge. We bring our experience or experiences as leaders, because every woman is a leader whether she accepts that role or realizes that it has fallen to her to be a leader. We bring our personal experience as leaders to the table. We bring an advocacy spirit to the table (Jaha, federal government employee).

> The HIV movement has been led by Black women. We brought compassion as mothers, sisters, grandmothers, wives, and daughters to the community that had to take care of the dying. We brought compassion and integrity, especially in the early days of HIV/AIDS. Women helped to open up the idea that the Black gay men belonged to family. They were our brothers, fathers, uncles, lovers and we the Black women loved them. There was an unconditional love infused into the hatred that was in the Black community directed at gay men and fueled by homophobia (Imani).

Bridge Builders

Much like community builders, bridge builders were Black women who continued to "reach across the aisles," in a nonjudgmental way, to educate themselves and gather resources on behalf of the community. They met the need where they found it. As bridge builders they "stood in the gaps" and filled them with resources for those who were unable or who wouldn't step up to lead. This gap often included other women, their children, families, faith communities, Black heterosexual men, and others from the gay and lesbian community.

As bridge builders Black women acknowledge their skills as mothers and nurtures to address the hurt and pain caused by the HIV/AIDS epidemic. Their willingness to step into leadership in the absence of others was also predicated by professional and lay activities in the community. Building bridges to other communities met stepping outside of the issues of homophobia an immorality to embrace all those who were suffering, and to collectively develop strategies to address HIV/AIDS on behalf of the Black community.

Whether as a community builder or bridge builder, neither role is conceptualized exclusively. Each conceptual theme seemed to drive home the value that Black women bring to the fight around HIV/AIDS and why their contributions as leaders are important to the ongoing community work around this epidemic. In the absence of formal of leadership, strategies, and resources Black women relied on their past and ongoing work in the community and as caregivers to develop their leadership abilities.

> There's no question that we bring value. I think the value that we bring again is working with all types of people in a nonjudgmental way—meeting people where they are. We bring innate sense of nurturing and mothering to what we do. It's easier to build relationship and to establish trust when people feel that you are genuine, that this is more than a nine to five and a paycheck. That's what I think we bring value of (Zuri).

When it came to women diagnosed with HIV/AIDS bridging the gap between racism, sexism, and gender, Black women worked across the aisles, because we didn't have models of our own to work from. How do you address this issue of sexuality and sexual expression and sexual decision making? We've not been necessarily intentional about those issues in our own lives. But most importantly because we occupy so much disproportion of the epidemic, nobody is going to save us but us. And if we don't do it, we don't survive (Thandeka).

In our communities and especially our urban communities there are a disproportionate number of female headed households with no male partners. In our schools, our children are disproportionately taught and administrated by Black women. Our churches are worked, coordinated, the ministry work, and congregations are mainly represented by Black women. In the workplace women of color do the majority of the back breaking work which is the hardest of the organization. Just by the fact that every aspect of daily living and building communities is dependent on the resources of women of color and Black women, then by in large we have the greatest opportunity and power to create change in all those spaces. And what's even more important about why Black women are so necessary is that where homophobia and heterosexual have their place in pressing forward the HIV/AIDS epidemic, Black mothers have always known what to do! (Thandeka)

Birthing

They remained hopeful, consistent, and confident that while they might not see the end of AIDS, they were in the fight for the duration. Terms such as resiliency and sustainability were used to describe their individual determination as well as their willingness to build organizations that would continue the work long after their departure. There was a consensus that they needed to be as committed to the HIV/AIDS fight as other pioneering women who had made tremendous sacrifices and contributions. They were diligent and unyielding regarding their ability to make a difference. While they acknowledge that the work was difficult, there was sense that their presence alone was significant, and lessened the burden on others.

> ... the economy is bad and it is hard, but I continue to do this work because I am committed to doing it. This could be my sister, my daughters, my grandchildren, my great grandchildren. I believe if not me then who? Whatever little bit I can contribute to this work, I'm going to continue to do it as well as some of the sisters that I know, I think about people like Dazon Dixon, and Sandra McDonald—the forbearers in this work and how they started out in this work. Sandra used to talk about starting out in her car—from the trunk of her car. They weren't being paid. We weren't getting the grants. We still don't get the grants. If these women sacrificed their lives for this work, then who am I to do any less? I believe that we are more than our brothers' and sisters' keepers. We are our brothers and sisters so what happens to one of us I think affect us all. That's why I'm still sitting here, trying to do what I do. At 64 years old, wanting to retire; but this disease isn't retiring yet (Zuri).

God Talk

Their spirituality fed into their self-renewal, regeneration, informed and guided their leadership activities. Through the demographic survey eight out of ten of the women indicated a membership in a local house of worship (Davison, 2010). While not everyone saw their spirituality as connected to a formal religious affiliation, all of the women recognized a connection to a higher presence that supported and grounded their behavior and intentions in their community work. There was a sense of humbleness, humility, and a servant attitude that threaded their idea of leadership. The women used phrases such as, "Co-creator of life," "The Lord knows me by name," "I see it as a blessing" and "that's what God put on my path." The role of women was described as being a unique position of power, and working with women to influence their health was "a blessing" and "a gift" to serve.

Spirituality was part of the call and response of their experiences. Their Creator called them to the work. Their response was to unquestionably stay committed to the fight until the end. Their rationale for doing HIV/AIDS community; "I'm supposed to." Through a burning passion that humbled them in service, without hesitation, they claimed their duty of leadership. Repeatedly, they reflected; "If not me who?", "If I walk away, then who?" or "What else would I do?" Commitment was also expressed in kinship to those infected with HIV/AIDS, "those are we," "that could be my mother, daughter, sister, grandmother." But most of all, they engaged in God talk about their spiritual path and purpose; "this is my calling," "this is my path," "I'm supposed to be," "by the grace of God," "The Lord keeps me in this."

> Well it seems like there's no other hands! I think for me to be able to be in a position of service and to serve people that are—just to serve humankind and then more specifically women being that I am woman, being that "those are we" have close ties to one another and we're here to create life. To co-create life of course but we definitely are the component of the co-creators of life and we are really powerful. So if I see there's a place I can be of service to something that is here to create life and keep life going then that's like, Wow, what a blessing! I see it as a blessing and opportunity and it's also been such a gift to be in this position to have influence and care of women that I've learned so much about who I am as a woman, who I want to be as a woman and who I don't want to be and how to—I'm always challenged on how to become a better woman regularly. So there's so much I get out of this—in this place since day one (Asha).

> Because it's my calling! That's what God put in my path and it's the only job that I ever engaged in where I still get up and I love what I do, there's always something new; there's always something different. I get to meet all kinds of people; help all kinds of people; change systems; change perceptions of leadership; I can see the fruits of my labor; both from a client perspective as well as a systems level and a lot of people don't get the opportunity to say that. I believe

that leadership moves beyond just your vocation. And that everybody should do something to change their community period (Ngozi).

Because, I'm supposed to! I don't have a choice. I don't think about how I do this—if I did I'd probably be overwhelmed and paralyzed. So I don't think about how. But I do know the why-This is my given purpose it is what I'm supposed to do with this life that I have as a gift. No matter what it is if I'm not working here, it will still be on this path of seeking as much change and justice as possible to change the quality of life for Black women and girls and people in general. If I ever stepped off that path, I don't think my blessings would be the same. On a more practical level, I have to make sure that my ideas have the infrastructure so that they are sustainable. So that's how I do it. I stay focused on where we've got to go, as they say "I believe I'll run on and see what the end is going to be"! (Thandeka)

Girl, the Lord keeps me in this! My life is invested at this point. What else would I do? It is not just about HIV/AIDS but the health of the community. We are so far away from our center as an African community. Issues around sexuality, for both our youth and elders are a manifestation of this. Our young girls are out of control with their lack of self-esteem. Our young men won't pull their pants up. Our seniors are experiencing a sexual liberation due to new pharmaceuticals that is reflective of the seventies. AIDS is the result of decades of our stuff, our discovery, our doing our own "thang." We are so far away from our center. The disease is just a catalyst for the enfoldment of many issues. Our center is grounded in our values as Africans (Imani).

Discussion

Black feminist epistemology was the guiding theoretical framework of the study which was incorporated into the development of the research questions, the implementation of the research methodology, and throughout the data analysis including the interpretation of the findings. Overall, the women embraced the principles of Black feminist epistemology through an open demonstration in their leadership and community work. Their collective action as women activists who developed paths and provided direction from the intersections of race and gender, while demanding a voice for other Black women, is described as Black feminist leadership (Hall, et.al, 2007).

Mobilization on behalf of the community was a commitment to social action that is best described as "maternal activism" and "activist mothering." As pioneers in the epidemic, amongst the fear and chaos, they used their professional and personal relationships to develop a response. They felt deeply that God had called them to address the dying and suffering of the community. As women, their innate sense of caring, compassion and unconditional love yielded an inclusive style of problem solving. For several of them this meant, giving birth to new agencies that could speak to the unique station of their experiences as Black women.

Black women in HIV/AIDS leadership are engaged in various aspects of the fight which include direct services, such as community outreach, as healthcare providers, public health officials, and as Executive Directors of their own agencies. Their work involved supporting and encouraging other Black women to develop the internal and external resources to address social injustices, but especially HIV/AIDS. Each participant expressed commitment to the value of naming and addressing inequities that impacted their families and communities, making no distinction between the two.

Conclusion

This study examined the nature of Black feminist leadership in HIV/AIDS community work. Black feminist epistemology (Collins, 2000) provides the filter through which Black women experience leadership at the intersection of race/gender/power. As a result of these lived experiences, including being in service to others in their homes, churches, and schools, Black women learned how to transfer the skills of caregiving in their domestic roles as mothers, to an "elevated motherhood public role of providing service to the community and nation. Having observed it from their grandmothers, mothers and othermothers in the community, *leadership through service* was the chosen modus operandi. (Ngunjiri, 2007; p.13). Transferring mothering skills to a public domain meant being more sensitive to the needs of marginalized members of their community and communities with parallel issues of oppression, stigma, and discrimination.

Black feminist leaders in HIV/AIDS community work led the AIDS movement on national and international fronts, but most importantly in their local communities. Their collective work and shared responsibility sought value in everyone's contributions, regardless of formal education. The women spoke of the ongoing self-sacrifice that is a part of their "calling" and their "response."

The study therefore concludes that the nature of Black feminist leadership in HIV/AIDS work is based on the historical roles of Black women in their community. It is a product of their lived experiences as leaders within the community as educators, churchwomen, and caretakers that provide them the skills to nurture and love unconditionally. Family values of community unity and liberation as the result of historical segregation also factored in their need to uplift the community. Their spiritual relationship with a higher power humbled them to understand that leadership was less about one and more about creating an inclusive space for all. The intersection of race and gender sometimes meant being faced with microaggressions internally and externally to the community. However, as Black women they felt this gave them a way of knowing how to reach out and build bridges to other marginalized communities in order to better build their community. Black feminist leadership in HIV/AIDS work meant developing an agenda where all persons regardless of skill level and position had a voice to be heard and means to access social services. Their leadership required collaboration with multiple professionals and nonprofessionals who could collective use their talents and intellect to better the Black community.

Implications

Within the Black community, we occupy simultaneous positions of power as intergenerational mothers and daughters, teachers, pastors, administrators, health providers, and as elected officials. We control decision making and resources from our kitchens to the collective tables of the community. Our meager or plentiful resources have been utilized to feed our households and the masses. The pan- epidemic of AIDS has forced us to extend our mothering skills to address the needs of the Diaspora community.

Black women have a historical legacy of tackling social issues such as poverty and health disparities in the face of race and gender discrimination. Black feminist epistemology provided the theoretical frame to examine the work of these pioneering women at the intersection of multiple oppressions. Their stories yield a "means of knowing" (Collins, 2000) how to address the issues that impact the Black community's quality of life and mortality. As pioneers in the HIV/AIDS fight, their leadership development came from family values, their community and church involvement, and their experiences of being in communal relationship with others. Their collective commitment to each other as community leaders was emphasized as they talked about being side by side with other commitment sisters who were in a reciprocal peer mentorship that provided a safe space for them to strategize, take risk, vent, and celebrate. Thus Black feminist epistemology, offers a framework that attends to the lived experiences of women of African ancestry, and offers an opportunity to develop leadership that builds on the strengths of our historical and contemporary knowledge.

One of the most profound statements that emerged from the interviews, "Black mothers have always known what to do," focused on how Black women's ability to insert humanity and love into a disease that is stigmatized by hatred, blaming, and victimization, also repositioned these women's leadership from being at the fringes to being the center component that created a space for everyone to be a part of the solution process. This type of "activist mothering" and "community mothering" is referenced in the community work that Black women have historically done on behalf of the community (Gilkes, 2001). Nurturing each other and relying heavily on their faith is what sustains us in our efforts to fight for resources on behalf of the community. For some of them, this included birthing organizations that prioritized Black women and their extended families.

Finally, Black women's leadership in HIV/AIDS borrows from the efforts of the liberation and uplift work of the Black Clubwomen of the 19th century, as well as the Black communal leadership of the Civil Rights Era, to address the social injustices of HIV/AIDS. The integration of theoretical frameworks that are inclusive and affirming to Black women's lived experiences may be a renewed opportunity to significantly improve the life of those infected with HIV/AIDS, while simultaneously adding to their self-determination. Examining the historical content of indigenous leadership, such as Black feminist leadership can provide a blue print for the development of future leaders in the HIV/AIDS fight and social services.

References

Abdullan, M. R. (2007). The emergence of Black feminist leadership model: African American women and political activism. Black women's intellectual traditions: Speaking their minds. In Waters, K. & Conawy, C. B. editors. University of Vermont Press. Burlington, Vermont, 328-346.

Allen, B. (1997). A Re-articulation of Black female community leadership: Processes, networks and a culture of resistance. *African American Research Perspectives*, 7:61-67.

Banks-Wallace, J. (2000). Womanist ways of knowing: Theoretical considerations of research with African American women. *Advances in Nursing Science*, 22(3) 33-45.

Barrett E.J. (1995). The policy priorities of African-American women in state legislatures. *Legislative Studies Quarterly*, 20 (2): 223-247.

Bass, B., & Avolio, B. (1997). *Full range of leadership manual for the multifactor leadership questionnaire*. Palo Alto, CA: Mind Garden.

Brice, T.S. (2005). "Disease and delinquency know no color: Syphilis and African American female delinquency. *Affilia*. Fall, 20(3), 300-315.

Collins, P.H. (2000). *Black feminist thought: Knowledge, consciousness, and the politics of empowerment*. (2nd ed.). New York, Routledge.

Collins, P. H. (2007). The politics of Black feminist thought. In Waters, K. & Conway, C. B., (Eds). *Black women's Intellectual Traditions: Speaking Their Minds*, (pp. 393-418). Burlington, Vermont: University of Vermont Press.

Carlton-LeNay, I. ed. (2001). *African American leadership: An empowerment tradition in social welfare history*. NASW Press.

Carlton-LaNey, I (1999). African American social work pioneers, response to need, *Social Work*, 4(4), 311-321.

Davison-McLane, D. (2010). An exploratory phenomenological study of Black feminist leadership in HIV/AIDS community work . ETD Collection for Robert W. Woodruff Library, Atlanta University Center. Paper 163.

Davis, S., Williams, A.D., Akinyela, M. (2010). An Afrocentric approach to building cultural relevance in social work research. *Journal of Black Studies*. 41(2), 338-350.

Eugene, T.M. (1995). There is a balm in Gilead: Black women and the Black church as agents of a therapeutic community. *Women & Therapy*. 1995. 16 (2/3) p55.

Few, A. L., Stephens, D. P., & Rouse-Arnett, M. (2003). Sister-to-sister talk: Transcending boundaries and challenges in qualitative research with Black women. *Family Relations*, 52(3), 205-213.

Gaetane, J.M.(2006). Welcoming the unwelcomed: A social justice imperative of African American female leaders at historically Black colleges and universities. *Educational Foundations*, 20 (1-2) 85-104.

Gilkes(2001). *If it wasn't for the women*. New York: Orbis Books.

Gilkes,C.T. (1980). Holding back the ocean with a broom: Black women and community work. In L. Rodgers-Rose(Ed). *The Black Woman*. New York: Sage.

Gilkes, C. T.(1985) Together and in harness: Women's traditions in the sanctified church. *Signs*, 10(4), 678-699.

Gordon, J. U. (2000). *Black leadership for social change*. Westport, CT: Greenwood Press.

Grayson, D.R.(1999). Necessity was the midwife of our politics: Black women's health activism in the "post"- civil rights era 1980-1996. In Springer, K. (ed.). *Still Climbing: African American women's contemporary activism*. (pp. 131-148). New York: New York University Press.

Green-Powell, P. (1997). Methodological considerations in field research: Six case studies. In K.M. Vaz (Ed.). *Oral Narrative Research with Black Women* (pp. 197-223). California: Sage Publication.

Greenewald, T. (2004). A phenomenological research design illustrated. *International Journal of Qualitative Methods*, 3 (1) 1-26.

Hall, R. L., Garrett-Akinsanya, B., & Hucles, M. (2007). Voices of Black feminist leaders: Making spaces for ourselves. In Chin, J. L., Lott, B., Rice, J. K., & Sanchez-Hucles, J. (Eds.), *Women and Leadership: Transforming Visions and Diverse Voices* (pp. 281-296). New York: Black well Publishing.

Hamilton-Howard, M. F. (2003). Theoretical frameworks for African American women. *New Directions for Student Services*, 104, 19-27.

Henry, A. (1992). African Canadian women teachers' activism: Recreating communities of caring and resistance. *Journal of Negro Education*, 61, 392–404.

hooks, b. (2000). *Feminist theory: From margin to center*. 2nd edition. Cambridge. M.A.: South End Press,

King,T.C & A. Ferguson, eds. (2011). *Black womanist leadership: Tracing the motherline*. State University of New York Press, Albany.

Martin, J. M., & Martin, E. P. (1985). The helping tradition in the African American family and community. Washington, DC: National Association of Social Workers.

McDonald, K. B. (1997). Black activist mothering: A historical intersection of race, gender, and class. *Gender and Society*, 11(6), 773-795.

Nance, T.A.(1996). Hearing the missing voice. *Journal of Black Studies*. 26(5)543-559.

Ngunjiri, F. W. (2007). Motherhood deconstructed: African women finding fulfillment in serving humanity. Paper presented at the NCA Conference, Chicago.

Parker, P.S. (2005). *Race, gender, and leadership: Re-envisioning organizational leadership from the perspectives of African American women executives*. Mawhah, New Jersey: Lawrence Erlbaum Associates, Publishers.

Perry, T. E., Davis-Maye, D., & Onolemhemhen, Durrend, N. (2007). Faith, spirituality, fatalism and hope: Ghanaian women coping in the face of HIV/AIDS. *Journal of HIV/AIDS & Social Services*, 6(4), pp. 37-58.

Reeder, G. D., Davison, D. M., Gipson, K. L., & Hesson-McInnis, M. (2001) Identifying the motivations of African American Volunteers Working to Prevent HIV/AIDS. *AIDS Education and Prevention: An Interdisciplinary Journal*, 13(4), 343-354.

Radford-Hill, S. (2000). Feminist leadership for the new century. Further to Fly: Black-Women and the Politics of Empowerment. Minneapolis: University of Minnesota Press, 81-94.

Riggs, M. Y. (1994). Awake, arise and act: A womanist call for Black liberation. Cleveland, OH: Pilgrim Press.

Rodriguez, C. (1996). African American anthropology and the pedagogy of activist community research. *Anthropology & Education Quarterly*. 27 (3), 414-431.

Roth, B. (1999). The making of the vanguard center: Black feminist emergence in the 1960's and 1970's in Springer, K. (ed.). *Still Climbing: African American women's contemporary activism*. (pp. 70-91). New York, New York University Press.

Sanders, C. J. (Ed.). (1995). *Living the intersection: Womanism and Afrocentrism in theology*. Minneapolis, MN: Fortress Press.

Sanders, C. J. (1995). *Empowerment ethics for a liberated people: A path to African American social transformation*. Minneapolis, MN: Fortress Press.

Simien, E.M.(2004a). Black feminist theory: Charting a course for Black women's studies in political science. *Women & Politics*, 26(2)81-93.

Simien, E.M. & R.A. Clawson. (2004). The intersection of race and gender: An examination of Black feminist consciousness, race consciousness, and policy attitudes. *Social Science Quarterly*, 85(3) 793-810.

Slevin, K.F.(2005). Intergenerational and community responsibility: Race uplift work in the retirement activities of professional African American women. *Journal of Aging Studies*, 19, 309-326.

Smith, S. L. (1995). Sick and tired of being sick and tired: African American women's health activism in America, 1890-1950. Philadelphia: University of Pennsylvania Press.

Tate, G.T.(2003). Unknown Tongues: Black women's political activism in the antebellum era, 1830-1860. East Lansing: Michigan State University Press.

Taylor, J. Y. (1998). Womanism: A methodologic framework for African American women. *Advances in Nursing Science*, 21(1), 53-64.

Vakalahi,H.O, Starks, S.H. & Oritz-Hendricks, C. (2007). Women of color as social work educators: Strengths and Survival. Alexandria, VA: CSWE Press.

Watkins, R.N. (2008). The southern roots of Ida. B. Wells-Barnett's revolutionary. *Southern Quarterly*.

Wilson, S. (2008). Research is ceremony: Indigenous research methods. Canada: Fernwood Publishing.

Chapter Ten
What *Mami* Taught Me about Empire
Elizabeth Huergo

Introduction

At the age of seven, I started coming home in the afternoons, my arms and legs bruised and scratched, something my mother questioned and I shrugged off for as long as possible. When the bruises and scratches became too regular, my mother's questions turned into an eyeball to eyeball interrogation, and I confessed, blurting out the words as if the sin were mortal and exclusively mine: I was being bullied. Soon after, my mother dragged me to a shoe store and introduced me to the biggest, ugliest shoes I had ever seen. They were made of leather, black and white, with black shoe laces and a heavily crimped, sown edge that ran their perimeter. Those were the shoes my mother started putting on my feet every morning before school, firmly pulling the laces into a tight bow. "If you hit a boy here," she said, dropping one hand down to her lap, "it hurts very, very much. Are you listening?"

I wasn't. I was wondering why it would hurt more than if someone kicked me there. "The next time he tries to hit you," she insisted, "grab his hair and kick him. Right here." I complained that the shoes were heavy and ugly, and she took me by the shoulders, her eyes on fire: "I'm going to be waiting at the fence with the other mothers. When I see you kick him, I'm going to start shouting to you to stop. Don't stop. Not until he stops." So I trudged to school that day with those iron armadillos on my feet, praying and hoping to avoid the bully, but when the final bell rang, there he was, fists clenched. He lunged at me. I grabbed him by the hair and kicked him in just the spot my mother told me. She was right; one kick and he collapsed, coiled in pain. "*Lee-see, eh-stop! Eh-stop!*" my mother called out to me. I could hear her in the distance, her voice cleaving through the fog of my fear and adrenaline.

Clearly, what *mami* taught me that day was to stand my ground and fight my own battles. However, as the decades passed, my sense of the complexity of that moment deepened. As an adult, it became clear to me that the story was as much about my mother as it was about myself, a story she knew viscerally long before I was able to piece it together. That little boy had recognized me as "Spanish." This was the difference that propelled his fists and fueled the taunts, prelude to every assault: "Hey, spic!" So in that long-ago moment, standing on the perimeter of the school-yard fence and the perimeter of an alien culture and language, my Cuban immigrant mother, left exhausted and bereft by US colonialism, had conveyed to her immigrant daughter an unwavering sense of how the world worked. It wasn't simply a lesson in self-reliance, as I had thought for so long, but part of a larger story about the difference between how others saw me and how I saw myself.

"*Lee-see, eh-stop! Eh-stop!*" she had called out to me in heavily accented English. And I remembered my mother that day, neatly dressed in matching hat and gloves and handbag, her head held high, studiously ignoring the bully's mother, who was standing nearby—fuming, enraged at what I had done to her angelic little man. My mother stood her ground, her voice, her use of my family nickname forming a life-line that encircled and drew me to safety, reassuring me that, though appearance and reality all too often diverge and sweet little boys can also be terrifying bullies, in fact skinny, soft-spoken little beige girls can hit back. She had given me shoes, instructions, support; most important, she had given me the gift of a very different story about myself than the one I had learned and come to believe in the school-yard. There was a clear line between defense and offense, and I was smart enough to know the difference. I wasn't a victim, but someone who was rooted, certain, capable.

Born in 1930, my mother had lived through (one phase of) the political and social convulsions of US colonialism. The era of Machado, a U.S.-backed dictator, began in 1925 and ended in 1933, after FDR had dispatched Sumner Welles, Ambassador Extraordinary and Plenipotentiary, to fix things, which meant letting Machado flee to the US in fear of his life and Welles (the White House) giving their nod of approval to the provisional presidency of Céspedes. It didn't matter to them that so many Cubans were opposed to this rather undemocratic, self-serving intervention or that this intervention would soon lead to revolt and the establishment of the *Pentarquía*, a junta of five rebels whose "communistic" tendencies did not appeal to the extraordinary and plenipotent ambassador. FDR, too, was displeased. Though he had been diligently marketing his "Good Neighbor Policy" to Latin America, he listened to Welles, then sent some 30 warships to surround Cuba. In the teeth of US opposition, Ramón Grau San Martín, one of the five members of the *Pentarquía* was appointed president, but soon overthrown (with US backing) by Fulgencio Batista, whose brutality and repression would eventually lead to Fidel, the Revolution of 1959, and more than 50 years of exile.

So for the first 29 years of her life, my mother had experienced more insurrection, torture, killing, and economic and social instability than the average citizen of the US does in a lifetime. Yet how many US citizens, well-educated and well-fed, know this "cultural script," this history of imperial intervention that finds its quotidian parallel in a school-yard bully? Who can tell this story above the roar of the narrative of American exceptionalism? My mother told it from the margin, standing on the other side of a chain-link fence. She refused the third-person narrative she had lived repeatedly in her homeland and had now encountered in exile. She pitched her "counterstory" across the open space of that school-yard to me that day, "a story that resists an oppressive identity and attempts to replace it with one that commands respect" (Nelson, 2001, 6).

My mother had repudiated the bully's misrepresentation of me as a passive victim, and done everything she could to help me form a different story, one that did not include accepting either fear or helplessness. As feminist philosopher Hilde Lindemann Nelson explains in *Damaged Identities, Narrative Repair*, "[t]he counterstory positions itself against a number of master narratives: the stories found lying about in our culture that serve as summaries of socially shared understandings" (6). For Nelson "[b]oth others' recognition that I am a morally responsible person and my own sense of myself as a morally responsible person, then, are required for the free exercise of moral agency" (22). Thus moral agency is composed not of one but two narrative lines: one that emerges from family or community as a "counterstory," a first-person narrative that has been internalized and become integral to how she sees herself; and the broader "master narrative" of the culture, a third-person narrative that, as Nelson points out, does not have to be destructive or pejorative, though it often is and can even lead to "infiltrated consciousness," drastically circumscribing how the subject sees herself and her ability to act in the world (22).

The presence and weight of this third-person narrative is a difficult concept for most Americans to grasp fully since it contradicts perhaps the central tenet of the master narrative of American exceptionalism: that any individual can rise from the meanest circumstances if only he (and it is usually a "he") works hard and follows (some of) the rules that apply to (some) men here in the land of the free and the home of the brave. (No one else in the world is free or brave, of course.) We understand ourselves, our ability to act, in relation to a social and cultural nexus, despite the frequent insistence that there is no such nexus, no fine ideological web that engirths and enmeshes us all. Our decisions, and the way we imagine the depth and scope of our actions, are also caught within and contained by that nexus. The destructive master narrative that "infiltrates consciousness" teaches us (silently and invisibly) that men are stronger, white is prettier, English more expressive, and then with a sleight of hand and tongue renders invisible the next and most dangerous of inferences: that those who are culturally, racially, and linguistically "superior" have a tacit, often God-given right, to bully everyone else into submission.

"A person's identity," writes Nelson, "is twice damaged by oppression when she internalizes as a self-understanding the hateful or dismissive views that other people have of her" (21). A "damaged identity," then, occurs in the traumatic intersection between those two lines of narrative—self and other, first-

and third-person, when "the master narratives used by a dominant group to justify the oppression of a less powerful group distort and falsify the group's identity by depicting the group—and therefore also its members—as morally subnormal" (106). Interestingly, master narratives draw from the elements of fiction: "stock plots and readily recognizable character types of master narratives characterize *groups* of people in certain ways, thereby cultivating and maintaining norms for the behavior of the people who belong to these groups, and weighting the ways others will or won't tend to see them" (106, italics original). Though Nelson clearly stipulates that "[i]dentities can be damaged and made incoherent or painful in all kinds of ways that have nothing to do with unjust social group relations" (106), her argument about how "oppressive master narratives cause *doxastic* damage—the damage of distorting and poisoning people's self-conceptions and their beliefs about who other people are" (106, italics original), is of special relevance to the push by "minority" writers to tell that traumatic intersection between first-person experience and a third-person "master narrative" that either distorts or renders their experience invisible.

Nelson describes "three levels of resistance" that bear on the drive to reconceptualize narrative form: refusal, which is basically a simple denial of the master narrative; repudiation, which uses a fragmented or disjointed counterstory to resist the master narrative; and contestation, which uses a fully and coherently developed counterstory to "oppose [the master narrative] ... both publicly and systematically" (169). Certainly, the transit through that traumatic intersection aestheticizes their experiences, though their full resistance and contestation of the master narrative is most evident in their re-conceptualization of narrative form. These fractured and often hybrid counterstories work less to aestheticize than to draw our attention to "pernicious cultural scripts and personae, rightly emphasizing the power that these narratives have over our imaginations" (85).

Refusal, repudiation, contestation—there is a narrative arc tacit in this cluster of responses to what Diana Tietjens Meyers terms in *Subjection and Subjectivity: Psychoanalytic Feminism and Moral Philosophy* "culturally normative prejudice" (cited in Nelson 85), a plot that drives the oscillation between first- and third-person narrative. And I think of my mother that day, standing on the perimeter of that school-yard, and realize with the fullness that only time can render, that the confrontation with the bully was as much hers as it was mine; that what she had repudiated was not only the story of her daughter as a victim, but the story that we, recent Cuban immigrants, would be subsumed in the master narrative of empire. My mother, who had never had the opportunity to finish high-school, did not need anyone to explain to her who Caliban was or why he cursed Prospero.

Responses to "culturally normative prejudice" (Meyers' phrase) abound. The question is, who is willing to hear those responses and be shaken to the very foundations? And who, having heard the story, is willing to relinquish the white-knuckle grip on power? If we want to hear, the praxis of feminism becomes clear, constituted as it is through counter-narrative—the stories our mothers tell in the spaces between the normative and the monstrous. Once heard, the illusion that men and women share the same moment of history shatters as the "relational" reading of social developments reveal how institutions promote one sex and hobble the other (Kelly-Gadol, 1976, 432-3). The idea finds its analogue in the desire of the imperial north to annex the south. We share the same moment of time, as García Marquez contests, carefully reframing the bloody and barbaric history of Europe, but we do not share the same moment of history: "The interpretation of our [Latin American] reality through patterns not our own, serves only to make us ever more unknown, ever less free, ever more solitary. Venerable Europe would perhaps be more perceptive if it tried to see us in its own past" (1982). Less known, less free, less connected to our common humanity: historical narrative has the power to tether us to unquestioned assumptions about the imperial projects of the moment and to rationalize every cultural difference as indicative of a lower order of being, an alignment that makes conquest morally worthy and "natural."

Sir Leslie Stephen's biographical essay on the life of Mary Wolstonecraft in the 22nd volume of the *Dictionary of National Biography* and the response of his daughter, Virginia Woolf, reveals the insidiousness of master narratives and their use of "stock plots and readily recognizable character types" (Nelson, 2001, 106); of how we can learn to contest historical narrative. Stephen, the editor of the *DNB* from 1882 to 1891, describes Wollstonecraft as the wife of Godwin and a "miscellaneous writer" (60). Given Wollstonecraft's racial and ethnic lineage, Stephen seems to ask, how could she ever have amounted to much? She was, after all, the "granddaughter of a rich Spitalfields manufacturer of Irish extraction," and "[h]er father, Edward John Wollstonecraft, spent the fortune which he had inherited, tried farming, took to drinking, bullied his wife, and rambled to various places, sinking lower at each move" (60) The selected details of Wollstonecraft's life are fitted into the stock plot of the fallen woman, the one who "scandalized her sisters" (61) with the publication of *Vindication of the Rights of Woman*; fell in love with Fuseli, a married man; tried to please Fuseli by getting "rid of her previously slovenly habits of dress" (61); left for Paris, where she fell in love with Gilbert Imlay, an American soldier, and "agreed to live with him as his wife—a legal marriage for an Englishwoman being probably difficult at the time, and not a matter of importance according to her views" (61).

She then gave birth out of wedlock to a child, Fanny; followed Imlay across Europe even after he had abandoned her and Fanny; tried to commit suicide by drowning herself; met Godwin; got pregnant; married Godwin because she was pregnant, (despite the fact that neither of them entirely approved of marriage); and died a few days after giving birth. Reading the story of Wollstonecraft's life, as Stephen tells it, we recognize both the stereotypical whore and the moral lesson—the stern warning of what happens to women who refuse the patriarchal master narrative that describes and delimits their role in the world. Stephen cannot seem to understand Wollstonecraft as anything other than what the master narrative renders her. From his third-person perspective, she is an Irish mongrel who "had much talent, though little education" (60) and a harlot. Her "slovenly habits of dress" (61), which derived from her refusal to wear a corset, served as an unequivocal indicator of her moral laxity, the loose habit(s) of a harlot.

In Virginia Woolf's essay on Mary Wollstonecraft in *The Second Common Reader*, published in 1932, Woolf responds to her father, countering his master narrative of the fallen woman. Of interest is not only the heartfelt identification that Woolf seems to have with Wollstonecraft, a woman whose intellect and iconoclastic posture toward the manners and morals of her time Woolf appreciates and shares, but the way Woolf's essay moves from first- to third-person, her identification with Wollstonecraft so clear despite time and social class, as she pitches it out across the open space between herself and a future she can only imagine. Woolf begins her essay on Mary Wollstonecraft by taking on the project of a third-person biographical narrative. Read side by side with her father's essay, however, the differences are striking. It isn't Wollstonecraft's ethnicity or social class but rather the broader historical context of her life that interests Woolf.

"Great wars are strangely intermittent in their effects," Woolf begins, explaining how "[t]he French Revolution took some people and tore them asunder; others it passed over without disturbing a hair of their heads" (156). Jane Austen, Charles Lamb, Beau Brummell—for these figures, the Revolution was of no importance (156). "But to Wordsworth and to Godwin it was the dawn; unmistakably they saw 'France standing on the top of golden hours, / And human nature seeming born again'" (156). Unlike her father, Woolf situates Wollstonecraft within an intellectual and historical frame, drawing our attention to the parallel between "a picturesque historian" and the frivolous Beau Brummel, both of whom are interested in what is fashionable and superficial, and the young, badly dressed, middle-class men (and woman) who were engaged in the highest principles of the French Revolution—liberty, fraternity, equality:

> Thus it would be easy for a picturesque historian to lay side by side the most glaring contrasts—here in Chesterfield Street was Beau Brummell letting his chin fall carefully upon his cravat and discussing in a tone studiously free from vulgar emphasis the proper cut of the lapel of a coat; and here in Somers Town was a party of ill-dressed, excited young men, one with a head too big for his body and a nose too long for his face, holding forth day by day over the teacups upon human perfectibility, ideal unity, and the rights of man. There was also a woman present with very bright eyes and a very eager tongue, and the young men, who had middle-class names, like Barlow and Holcroft and Godwin, called her simply 'Wollstonecraft', as if it did not matter whether she were married or unmarried, as if she were a young man like themselves. (156-7)

Which will you choose? Woolf demands. The fop or the philosopher? What will you stand for, the monarchy or the rights of man? "Such glaring discords among intelligent people—for Charles Lamb and Godwin, Jane Austen and Mary Wollstonecraft were all highly intelligent—suggest how much influence circumstances have upon opinions." (157)

Woolf points to the social and cultural nexus, that fine ideological web of "circumstances" that engirth and enmesh, that "infiltrates consciousness," even the consciousness of "highly intelligent" people. Put differently, our opinions are contingent on our circumstances; change the circumstance, and the opinion and the narrative that sustains that opinion will change:

> If Godwin had been brought up in the precincts of the Temple and had drunk deep of antiquity and old letters at Christ's Hospital, he might never have cared a straw for the future of man and his rights in general. If Jane Austen had lain as a child on the landing to prevent her father from thrashing her mother, her soul might have burnt with such a passion against tyranny that all her novels might have been consumed in one cry for justice. (157)

Woolf's third-person narrative shifts, becoming less about the life of Wollstonecraft and more an expression of empathy that teeters on becoming a first-person narrative. Woolf, a woman of privilege, identifies with Wollstonecraft instead of her own class; sees herself on the same social and moral perimeter as Wollstonecraft, trying like Wollstonecraft to transit the space between "Women and Fiction" at a time when the drive to write made her a manx cat, the image she uses in *A Room of One's Own* (2005, 11); made her as monstrous as Wollstonecraft, the "hyena in petticoats" as Horace Walpole called her, a creature whose gender was believed to change with every new moon.

Like her father, Woolf proceeds to tell the same tragic arc of Wollstonecraft's story, but she substitutes the stock plot of the fallen woman with specific, pivotal ideas that develop as a result of Wollstonecraft's experiences. Wollstonecraft's experiences are not the cause of her fall; instead, every pivotal experience is yoked to a revelation, the deepening of a moral philosophy:

> The staple of [Wollstonecraft's] doctrine was that nothing mattered save independence. 'Every obligation we receive from our fellow-creatures is a new shackle, takes from our native freedom, and debases the mind.' Independence was the first necessity for a woman; not grace or charm, but energy and courage and the power to put her will into effect, were her necessary qualities. It was her highest boast to be able to say, 'I never yet resolved to do anything of consequence that I did not adhere readily to it'. Certainly Mary could say this with truth. When she was a little more than thirty she could look back upon a series of actions which she had carried out in the teeth of opposition. (157-8)

What follows is a recitation of the same events that Stephen had noted, only in this counterstory Wollstonecraft appears as Delacroix's bare-breasted Liberty, standing at a barricade and leading her people, an early nineteenth-century Joan of Arc. And as for the contradictions and inconsistencies of Wollstonecraft's life that troubled Stephen, these are for Woolf an integral part of Wollstonecraft's intellectual quest: "Every day she made theories by which life should be lived; and every day she came smack against the rock of other people's prejudices. Every day too—for she was no pedant, no cold-blooded theorist—something was born in her that thrust aside her theories and forced her to model them afresh" (159).

As Woolf explains, even such a deeply personal decision as marrying Godwin "was an experiment, as Mary's life had been an experiment from the start, an attempt to make human conventions conform more closely to human needs" (163). The master narrative of the fallen woman ends in shame, death and historical oblivion, but in the counter-story Wollstonecraft "has her revenge," (163) and so does Woolf, who turns Wollstonecraft's early demise at the age of thirty-six into a victory. Wollstonecraft's life, consciously led and recorded, render her immortal:

> Many millions have died and been forgotten in the hundred and thirty years that have passed since she was buried; and yet as we read her letters and listen to her arguments and consider her experiments, above all, that most fruitful experiment, her relation with Godwin, and realize the high-handed and hot-blooded manner in which she cut her way to the quick of life, one form of immortality is hers undoubtedly: she is alive and active, she argues and experiments, we hear her voice and trace her influence even now among the living. (163)

Woolf tells the metamorphosis of Wollstonecraft, mythologizing her for a larger community of women across the centuries in a manner that (to use Nelson's term) serves as a repudiation—an ancient story of revolt and rebellion, a Promethean story by which Wollstonecraft defines herself; and a story her daughter, Mary Wollstonecraft Shelley, would tell in the pages of *Frankenstein; Or, the Modern Prometheus*. History matters—and Woolf knows that. To her father's dismissive summary of Wollstonecraft's life and work, she responds, positioning Wollstonecraft with a circle of free-thinking intellectuals, and later giving Wollstonecraft "one form of immortality [that] is hers undoubtedly: she is alive and active, she argues and experiments, we hear her voice and trace her influence even now among the living" (163). Stephen's narrative of Wollstonecraft's life has been transformed into a counterstory extrapolated, serving to heal (to use Nelson's term) "damaged identities," providing Woolf with a narrative of her own, one that stages again that same transformative oscillation between third- and first-person.

In 1928, Woolf had recorded the intimate process of building the connective, transformative arc between "Women and Fiction," the topic of two lectures that would become *A Room of One's Own*. Here, however, idea and story are complicated by the absence of the tacit plot in her essay on Wollstonecraft—the chronology of Wollstonecraft's birth, life and death. In *A Room of One's Own*, the seemingly straightforward topic of "Women and Fiction" became "inextricably mixed" (3). Does the topic refer to "women and what they are like," "women and the fiction that they write," or "women and the fiction that is written about them" (3)? She decides to pursue a mix of all three, despite the "fatal drawback" of that approach; namely, that "I should never be able to come to a conclusion. I should never be able to fulfill what is, I understand, the first duty of a lecturer—to hand you after an hour's discourse a nugget of pure truth to wrap up between the pages of your notebooks and keep on the mantel-piece for ever" (3-4). The degree of certainty you are used to, Woolf tells us, is an illusion, as is the possibility of eliminating the hybridity of the topic. Put differently, to say anything about "Women and Fiction," we have to recognize the distance between fop and philosopher, "how much influence circumstances have upon opinions," and the need of a woman writer to see herself and to be seen by others as a moral agent.

What she can do, and the offer seems coy indeed, is present us with this solitary opinion: "a woman must have money and a room of one's own if she is to write fiction" (4). The master narrative about women and fiction is rooted in a denial of material circumstance: change that circumstance and the "unsolved problems" (4) of women and fiction will not need resolution. They won't even need articulation because "in a hundred years," when "women will have ceased to be the protected sex…. All assumptions founded on the facts observed when women were the protected sex will have disappeared…" (40). The "damaged identity" situated between those two lines of narrative—self and other, first- and third-person, will no longer be distorted and misrepresented. "Imaginatively [woman] is of the highest importance; practically she is completely insignificant. She pervades poetry from cover to cover; she is all but absent from history" (43).

This "odd monster," "a worm winged like an eagle; the spirit of life and beauty in a kitchen chopping up suet" (44) represents the same discrepancy Woolf observed and responded to in her essay on Wollstonecraft. The imaginative or fanciful rendering of woman by poets and historians as either ideally spiritual or grossly material finds its parallel in the persistent illusion about "realism" as a literary trope. It, too, is an "odd monster," as Woolf and her intellectual circle understood, as aestheticized and fetishized as the Victorian obsession with the image of Shakespeare's Ophelia floating under the water's surface, at some elusive point after her last breath but before her physical decay. What we represent to ourselves as the linearity of history is an illusion, a highly selected and aestheticized narrative that serves to support certain configurations of power and privilege. What we represent to ourselves as "realism" is a series of historically bound narrative or painterly conventions. Unable to see the contingency of "realism" as a trope, we might also find "magical realism" problematic or puerile.

"Call me Mary Beton, Mary Seton, Mary Carmichael" (5), Woolf insists. Her transit from Oxbridge to river's edge to Fernham to British Museum to window—this is the transit of an allegorical figure, one and many simultaneously, struggling to understand two categories, Women and Fiction, that have been purposely situated outside her immediate grasp: "Women have served all these centuries as looking-glasses possessing the magic and delicious power of reflecting the figure of man at twice its natural size" (35). The representation of a woman's agency as a flat, reflective surface is an illusion. Or, to quote Diana Tietjens Meyers in *Gender in the Mirror: Cultural Imagery and Women's Agency*, "[t]he mirrors that give women their self-images lie" (2002, Preface). Cultures, as Meyers argues, "promote" or "suppress" agency depending on the social roles they want certain groups of people to play (2002, 24). Woolf is clear about the role of women being promoted within the culture that surrounds her: "Whatever may be their use in civilized societies, mirrors are essential to all violent and heroic actions. That is why Napoleon and Mussilini both insist so emphatically on the inferiority of women, for if they were not inferior, they would cease to enlarge" (35-36).

She is clear, too, that this misrepresentation of women's moral agency is a way of tethering them to the patriarchal project, which is all too often also the project of empire. "It is one of the great advantages of being a woman," she comments later in her essay, "that one can pass even a very fine negress without wishing to make an Englishwoman of her" (50). By eschewing the desire to subordinate others, women set aside the easy path to self-confidence, that "imponderable" and "so invaluable" quality (35), which we derive "[b]y thinking that other people are inferior to oneself. By feeling that one has some innate superiority ... over other people" (35). The mirror that stands for the monumentalism, the fanatical monological narrative of fascism is a symbol of an easy and ultimately false self-confidence, one fueled by the barely disguised and inexplicable rage against women that Woolf cites throughout her essay. Sitting at the cross-roads of a seemingly interminable historical trauma, positioned between those two lines of narrative—self and other, first- and third-person, the difficult process of healing lies in transiting across and through that wound that has so distorted and limited women's moral agency.

Woolf understands this, which is why she argues somewhat clumsily for the "androgynous mind," its incandescence signifying not simply great intellect but a sense of the contingent. Which will you choose? Woolf demands. The fop or the philosopher? What will you stand for, the monarchy or the rights of man? She is drawing our attention after the fact to "how much influence circumstances have upon opinions." Opinions and the narratives that sustain those opinions will change under the influence of time and circumstance, of history. "With the eye of the imagination," Woolf explains, "I saw a very ancient lady crossing the street on the arm of a middle-aged woman, her daughter, perhaps" (87):

> The elder is close on eighty, but if one asked her what her life has meant to her, she would say that she remembered the streets lit for the battle of Balaclava, or had heard the guns fire in Hyde Park for the birth of King Edward the Seventh. And if one asked her, longing to pin down the moment with date and season, but what were you doing on the fifth of April 1868, or the second of November 1875, she would look vague and say that she could remember nothing. For all the dinners are cooked; the plates and cups washed; the children sent to school and gone out into the world. Nothing remains of it all. All has vanished. No biography or history has a word to say about it. And the novels, without meaning to, inevitably lie. (87-88)

Neither biography nor history can capture the quotidian reality of this elderly woman's life—of any life that is relegated to the unimportant, to that outside of the economy of images and roles that matter within a patriarchy. And novels, which aestheticize the subject, "inevitably lie."

Here is the same problem Woolf articulated earlier: "is the charwoman who has brought up eight children of less value to the world than the barrister who has made a hundred thousand pounds" (39)? The question is pointless, she concludes, because "[n]ot only do the comparative values of charwomen and lawyers rise and fall from decade to decade, but we have no rods with which to measure them even as they are at the moment" (39-40). Here the equation between the second-class status of woman and native, of the project of misogyny and empire, is echoed in the words of García Marquez as he contests a compensatory reading of Latin American history, political and aesthetic:

> [I]t is understandable that the rational talents on this [European] side of the world, exalted in the contemplation of their own cultures, should have found themselves without valid means to interpret us. It is only natural that they insist on measuring us with the yardstick that they use for themselves, forgetting that the ravages of life are not the same for all, and that the quest of our own identity is just as arduous and bloody for us as it was for them. (1982)

For Woolf, the "comparative values" are not only contingent, but there is no institutional interest in representing the consciousness of that elderly woman. The allegorical figure of Mary Beton, Mary Seton, Mary Carmichael has transited from one space to another, and within each space there is some resolution, some revelation that moves toward understanding. Her transit pushes the formal edges of this essay, making it hybrid: she is not only "essaying" or "testing" an idea, she is also telling a short story about Everywoman. Yet she returns to this problem of transiting from domestic to public sphere, from reflective surface to moral agent without resolution. Everywoman does not seem to find the traction necessary to contest the master narrative about women, "[f]or we think back through our mothers if we are women" (75), and history, which could serve in the creation of a counterstory, instead silences, contributing to the literary narratives that aestheticize or, as Woolf puts it, "inevitably lie." Woolf wrote in the teeth of that institutionalized silence, tossing her counterstory out across an open space she could only imagine, a time when women would be equal to men.

Seen from the distance of years, Emerson writes, the journey of a thousand tacks is actually one straight line. "Your genuine action" in the world, he continues, "will explain itself and will explain your other genuine actions. Your conformity explains nothing" ("Self-Reliance," 1926, 42). Emerson's words console me in a way that people who have never felt the blunt force of history's dislocations perhaps might not understand—for exile is a deeply internalized dislocation, the result of an interminable chain of causes and effects that lie far out of any one individual's grasp or reach. Fidel descends from the *Sierra Maestra*, symbol and agent of a counter-revolution that itself springs from a nexus of social injustice and foreign colonization; and like so many others I lost my homeland, the trajectory of my life, and the lives of my family, inflected permanently.

I grew up listening to my mother's stories about Cuba. Telling and listening became the sole redeeming qualities of being exiled. And within the context of so great a loss, story had less to do with entertainment than transformation, the ability to create a space within ourselves in which the very things that had become impossible and inaccessible were real again, if only in the space of the imagination. The brittle, yellowed birthday telegrams; the voices distorted by static on the telephone line; the few creased black-and-white photographs: my mother's stories changed what was flat, brittle, and broken and made my family real to me. Her stories populated the emptiness of exile. More important, her will to tell stories forced open a space that exile had occluded, and it was in that space that I learned about grit, the will to *sobrevivir* the blunt force of history's dislocations.

"Who cares?" In the idiom of American English, what happened yesterday—well, "that's history," the phrase suggesting a habit of mind, how history is preferably forgotten, set aside in favor of the ever brightly approaching and limitless future. Yet it is history that has given me my "double perspective." Edward Said uses the term in *Representations of the Intellectual* to describe how the exile never sees anything in isolation, but rather always in counterpoint to what has been lost (1994, 60). For Said one of the advantages of exile is that it helps us "[l]ook at situations as contingent, not inevitable, [to] look at them as the result of a series of historical choices made by men and women, as facts of society made by human beings, and not as natural or god-given, therefore unchangeable, permanent, irreversible" (60-61). Thus every situation is contingent and made—capable of shattering, but capable also of being gathered, reconstituted, actively shaped again. Seeing all social systems as contingent, the exile serves not the interests of the most elite sectors of a given society, but chooses instead to question what is represented as orthodoxy, and to represent, as Said insists, "all those people and issues that are routinely forgotten or swept under the rug" (11).

The "double perspective" situates the exile especially well, providing the traction necessary to transit that space between first- and third-person narrative, reinforcing the counterstory's ability to contest the master narrative "publicly and systematically," to use Nelson's words. The idea of the "double perspective" echoes the point made by Paulo Freire and Donaldo Macedo in *Pedagogy of the Oppressed* between how one reads the world and how one reads the word; between the actual cultural, social and political practices in which we all engage and the language we use to describe those practices; between what we actually do and how we insist on representing those actions to ourselves. That same distinction can be used to define the educator as one who retains a sense of contingency, who refuses to be co-opted. It is a distinction shaped by conscious choice, though certainly the blunt force of historical events can often catalyze this type of seeing, which seems to come more readily, though not exclusively, from someone who experiences political exile or whose *mestizaje* (and Gloria Anzaldúa immediately comes to mind) literally embodies the clash of empires, rather than from someone comfortably ensconced within an elite class. This ability to "read the world" is described by Freire and Macedo as a "critical comprehension of reality," a process that involves not just seeing distinct objects, but the web of "complex relations among objects," "the memories, beliefs, values, meanings," those nuanced semantic fields that can be so easily rendered invisible or turned into propaganda.

The idea that there are people who need to be dominated, their very consciousness split open, divided against itself for their own good, for the good of one or another's economic self- interest, still has the upper hand, even in this new century, and after the bloodiest century in recorded human history. Within every institution of higher education across the country are the victims of those terrible dislocations, myself included. Yet the historical narratives that would render the reasons for our presence here, in this alien culture and language, are invisible, silent. The installation of Fulgencio Batista's puppet government in Cuba; the removal of Mohammad Mosaddegh in Iran; the trade embargoes against Cuba and Iran; the war in Vietnam; the overthrow of the Bosch government in the Dominican Republic; of Nkrumah in Ghana; of Salvador Allende in Chile; the invasion of Panama; the weapons and training provided illegally to the Contras of El Salvador—sadly, these are just a few of many examples.

Look across every classroom: we are the unrecognized, the invisible "blowback," and we will remain just that until the complexity of those historical narratives is told and heard. We are not here because we hate our countries, our languages and cultures, or because we consider our homes inferior. We are not here to skulk along the margins, to steal jobs, or to tarnish the pristine racial and ethnic mix of the US. Our presence can be understood only in relation to a series of historically contingent decisions that remain for the most part unspoken by the master narrative of US history. Each of us, with varying degrees of consciousness, through a range of mediums, inhabit this traumatic space, giving testimony to the human cost of residing between cultures, between languages. Within the act of testimony, however, begins the counterstory—the promise and the practice of making ourselves whole again through a collective story that develops from the questions we are willing to ask.

What Woolf accomplished in her retelling of Wollstonecraft's life and in *A Room of One's Own* is an act of testimony that lets us "think back through our mothers" (75) and provides a space from which to begin contesting women's "deprivation of opportunity" and engaging in a process of "narrative repair" (Nelson, 9). Her testimony gives the lie to patriarchal master narratives about women and natives; and in *A Room of One's Own*, the hybridity of that essay/story, the difficult associational pattern that eschews simple chronology provides insight into the difficulty of shaping a counterstory in the teeth of that illusory void created by the master narrative. At the end, she provides a coda that is logical, succinct, and linear—as if to remind us that we should not dismiss her as an obtuse or flowery writer, but as someone who consciously stages for us that monstrous, hybrid form that is one possible shape for a consciousness that has no history except the compensatory narrative that has been reified as history.

Look at James Baldwin's "Sonny's Blues" and Sandra Cisneros' *The House on Mango Street* and see how the first-person narrative pushes the edges of consciousness until the literary form of the short story and the novel is reflective more of each writer's way of seeing than of a standardized aesthetic form, and yet the narrative is not solipsistic. It is a testimony that beckons the world to listen. In "Sonny's Blues" the story jettisons realism at just the point when the music, so purely abstract, touches the invisible well-spring of repressed sorrow in the narrator; yet at the point of greatest individuation, his consciousness becomes historical, the story of the brutality perpetrated against African Americans in this country. In *The House on Mango Street* there are similar moments. When, for example, Esmeralda begins naming the clouds, the game is a demonstration of her intelligence; but when the clouds are given children's names, we begin to understand Esmeralda's game as testimony, as the history of the lives of children who are in relation to majority culture expendable, their lives as evanescent and unimportant as a passing cloud.

In that long-ago moment, standing on the perimeter of the school-yard fence and the perimeter of an alien culture and language, my Cuban immigrant mother, left exhausted and bereft by US colonialism, conveyed to me an unwavering sense of how the world works, of how power yields ultimately to resistance, and how resistance is an exercise in seeing myself within a context that is completely invisible to most of the people around me. That day, as my mother called out to me from the fence, I had my first glimpse of the two edges that form the first- and third-person narrative; the edge of the devouring "master narrative" about gender, culture and color, (a narrative amplified, extended like tentacles to every ideological horizon), and the edge of a counterstory that my mother extended to me across the space of that school-yard from the well-spring of her own anguish and loss, the best weapon she had at hand. And I am eternally grateful to her.

References

Emerson, R. W. (1951). Self-Reliance. In R. W. Emerson, *Essays by Ralph Waldo Emerson* (pp. 31-66). New York: Harper and Row.

Freire, P. (2001). *Pedagogy of Freedom: Ethics, Democracy, and Civic Courage*. New York: Rowman and Littlefield.

"Gabriel, Garcia Marquez—Nobel Lecture: The Solitude of Latin America." Nobelprize.org. 3 Mar 2013.

Meyers, D. T. (2002). *Gender in the Mirror: Cultural Imagery and Women's Agency*. New York: Oxford University Press.

Nelson, H. L. (2001). *Damaged identities, Narrative Repair*. Ithaca: Cornell University Press.

Said, E. W. (1994). *Representations of the Intellectual: The 1993 Reith Lectures*. New York: Vintage Books.

Woolf, V. (1953). Mary Wollstonecraft. In V. Woolf, *The Common Reader, Second Series*. New York: Harvest.

Woolf, V, (2005). *A Room of One's Own*. New York: Harcourt.